To my wife, Susan, for her unflinching support and invaluable advice.

To my children, Robert and Jennie, for being my biggest fans.

To my brothers, for their insightful criticism.

To my mother, for encouraging adventure and forbidding excuses.

To my father, for teaching me very little, insisting that one should discover things for oneself; in other words, for teaching me quite a lot.

Jonathan Ochshorn

BUILDING BAD

How Architectural Utility is Constrained by Politics and Damaged by Expression

LUND
HUMPHRIES

First published in 2021 by Lund Humphries

Lund Humphries
Office 3, Book House
261A City Road
London EC1V 1JX
UK

www.lundhumphries.com

ISBN: 978–1–84822–466–7

A Cataloguing-in-Publication record for this book is available from the British Library.

Copy edited by Pamela Bertram
Designed by Jacqui Cornish
Proofread by Patrick Cole
Set in Arnhem Pro and Apercu
Printed in China

CONTENTS

PREFACE

This book grew out of my longstanding interest in developing an objective theory of architecture, one that accounted for architecture's subjective dimension without succumbing to the siren's song of stylistic advocacy. Ultimately, my target became focused on the nature of utilitarian function in architecture and, in particular, how such functionality is constrained by political and economic forces, while also effectively undermined by forms of expression.

There are other books that more systematically list utilitarian and expressive functions of buildings, or explain their historic evolution, or promote strategies and styles to make buildings "better." My intention, in contrast, is the "ruthless criticism" of functionality in contemporary architectural practice, analogous to Marx's comments in a letter to Arnold Ruge written in 1843: "If we have no business with the construction of the future or with organizing it for all time, there can still be no doubt about the task confronting us at present: the *ruthless criticism* of the existing order, ruthless in that it will shrink neither from its own discoveries, nor from conflict with the powers that be."[1] Thus, there is both humility and arrogance in my approach: humility in that I refrain from promoting any particular style of architecture, least of all my own; arrogance in that I subject a wide range of contemporary architectural discourse and production to unapologetic criticism. This book therefore fills a rather unique niche, which I believe will be of interest to many readers both inside and outside the discipline of architecture.

In 1983, as a young adjunct professor of architecture at the City College of New York, I submitted an article on "Fashionable Building" to the *Journal of Architectural Education*. In rejecting the submission, the executive editor explained that "the target is too big, and you used a shotgun." More than 35 years later, the present book elaborates on the notions first outlined in that unsuccessful 1983 submission. If I'm still using a shotgun, it's precisely because the target *is* big and spread over quite a few intellectual domains. While this weapon might not kill the beast, I'm hoping to at least get its attention.

INTRODUCTION

Architecture consists of form—the totality of the shapes of its various constituent parts—and also the spaces thereby defined. These parts may be separately understood as structure (the columns, beams, walls, slabs, and connectors that provide strength, stiffness, and stability); as enclosure (the surfaces that, through their continuity and specific physical properties, create an interior domain differentiated, and protected, from outside elements—and vice versa); and all the myriad interior elements—partitions, doors, toilets, ducts, conduits, pipes, stairs, elevators, and so on—at least inasmuch as they reveal themselves by virtue of their visible surfaces, their tactile qualities, their interaction with sound, their radiant attributes, and their smells.

These are the objective qualities of architectural form, such that buildings can be described, bid on, and built, ending up pretty much as they were envisioned by their designers. Forms, and the spaces they contain, are intended to afford, or enable, certain actions and activities—living, sleeping, teaching, shopping, impromptu interactions, and so on—which are the *utilitarian functions* of architecture. Yet the same forms and spaces have subjective dimensions or qualities which, as is the nature of subjective things, are not as easily defined. A house may be understood as a symbol of having attained a certain social status; or, by some other observer, as a vapid cliché representing nothing but kitsch sensibilities. It may be admired as an avant-garde composition or despised as a blight on the neighborhood.

Still, in listing subjective interpretations of formal things, one cannot help but notice that such interpretations also constitute functions of architecture: to reinforce social status, to shock or offend, to symbolize state power or private wealth, to instill awe, fear, or reverence. This book aims to disentangle the utilitarian and expressive functions of architecture, to elucidate their political dimensions, and to show how utility is constrained by politics and threatened by expression.

The categories constituting the functions of expression and utility are quite analogous to what is often called the "art and science" of architecture: on the one hand, the expressive, artistic, or symbolic function of buildings (Vitruvius's *venustas*) and, on the other hand, the utilitarian function of buildings (*utilitas*, combining the Vitruvian categories of *utilitas* and *firmitas*).[1] Within the *venustas* category—hereafter referred to simply as "expression" or "fashion"—one can also identify a kind of *meta*-function that seeks to understand and explain the overarching purpose of architecture within its economic and cultural setting.

It is not always possible to be precise about which functional aspects of buildings belong within each category, so certain concepts appear in more than one chapter. For one thing, the function of "beauty" or "pleasure"—what to Jean-Nicolas-Louis Durand is "no more than the frivolous advantage of delighting the eye"[2]—can often be difficult to distinguish from pure utility. For example, if one function of a window is to provide a "quality view" in order to "give building occupants a connection to the natural outdoor environment,"[3] then would such a function be classified as purely aesthetic ("frivolous," per Durand) or, to the extent that such views improve worker productivity, qualify as utilitarian?

This question was considered by Henry Ford, who viewed the conditions that improved productivity in his factories—including daylighting and adequate ventilation—as purely utilitarian: "To a stranger [our machines] may seem piled right on top of one another, but they are scientifically arranged, not only in the sequence of operations, but to give every man and every machine every square inch that he requires and, if possible, not a square inch, and certainly not a square foot, more than he requires."[4] Yet the same types of windows or skylights that create Ford's "well-lighted" factory may lead to excessive heat loss or heat gain, thereby coming into conflict with an evolving politics of energy conservation and global warming mitigation. At the other extreme, they may be deployed as part of an expressive system in which glazing is valued, not for its objective physical qualities, but rather as symbol and metaphor. Politics and economics, in other words, establish lower and upper bounds for all utilitarian functions, whose costs and benefits are continually assessed on the basis of the profitable accumulation of wealth within a competitive global economy. Even so, the ideal of utilitarian functionality is even more seriously threatened by an artistic sensibility, also driven by competition, that seeks to defamiliarize (make strange) conventional formal-utilitarian strategies and that increasingly relies on a type of modernist abstraction in which conventional building elements—for example, wall and window, roof and room—are radically reconceived, reduced to conceptual surfaces and voids, solids and space. Thus, to the extent that utility is both constrained by politics and attacked by expression, buildings—especially those that aim to be fashionable and avant-garde—experience various degrees of utilitarian failure.

These factors affecting architectural utility—on the one hand, the constraints set by politics and, on the other hand, the threats posed by expression—are separately examined in the two parts of this book. The chapters in Part I illustrate how utilitarian function is both informed and constrained by political considerations within modern capitalist states, while the chapters in Part II show how expression, driven by competition, can also compromise utility. Some of the utilitarian functions discussed in Part I—in particular, those involving structure, sustainability, light, and air—reappear in Part II, but in their expressive guise. As Lewis Mumford argued in 1951, "Functions permanently invisible, like those performed by the foundations or the heating apparatus, may remain outside the architectural picture; but every function that is visible contributes in some degree to expression."[5]

An epilogue takes a look at architectural education. First, characteristics of typical architectural curricula are identified: the division into distinct subject areas, the open-ended nature of design studios, and the superficial treatment of technical subjects. Next, these characteristics are explained as a logical response to the contradictions between utilitarian and expressive functions (and especially architecture's meta-function) explored in the prior chapters. I conclude that architectural pedagogy—increasingly alienated from technical, social, and practical concerns—has become complicit in the creation of bad buildings.

PART I

THE FUNCTION OF UTILITY

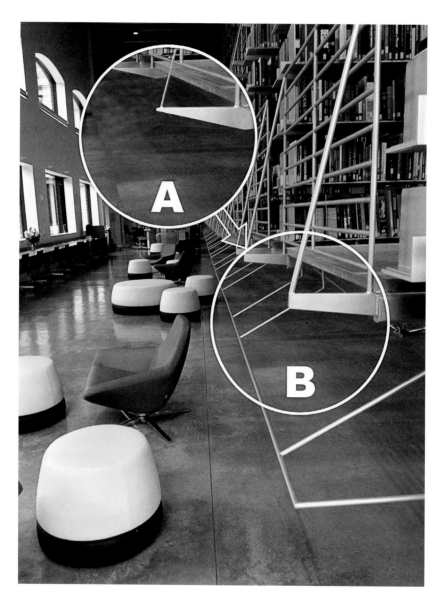

1.1　The schematic proposal for a Fine Arts Library at Cornell University, designed by Wolfgang Tschapeller, contained illegal protruding objects with knife-like edges, shown photoshopped in circle "A," based on the architect's published schematic renderings. The actual as-built condition blunts the knife-edges and adds a continuous cane-detection rod below, as shown in circle "B."

1
HEALTH, SAFETY, AND WELFARE

Monty Python, in their "Architects Sketch," describe a building proposal in which the universal functions of health, safety, and welfare in buildings are turned upside-down: "The tenants arrive here and are carried along the corridor on a conveyor belt in extreme comfort, past murals depicting Mediterranean scenes, towards the rotating knives."[1] The sketch is funny not because it is so far off base as to be ridiculous, but precisely because it captures, and exaggerates, a plausible architectural attitude towards health, safety, and welfare. Figure 1.1, for example, shows a real architect's schematic proposal containing dangerous "protruding objects" that, while not exactly "rotating," have a knife-like appearance and a knife-like effect.[2] Occupants with vision disabilities (or even distracted students without such disabilities) can collide with such projecting elements whose leading edges are not within the so-called cane sweep or cane-detection zone. Building codes prohibit such designs (see discussion in Chapter 4), yet they proliferate in architect-designed buildings and exhibitions.

Although it is clearly not possible to anticipate all the ways in which architects can make their buildings dangerous and then compile a comprehensive "negative" list of what to avoid (e.g., "rotating knives"), it is also clear that simply advising architects to make their buildings healthy and safe without providing more specific guidance is not effective. Remedies outlined in the Code of Hammurabi (c.1740 BC), which suggested that if "a builder builds a house ... and the house ... collapse[s] and cause[s] the death of the owner of the house [then] that builder shall be put to death," have long been superseded by prevailing standards of care and the prescriptive mandates found in building codes and zoning ordinances.[3] Put another way, many utilitarian architectural functions in the health, safety, and welfare category cannot be adequately addressed by relying on common sense or moral invocations, or even by issuing voluntary standards. The historical record makes it clear that only governmental intervention, embedding minimum health, safety, and welfare standards within legally mandated codes and ordinances, has a chance of overcoming the reluctance of individual building owners to constrain the freedom of their designers or increase the cost of construction.

Building codes regulate health, safety, and welfare in several categories: structural strength and stability, fire safety, the provision of adequate light and air, accessibility, sustainability, electrical systems, mechanical systems, and plumbing systems. Zoning ordinances, on the other hand, regulate the provision of light and air more indirectly, by constraining the size and shape of buildings, yards, and courtyards. Architects in the U.S. are also compelled to take continuing education courses related to health, safety, and welfare (HSW) in buildings not only to meet the requirements of voluntary professional organizations such as the American Institute of Architects, but also to maintain their architectural licensure in most (but not all) states in the U.S.

Providing health, safety, and welfare in this context is, of course, relative, and a more accurate statement would acknowledge that codes and ordinances are not concerned with the ideal of an absolutely safe and healthy environment (which, in any case, cannot be achieved), but instead are intended to bring about a politically and economically *appropriate* level of safety. This occurs when the added value attributed to governmental regulation (e.g., reduced damage from fire, or lower incidence of building collapse) exceeds the costs expended to comply with such regulation (e.g., due to requirements for additional fire-resistive material or sprinklers; or for increased structural strength to resist low-probability events such as earthquakes and hurricanes).

Governmental intervention to enforce functional requirements involving issues of health, safety, and welfare within privately owned buildings may seem both necessary and appropriate, yet the legal basis for restricting what property owners can do with their property has proven to be quite contentious in U.S. practice. The problem comes about because of the apparent contradiction between the ideal of *freedom*—that is, the freedom to use one's property as one desires and to exclude others from it—and the state's interest in maintaining that freedom *by restricting it*. The constitutional basis for this ideal of economic freedom can be found in the Fourteenth Amendment, which says in part that no state shall "deprive any person of life, liberty, *or property*, without due process of law."[4] Yet governmental intervention to restrict precisely that freedom, in order to protect public health, safety, and welfare (as well as public morals, but that's another story with less obvious application to questions of architectural function), also has a legal basis—albeit less clearly articulated in the Constitution—in the legitimate exercise of police power:

> The most obvious power of states that follows from the original meaning of the Privileges or Immunities Clause [also in the Fourteenth Amendment] is the power to prohibit any violations by some citizens of the liberties or rights of other citizens. In addition to the power of *prohibiting wrongful* conduct, the power of states may also properly include the power of *regulating rightful* behavior. It is no coincidence, then, that this very conception of state power came to be advocated by courts and commentators seeking to respect and protect the background rights of the people. This power was called the power of police or the 'police power' of the states. It is notorious for being difficult to define and limit.[5]

Though the discovery of this contradiction between freedom and public welfare is hardly new, specific boundaries between, on the one hand, the rights of building owners to do whatever they want with their property and, on the other hand, governmental intervention to constrain those freedoms by issuing regulations regarding health, safety, and welfare, are always in flux. As but one example, the constitutionality of zoning to regulate land use was not settled in the U.S. until 1926. Yet even the Supreme Court opinion in "Village of Euclid v. Ambler Realty Co.," while asserting that such laws "must find their justification in some aspect of the police power, asserted for the public welfare," nevertheless admitted that the "line which in this field separates the legitimate from the illegitimate assumption of power is not capable of precise delimitation. It varies with circumstances and conditions. A regulatory zoning ordinance, which would be clearly valid as applied to the great cities, might be clearly invalid as applied to rural communities."[6]

The fight over this contested boundary—between property rights and public welfare—determines, at least provisionally, which utilitarian functions become mandated in buildings. And although these functions can be loosely grouped under the categories of health (e.g., minimum requirements for light and air), safety (e.g., minimum requirements for structural strength or fire resistance), and welfare (e.g., minimum requirements for accessibility), there is an underlying rationale that encompasses all such governmental regulations. This rationale resolves the apparent contradiction between property rights and the public good by requiring that all state intervention be undertaken, not out of some freestanding moral impulse, or to maintain order, but rather to promote the accumulation of private wealth. "As the ideal collective capitalist, the state provides . . . those necessary conditions *for* competition which are not reproduced *in* competition [and] preserves the class of competitors with *no* property, so that it can continue being useful as a means *for* private property."[7] In doing this, the state makes a series of calculations to maximize wealth, even explicitly mandating—at least since Ronald Reagan signed Executive Order 12291 in 1981—that "regulatory action shall not be undertaken unless the potential benefits to society from the regulation outweigh the potential costs to society."[8]

Thus, well-being of people or ecosystems is *not* the function of laws regulating health, safety, and welfare in buildings and environments, except to the extent that such well-being is consistent with the competitive needs of capital. Buildings are designed, constructed, and maintained within a competitive environment in which architecture firms, consultants, suppliers, contractors, owners, developers, and all other related businesses are compelled to find ways to lower their costs of production.[9] Confronted with workers who must be paid, and natural materials that must be exploited, both human and natural "factors" of production are routinely damaged due to the constant need felt by business entities to maintain a competitive position. The word "damage" is meant to be taken literally: workers are damaged by being exposed to unsafe or unhealthy work environments, and by receiving insufficient free time, wages, and benefits to exploit their own human potential. Environmental conditions are damaged due to cost-cutting measures, taken by businesses to maintain a competitive position, which impair the ability of the natural world to sustain life. Such damage is often noticed, especially when it affects the lifestyle of the elites themselves, or when it threatens the underlying basis of the capitalist system by preventing the reproduction of the class of workers or by destroying the natural world to such an extent that its profitable exploitation can no longer be guaranteed.

The necessity to maintain at least a minimum level of "health, safety, and welfare," and the requirement for some sort of governmental intervention to overcome the destructive tendencies of profit-seeking entities, is the never-ending subject of political debate. Within that debate, the reasons and strategies advocated for individual, not-for-profit, corporate, or governmental intervention take several forms. First, for owners of property and their advocates, the essential argument against any interference with the affairs of business is based on freedom to compete with one's property, and markets to organize social production and consumption, rather than explicit social planning or regulation. The idea that business interests and their moral counterparts develop different arguments about governmental intervention is hardly controversial. As Robert Pear reported in the *New York Times*: "Business groups generally argue that federal regulations are onerous and needlessly add costs that are passed on to consumers, while their opponents accuse them of trying to whittle down regulations that are vital to safety and quality of life."[10]

Second, arguments in support of state intervention typically include appeals for human rights and social-environmental justice, based on a moral standpoint. Morality is invariably misconstrued as an intrinsically human attitude, rather than as an ideological reflection on a particular type of economic and political rule. This can be seen in the way modern, moral citizens misunderstand both the world of competition in which they are actually situated, as well as the application of state power that sustains it. Unwilling to confront the reality of these economic and political conditions, they prefer to combine their own morality with an idealization of state power: "Citizens want the law for the sake of personal advantage, despite the fact that it also restricts them. To seek their advantage, then, they also have to want those restrictions imposed on themselves, and this is what morality is. Moral citizens justify their submission to a damaging power by citing the ideal of that power, adding their own private virtue to the force imposed on them."[11]

A third variant, combining the business mentality of the first with the idealism of the second, argues that human rights and social-environmental justice are not only morally desirable but are logical consequences of—although at the same time subservient to—private ownership and the competitive drive for profit.

These arguments appear in various forms where governmental intervention creates functional mandates for buildings. Even so, virtually every building function involving health, safety, or welfare has, in general terms, the same trajectory. First, a "problem" arises; it becomes noticed and placed on the political agenda to the extent that it either threatens or enables business productivity (or otherwise affects the lifestyles of the elites).

Next, those opposed to governmental intervention, because their own immediate interests would be negatively impacted, typically raise the specter of socialism or wax eloquently about freedom and self-sufficiency (see first argument above). Those negatively affected by the problem begin to agitate for remediation by articulating a moral position (see second argument above). At times, the third argument emerges: moral issues raised by the problem are not only considered legitimate, but at the same time seen as being subservient to market forces which, defying all actual evidence to the contrary, are presumed uniquely capable of determining an ideal course of action.

At this point, programs are implemented that mandate minimum standards for these building functions. But an actual resolution of any particular problem *for its own sake* is never on the political agenda. Instead, what is debated is the appropriate minimum level of intervention consistent with the accumulation of wealth in the form of private property. Moral arguments continue to be expounded by politicians and other activists, but the actual resolution of the problem comes about through a comparison of costs and benefits attributed to competing political proposals, including the default strategy of doing nothing. While such calculations cannot typically be as precise and certain as, say, those predicting the position of a comet in relation to the earth's orbit at a certain time; while special interests or other forms of corruption may sway, to some extent, the final results; and while politicians and newscasters never fail to deliver moral platitudes about serving the common good; the outcome always, nevertheless, has its basis in the government's fundamental interest in *facilitating the production of privately owned wealth* and, therefore, its own power. Conventional political science texts most often abstract from this relationship between private wealth and state intervention, arguing instead that the purposes of government consist of "maintaining order (preserving life and protecting property) and providing public goods [while also sometimes] promoting equality, which is more controversial."[12] Even so, the various mandated functions discussed in the chapters that follow—enforcing minimum standards of structural strength, protecting buildings from damage (security and fire safety), allowing people to participate in the workforce irrespective of handicaps or disabilities (accessibility), and reducing environmental damage attributed to building design (sustainability)—are all consistent with, and prerequisite to, this fundamental state interest.

2
STRUCTURE

A building's function always includes the provision of a safe and stable platform—the building's "structure"—to enable its other functions. Structure—describing the elements that support and define floors, roofs, and exterior walls—can be more or less efficient (e.g., measured by the weight of structural steel required for each square foot of floor area), can interfere with or facilitate building activities (e.g., columns in an auditorium or stadium that block sight lines from certain seats), can support or inhibit future changes in occupancy (flexibility), and can be more or less safe (although structures in advanced capitalist democracies generally achieve a fairly consistent level of safety, i.e., are designed to have an economically or politically tolerable probability of failure, consistent with the intended occupancy).

While it may seem self-evident which fixed elements constitute a building's structure, there is actually no rational way to distinguish structural from so-called non-structural elements. Any attempt to define structure in such a way that certain solid building elements are excluded will run into problems. Defining structural systems as "load-resisting" or "transferring loads," per Wikipedia,[1] is pretty much useless, since a carpet placed over a concrete slab also resists dead and live loads placed on it, and transfers those loads to the slab beneath it. Is that carpet really part of the building's structure? In the same way, a pane of glass in a window is also structure, since it resists wind loading, and transfers those wind loads to adjacent walls or to the building's structural frame. In fact, everything fixed in a building is structure since everything both resists and transfers loads, even if only its own self-weight. But such an all-inclusive definition is clearly unsatisfactory in this context. We need to limit the *firmitas* category by excluding carpet and similar things—those things labeled non-structural in common usage. The best way to do this is to define structure in a circular manner, as *those elements or systems in a building that have been designed by a structural engineer*.

This much can be said about the objective, or utilitarian, qualities of structure: now largely in the hands of engineering consultants (i.e., removed from the purview of architects), the structural function is informed by engineering science advanced through academic research and practical experience, codified in consensus-based protocols developed by not-for-profit organizations representing the major structural materials, and finally adopted within a political process as a part of actual or de facto national building codes. For this reason, the utilitarian function of structure in advanced capitalist democracies has become largely routine, employing a limited range of materials, shapes, and connections, and achieving a fairly predictable and consistent level of safety (or, put another way, a fairly consistent and politically acceptable probability of failure). This is not to deny the continual refinement and advancement of structural design (e.g., improvements of structural systems designed to resist seismic or wind loading) or the combination of routine structural elements into creatively outlandish systems consistent with the architectural forms they support, but only to emphasize the rational nature of such advancements or applications when examined solely from the functional standpoint of *firmitas*: providing adequate strength, elasticity, and stiffness.

The utilitarian structural function also has a *political* dimension since the design of all structural systems—based on government-sanctioned standards—presupposes a politically acceptable probability of failure. There are two aspects to this observation. First, it is not possible to create standards for structural systems that absolutely preclude failure. Uncertainties in three categories discussed below—that is, concerning the *design*, *manufacture*, and *construction* of structural systems—can be minimized, but never entirely overcome.

DESIGN

Numerical models for structural design only approximate the behavior of real structures; even the most sophisticated finite element methods, which subdivide the "real" structural system into a conceptual matrix of ever-smaller parts in order to better mathematically relate the behavior of the various parts to each other and thereby determine the distribution of stress and deflection under assumed loads, face *practical* limits in how small these parts can be, and face *theoretical* limits in how well the interaction between the parts can be modeled. The question of what loads to apply is even more fraught with uncertainty; actual loads are both non-stationary and dynamic in nature, far more complex than the static force vectors typically assumed in structural calculations. And extreme loading scenarios, especially those caused by seismic events (earthquakes) or high winds (hurricanes/typhoons), are not only inherently unique and unpredictable, but also have different probabilities of occurrence and different probabilities of exceeding certain magnitudes of acceleration (ground motion) or wind speed, depending on geographic location. Dead loads—consisting of the weight of the building and its fixed elements—can be anticipated with a high, but not absolute, degree of confidence; but that assumes that the building materials specified for the design remain in place forever, and are not replaced with heavier (or lighter) material. For example, heavy ceramic tile on a mortar bed may weigh four times as much as the hardwood floor it replaces, eight times as much as carpet, and up to 16 times as much as thin linoleum or asphalt tile. And while being heavier has obvious ramifications for structural safety, being *lighter* than designed can also be problematic, especially for tall buildings where adequate weight, bearing down in the vertical direction (i.e., through the action of gravity), may be necessary to prevent uplift or overturning tendencies triggered by horizontal wind loads. Live loads—those caused by things like people or moveable furniture—are, by definition, unpredictable. How could one possibly know in advance not only how many people will fill any given room or any given building on any particular occasion, but also how much they will weigh, whether they will all congregate on one edge of the structure or distribute themselves evenly throughout the building, whether they will be jumping or dancing in unison, imparting dynamic loads on a structure designed on the basis of static loading, and so on.

MANUFACTURE

Manufacturing processes have varying degrees of quality control. Wood elements, at one extreme, have huge variations in physical properties that cannot always be accurately determined after they are cut from trees and evaluated (graded); concrete strength, especially when elements are cast in place on site, has such a high potential for uncertainty that numerous samples must be shipped to testing labs and cured for four weeks before being crushed to confirm whether the specified design strength has, in fact, been met. Such tests may provide incentives for contractors and suppliers not to cut corners, but also may provide incentives for unscrupulous testing labs to fabricate results in order to save money.[2] Even the steel industry has had its share of scandals, for example, the disclosure by Kobe Steel "that some of its executives had known about fake quality data for years—in at least one case for decades," a problem attributed to "a companywide focus on profitability and weak corporate governance."[3]

CONSTRUCTION

Construction offers a final dose of uncertainty. Even if manufacture and design seem adequate, construction of the building's structure—involving innumerable acts of cutting, placing, adhering, connecting, and so on—may not conform to the design drawings and specifications. Wood elements may not be nailed or bolted as specified, or they may suffer unintended damage due to rain; adhesives may be applied to surfaces that are no longer clean, or used when the ambient temperature falls outside the manufacturer's specifications. Concrete reinforcement detailing may not correspond to the design drawings, or so-called honeycombing may result from improper consolidation techniques—discovered only after formwork is removed. Steel connections may not be properly executed: welds may be too porous or have the wrong bead profile. High-strength bolts may not be tightened to deliver the correct tension; and so on.

This is the bad news: many things can go wrong in the design, manufacture, and construction of structural systems. The good news is that structural design explicitly acknowledges such uncertainties, which brings up the second aspect to the observation that the utilitarian structural function has a *political* content. Once it is understood that structural failure is impossible to prevent absolutely, the following question arises: how safe should structures be? Unfortunately, any seemingly rational and objective mathematically based methodology that might possibly shed light on this question ultimately falls apart when confronting the only common metric recognized as valid within a free-market society—cost. Even though we might agree with J.G. MacGregor, the internationally renowned engineering researcher who argued in 1976 that the function of structural safety must account for the fact that "(a) the strengths of materials or elements may be less than expected, (b) overloads may occur, and (c) the consequences of a failure may be very severe,"[4] we must also acknowledge that none of these three issues can be addressed from a purely objective standpoint.

Skipping over, for a moment, strengths of materials and magnitudes of loads, the third issue—measuring and evaluating the "consequences of failure"—presents a unique challenge. Since the consequences—the "cost"—of injury and loss of life involve considerations of value that cannot simply be equated with the exchange value of ordinary commodities bought and sold in the marketplace, academics must twist and turn (and they do; see the discussion of fire safety in Chapter 3) to balance cost savings associated with decreased safety standards against the increased cost required to better protect against injury and loss of life. Yet while one finds plenty of academics willing to make such calculations and validate such numbers (including the value of a human life), final decisions impacting the cost of structures within a competitive marketplace are necessarily political, and so are made within legislative bodies.

In the U.S., at least since the consolidation of the major not-for-profit model code agencies under the International Code Council (ICC) and the issuance of the inaugural *International Building Code* in 2000, all 50 states have decided to forego competition on the basis of structural safety by agreeing to adopt the recommendations of the ICC, embodied in the ICC's suite of model codes—albeit with a few state-by-state modifications—and create a de facto national building code. This certainly does not remove the political dimension from the determination of how much safety is appropriate, since not only academics but also industry and business interests are represented in the voluntary consensus standards process through which such model codes are adopted in the first place. However, by leveling the playing field and by making any deviation from the national norm a competitive *dis*advantage (since businesses working across state boundaries value uniformity and certainty), the incentive for states to use decreased structural safety as a competitive bargaining chip is reduced, if not eliminated. What remains as a regulating agent, keeping both the risk of failure and the cost of construction within acceptable bounds, is the incremental accumulation of experience with structural collapse—in particular, the experience gained from ever-new terrorist, earthquake, and hurricane events—that provides not only raw data for advances in engineering knowledge but also two additional types of information that even politicians wary of imposing increased regulatory costs can comprehend: an awareness that their own lives and property, and the lives and property of the elites they represent, are in danger; and *real* (not merely modeled) measurements of economic loss in relation to existing standards that provide some insight into whether, and to what extent, expected future losses ought to be mitigated by adopting tougher codes.

With respect to the first two parameters listed by MacGregor— strength of materials, on the one hand, and magnitude of loads, on the other hand—the risk of structural failure is largely determined by the selection of factors of safety that effectively reduce material strength (in so-called *allowable stress design*) or, in more modern methodologies (*strength design* for reinforced concrete or *load and resistance factor design* for wood and steel), not only reduce the values assumed for material strengths (resistances), but also increase the values assumed for loads. Yet, since the choice of safety factors invariably affects the cost of building in relation to building safety, it, too, becomes a political question that involves exactly the same sort of considerations—about the value of life and property— raised when evaluating the consequences of failure independently of loads or material strength.

That the seemingly objective function of safety factors has a political content becomes evident when examining the historical competition between concrete and steel industry associations for market share. Many modern commercial or institutional buildings can equally well be built in steel or reinforced concrete, and the decision to use one material or the other often hinges not on esoteric questions involving structural or architectural expression, but rather on cost. Cost, in turn, is affected by the magnitude of safety factors, since safer buildings have larger, heavier, or more expensive components. Safety factors, in turn, are embedded in building codes which have been adopted through legislative processes; these codes, which are recognized as legal mandates, are based on non-binding model codes whose structural design requirements are, in turn, based on standards promulgated by the various structural material industry associations; and these competing associations—primarily the American Concrete Institute (ACI) and the American Institute of Steel

Construction (AISC) in the U.S.—do not necessarily cooperate with each other when developing their own structural recommendations.

All this is illustrated by the peculiar story of how more sophisticated and explicitly risk-based methodologies were first introduced into U.S. engineering practice. Traditional use of Allowable Stress Design (ASD), with its single safety factor, neither accounts for the full (ultimate) strength of materials nor the different risks presented by different types of loads and their combinations. While it is still being used, ASD is threatened by more sophisticated structural design methodologies that—because they more explicitly account for risk—have the potential to reduce the cost of structures that might otherwise be designed with unnecessary strength (or, in some cases, to increase the cost of structures that might otherwise be designed with inadequate safety).

Consider, for example, two structural columns, each supporting a weight of 1,000 (pounds, kips, kilograms: the units are not important here), but with column "A" supporting 750 units of live load and 250 units of dead load, and column "B" supporting 250 units of live load and 750 units of dead load. In ASD, both columns would be designed to have the same size and strength, since the total load in each case is the same. However, in a more sophisticated method, such as the strength design method used for reinforced concrete structures, separate factors of safety would be placed on live and dead loads, recognizing the higher degree of uncertainty in the specification of live loads compared with dead loads. Using strength design, since column "A" has a greater proportion of live load than column "B," it would be designed differently (and end up being stronger) than would column "B," but both columns would have the same, and an appropriate, risk of failure. In principle, then, a structure designed with ASD would be less efficient and more expensive than one based on strength design, since *both* ASD columns would need to be designed for the worst-case distribution of live and dead loads represented by column "A." Therefore, assuming that the ASD method was calibrated so that safety would be optimized for proportions of live and dead load found in column "A," column "B" would end up being safer, stronger, *and more expensive* than it needed to be. But if the calibration were based on some other assumed proportions of live and dead load—for example, if column "B" instead of column "A" turned out to be designed with an appropriate degree of safety—then column "A," having a greater proportion of live load but the same structural strength, would be cheaper, but *less safe*, than it should be. In other words, while there may be one "sweet spot" where the design of columns in ASD and strength design are precisely equivalent, any other proportion of live and dead loads would result either in the ASD version being more expensive (and too safe) or less expensive (but comparatively unsafe).

The strength design method (originally called "ultimate strength design") was pioneered by the American Concrete Institute in 1956 and, as illustrated above, incorporated separate load safety factors for each different kind of load, while also considering the ultimate (failure) stress, rather than relying upon a single "allowable" stress.[5] Nevertheless, an allowable ("working") stress design method remained the dominant methodology for many years because it was simpler to use. However, this latter method did not distinguish between uncertainties inherent in various load types (e.g., dead vs. live loads), and did not consider the actual (ultimate) strength of a structural element subjected to these loads.

By the early 1960s, strength design for reinforced concrete structures had matured to the point where both loads *and* resistances were given their own, independent sets of safety factors that were equivalent, at least in theory, to what many years later became known as load and resistance factor design (LRFD), eventually adopted by the wood and steel industries. While the traditional working stress design method was, at that time, still the featured methodology for the design of reinforced concrete elements, strength design gradually began to displace the older method. The first incarnation of strength design did not yet have explicit strength-reduction (resistance) factors and was presented somewhat tentatively in the 1956 edition of ACI 318, the "Building Code Requirements for Reinforced Concrete" that is updated by ACI every few years. A short note referred those willing to try this new method to the appendix, which contained a concise description of the requirements for "ultimate strength design." In 1963, working stress and strength methods achieved separate but equal status within the body of ACI 318. By 1971, strength design had become the featured method, with working stress design still included, but only as an "alternate design method." In 1989, working stress design no longer appeared in the main text of ACI 318 at all, but was moved to the appendix, where it remained as an alternate method for another decade. By the time ACI 318 was updated in 2002, working stress design had been consigned to a small note in the manual's commentary stating that anyone still interested in it would need to consult the appendix of the 1999 edition, where it had last appeared.

Remarkably, it took 30 years after strength design was first presented in the ACI Code before the steel industry adopted LRFD in 1986. For many years, however, load factors differed between steel and reinforced concrete. Those adopted by ACI had been calculated on the basis of "engineering judgment" rather than on more solid empirical studies and probabilistic research. Initial values from 1963, for example, included load factors of 1.5 and 1.8 for dead and live loads respectively; these were "adjusted" to 1.4 and 1.7 in 1971, where they remained for more than 30 years. Meanwhile, dead and live load factors for steel structures were set at 1.2 and 1.6 respectively, values that appeared in the very first LRFD edition of the American Institute of Steel Construction's (AISC) *Manual of Steel Construction* in 1986, and that have been sanctioned by the American Society of Civil Engineers (ASCE) in their *Minimum Design Loads for Buildings and Other Structures* since 1988 and by the American National Standards Institute (ANSI) in the precursor to this standard dating from 1982.

In principle, the lower load factors used for steel structures (1.2 and 1.6) compared with those used for reinforced concrete structures (1.4 and 1.7) would make steel structures both less expensive and less safe since they could legally be designed for smaller loads. However, because the new design methodologies contain not only load factors, but also strength-reduction safety factors affecting the assumed resistance of the structural material, the final degree of safety is determined not just by "design" loads placed on the structure, but by the combination of load *and* resistance factors. And while the steel industry allowed smaller loads to be used within the design process, the concrete industry was less conservative in determining the magnitude of its strength-reduction (resistance) safety factors.

Safety factors for loads ought to be completely independent of particular material properties, so it was something of an embarrassment for the concrete and steel institutes to be seen arguing in this way; and since concrete and steel elements are often used in the same building, the problem of constantly re-calculating, and potentially losing track of the magnitudes of design loads—for example, when the weight of a steel column bears on a concrete foundation pier—became not only cumbersome but dangerous. Therefore, it was something of a relief when the ACI finally gave in, reconciling their strength design load factors with those of the AISC and ASCE in the 2002 edition of ACI 318. In order to maintain a comparable level of safety with these newly reduced, and therefore less conservative, load factors, ACI 318-02 also adjusted its strength-reduction factors—that is, made them more conservative.

Thus, competition—between material-based industry groups seeking to lower the cost of their products and thereby increase market share; between individual states seeking to attract businesses on the basis of lower construction costs; and even between nations seeking to provide a more attractive "climate" for business by inadequately upgrading, or not properly enforcing, regulations that might otherwise increase costs of construction—is always a factor in the determination of structural safety. But while such competition tends to reduce the cost of construction and therefore reduce safety, the increased risk to life and property entails a countervailing cost, raising the same question we started with: how safe should structures be? Individual competitors cannot be relied upon to provide a satisfactory answer, especially in a probabilistic environment where cutting corners and reducing structural costs does not guarantee structural failure in any particular case. For example, builders constructing a reinforced concrete school in a country with ineffective, or corrupt, code enforcement may simply build cheaply and badly, especially if this is the way they are used to building, and if it is their experience that even such badly built buildings do not necessarily collapse. Everything works out just fine until, that is, a low-probability earthquake, hurricane, or tsunami strikes. In this way, individual, profit-driven decisions reveal their social/political dimension: for society as a whole, calculations about the risks to life and property can be assessed in the aggregate, and a level playing field can be established so that competition on the basis of reduced structural safety is no longer viable.

3
FIRE SAFETY

To varying degrees, reducing the risk of fire damage to both buildings and their contents is a function of all architecture. The problem originates in the use of carbon-based materials that, under the right circumstances, may enter into a state of rapid combustion. Fire is not something external to such materials, but rather an alternative state of being triggered by ignition and sustained by heat, in the presence of oxygen. Where carbon-based materials are used (ubiquitously in buildings), and where sources of ignition are plentiful (candles, matches, lightning, gas lamps or stoves, fireplaces and chimneys, boilers and furnaces, faulty electrical connections, and so on), it is not surprising that rooms, buildings, and entire sections of cities often burn.[1]

The function of fire safety in buildings has evolved over the years, following a trajectory involving increasingly greater control over both the initiation and spread of fire. Historically, the first significant functional fire safety goal was to prevent urban conflagrations, that is, to prevent fire spreading from a single *building* of origin to adjacent structures; the second goal was to limit fire damage to a building's *floor* of origin; and the third was to limit fire damage to the *room* of origin. To accomplish this, fire safety regulations governing the design of buildings have become increasingly rigorous and comprehensive, including requirements for more effective passive and active systems.

Passive systems refer, in general, to physical barriers that "compartmentalize" any given building into smaller zones from which a fire, having started, is not likely to transgress. The most basic compartment is the "story," created with continuous horizontal floor-ceiling assemblies that limit a fire to the floor of origin. Compartments can also be defined by continuous vertical elements, such as fire barriers and fire walls. Clearly, continuity of elements that define the boundaries of compartments is critical, so that openings in them must be limited and carefully designed.

Active systems refer, most commonly, to automatic sprinklers. On the one hand, these systems have proved to be incredibly effective in limiting fires to their room of origin, knocking them out in place before they have a chance to grow larger. The most common systems rely on water under pressure within a grid or loop of pipes placed just below the ceiling. On the other hand, fire sprinklers do not always work as intended. The National Fire Protection Association calculated a sprinkler failure rate of about 12 percent, taking into account both sprinkler operation and sprinkler effectiveness: "In fires considered large enough to activate the sprinkler, sprinklers operated 92% of the time. Sprinklers were effective in controlling the fire in 96% of the fires in which they operated. Taken together, sprinklers both operated and were effective in 88% of the fires large enough to operate them."[2] Thus, it is dangerous to rely entirely on sprinklers, and passive protection remains important. It is thus a fairly big deal that the historic trajectory of increasingly more stringent requirements for both passive and active protection has seemingly come to an end, as modern building codes have incorporated so-called sprinkler trade-offs that allow reductions in passive protection and increases in both floor area and building height when sprinkler systems are used.[3]

Both passive and active fire safety elements show up in building codes, but not always as absolute requirements. Instead, the mandated function of fire safety is accomplished by considering the risk of damage, death, and injury for each particular project, based on a number of fire science principles. First, the impact of "fuel" (combustible material consisting of the building itself or its contents) available for a fire must be considered. This can be done in several ways: by employing the basic passive strategy of compartmentation (i.e., using fire barriers, fire walls, horizontal assemblies, etc.) to subdivide a large space into smaller ones that have been separated from each other so that a fire is contained within the compartment where it starts; by adding active automatic sprinkler systems; and by enforcing floor area and height limits based on the occupancy of the space and the construction type of the building. The occupancy refers to the type of activity anticipated in the building, and activities that present a relatively greater risk of death or property damage—for example, assembly uses where lots of people gather in confined spaces, or storage/library stack areas where large quantities of combustible material such as books and magazines are intrinsic to the activity itself—have more stringent limitations on both floor area and height above the ground. The construction type refers to the materials used to construct the building and, in particular, whether they are combustible (e.g., made of wood, plastics, or other carbon-based materials), non-combustible (e.g., made of steel, reinforced concrete, or masonry), or protected with a fire-resistant covering. A building made with a more fire-resistant construction type can have greater floor area and building height. In fact, buildings with the most fire-resistant construction type (except when containing high-hazard occupancies) can be built with unlimited floor area and unlimited height, at least from the standpoint of fire safety—floor area and height may well be constrained by zoning ordinances that are based on considerations having nothing to do with fire safety.

Second, it is necessary to reduce the risk of fire spreading from a single building to adjacent properties. As the distance from a building's perimeter to its bounding property lines (its so-called *frontage*) increases, the risk of fire "jumping" from that building to adjacent construction is reduced, and additional floor area is permitted. On the other hand, to the extent that a building's exterior wall is constructed close to, or actually on, a property line adjacent to another piece of property, regulations regarding both the fire-resistance of that wall, as well as the amount and the required fire protection of openings in that wall, become more restrictive. At the extreme, it is common to prohibit all openings in exterior walls built on a side or rear lot line.

Third, it is necessary to reduce the risk of inadvertent ignition by regulating electrical installations and appliances that produce heat and fire (such as stoves). Societal trends that discourage (or even prohibit) smoking in buildings also help eliminate what remains a dangerous source of ignition, especially in residences: "Smoking materials, including cigarettes, pipes, and cigars, started an estimated 17,200 home structure fires reported to U.S. fire departments in 2014. These fires caused 570 deaths, 1,140 injuries and $426 million in direct property damage."[4]

Fourth, it is necessary to enable fire *suppression* by encouraging the use of automatic sprinkler systems and by providing access (including additional fire stairs in tall buildings) and water (including the installation of standpipes) to trained firefighting personnel.

Fifth, it is necessary to exhaust or otherwise control smoke originating from a fire. Smoke is the largest cause of death in building fires, and much of the logic of compartmentation has to do with restricting the movement of this deadly gas. The classic "violation" of the compartmentation principle would occur in multi-story atriums, except that special building code provisions have been developed to ensure that smoke originating from fires can be controlled and, usually, exhausted from the top of such spaces. Otherwise, building codes generally permit openings in floor-ceiling assemblies to connect no more than two adjacent stories.

Sixth, it is necessary to provide adequate and protected means of egress (exits), along with detection and alarm systems, so that people are aware of, and can escape from fire in buildings. The number of exits for a room, or for an entire building story, is determined by the number of occupants in that room or story. In U.S. practice, rooms with no more than 49 occupants generally need only one exit. Some entire buildings with low occupancy (and no more than one or two stories) can also be built with a single exit, but this is atypical: most buildings need at least two means of egress.

The function of fire safety is implemented in buildings, not because owners and architects think it's a good idea, but because the historic experience of fire damage (including loss of life, injury, and loss of property) has led to the evolution of laws mandating specific fire safety provisions. Yet there is a difference between fire science and fire codes. Where fire science seeks to explain how fires start in buildings, how they spread, what sort of risks they pose, and how they can be prevented, controlled, and suppressed, fire codes attempt to prescribe requirements for construction that reconcile the costs of fire (i.e., death, injury, and property loss) with the costs of fire safety measures. Fire codes are therefore political documents that use engineering and scientific knowledge to support political goals. Even so, we can take code requirements as the de facto functional prerequisites for fire safety, since—for society as a whole if not for every individual building—these requirements provide a politically acceptable level of safety. That a political decision-making process defines this architectural function—with the underlying fire science often obscured in the prescriptive text and, in any case, not well understood by architects and building owners—gives rise to numerous misconceptions about fire safety and results in various types of non-compliance with current regulations.

Fire safety requirements are the outcome of political decisions based on the consideration, if not explicit calculation, of costs and benefits. This argument can be best understood by examining how governments have historically intervened to limit damage from fire, starting with the periodic conflagrations that routinely destroyed entire urban areas, and continuing with efforts to find cost-effective means to reduce and control fire damage within individual buildings.

Urban conflagrations were hardly limited to those fires famous for their impact on the history of architecture, notably the Great Fire of London in 1666 and the Great Chicago Fire in 1871 (Fig.3.1). Virtually all

3.1   The Great Fire of London, 1666 (Old St. Paul's Cathedral burning in the Great Fire of London by Wenceslaus Hollar, *top*), and the Great Chicago Fire, 1871 (destroyed buildings, photographer unknown, *bottom*).

cities experienced major conflagrations, and the causes were well known: combustible materials used for building walls, floors, and roofs; narrow streets which allowed fires to spread easily from one building to another; flammable material stored near ignition sources; and so on. In London before 1666, "the greater part of the houses were still half timbered with pointed gables facing the street."[5] The London fire began as a

> strong east wind carried sparks from the burning timbers across the narrow lane on to hay piled in the yard of an inn opposite. The inn caught, and from there the flames quickly spread into Thames Street, then, as now, a street famed for its wharfingers. Stores of combustibles— tallow, oil and spirits—were kept in its cellars, whilst hay, timber, and coal were stacked on the open wharves near by.[6]

Conditions in Boston, immediately before the Great Fire there in 1760, were similar: wood frame houses with combustible siding and roofing materials were common. Large amounts of combustible material could be found inside buildings, including commercial products in residential contexts ("rented rooms doubled as piecework shops, and leather, petroleum products, and the raw materials for manufacturing textiles covered their floors"). Ignition sources including candles and "lard or whale oil lamps with on open wick" were present. Narrow streets allowed fires to spread beyond the building of origin; manufacturing technologies commonly relied upon fire, often operating immediately adjacent to combustible materials ("Breweries, glassworks, tanneries, forges, candle-makers, dyers, and potters all had to use ovens or open-pit fires. Next to the flames were fuel sources"). Barns contained straw and hay. Armories and forts contained gunpowder. Combustible materials were stored in shipyards (e.g., rope, tar, sails, etc.). Combustible soot was present in chimneys directly adjacent to thatch roofs. And flagrant violations of existing, enacted, fire regulations (e.g., those mandating tile roofs or masonry walls) were common.[7]

The potential damage from urban conflagrations was well known and well understood; and it was increasingly clear that economic costs of such fires exceeded the costs of remediation: "The evils of the old [i.e., London *before* the Great Fire] had been glaring, its critics legion. For many years, from the King downwards, men had striven to provide remedies."[8] What stood in the way of adopting safer building practices was not knowledge, but the unwillingness of individual property owners to transcend their own immediate interests: "Annual fire losses represented a waste of resources for the nation as a whole, but individuals were unwilling to shoulder the burden, in the form of more expensive buildings, to help reduce this loss."[9] In the case of the Boston fire described above, the economic motivation of individual owners to continue building with combustible materials was clear: "For all the damage the [earlier] Great Fire of 1711 caused and the handwringing that followed, Boston remained a wooden city because the cost of rebuilding in wood was lower than the cost of fireproofing."[10]

Strategies that required large-scale planning and regulation were only possible with state intervention. Yet, as can be seen in the aftermath of the London fire, proposals that require state intervention to correct problems *for their own sake*, that is, proposals coming primarily from an aesthetic, idealistic, or moral standpoint, are not generally successful. Christopher Wren's radical vision for central London, one among several plans submitted immediately after the fire, was famously rejected, according to Wren's grandson, because of "the obstinate Averseness of a great Part of the Citizens to alter their old Properties, and to recede from building their houses again on their old Ground & Foundations."[11] On the other hand, there were instances where private owners implemented voluntary standards for their own buildings, based explicitly on cost–benefit calculations—for example, taking into account the added costs of insurance for buildings that were not adequately fireproofed. Even so, while insurance costs may have had some effect on encouraging fire-safe practices, the idea that such a market-driven mechanism is sufficient to promote a rational allocation of resources to fire safety is questionable. As Sara Wermiel argues: "Unfortunately, the intense competition in the fire insurance industry made it difficult for companies to stick to a rate schedule, even if they wanted to. They were more likely to charge whatever it took to win or keep a customer."[12] In general, it is unlikely that individual building owners would spend money for technologies that improved fire safety but were not mandated by building codes.

In the case of fire safety, state intervention on behalf of overarching economic interests had to contend with two major obstacles: first, uncertainty about the scope of the problem (fires happen in a probabilistic context that makes precise calculations of costs difficult); and second, the resistance of individual owners who would experience higher initial costs. As a result, laws compelling owners to adopt fire safety measures originate at points of greatest certainty (i.e., where the recent experience of fire damage is unequivocal) and where the results of inaction are calculated to have unacceptable negative consequences. Thus, an initial proclamation issued only one week after the Great Fire of London established the basic conditions for preventing future conflagrations: "Rebuilding was to be carried out in brick or stone, and all 'eminent and notorious streets' so widened that a fire could not cross from one side to the other."[13] In an analogous manner, the notorious Triangle Shirtwaist Factory Fire of 1911 in New York City "proved to be a turning point in the history of fire safety practice."[14] As various technologies to promote fire safety are introduced in limited ways, it becomes possible to increase, or decrease, their application over a broader range of building types, depending upon the actual costs and benefits experienced in these trial applications.

For example, automatic sprinkler systems in the U.S. were first generally used in Associated Factory Mutual mill buildings in the late 19th century—one of several fire safety measures required for lower insurance rates—but were rarely used in any other context until they were first mandated in building codes. Initial sprinkler requirements were limited to theaters, and only for the proscenium opening and stage.[15] As evidence of their effectiveness became known, and experience with their use made costs of installation more predictable, it became possible to more convincingly cite their economic benefits for an increasing range of applications. Other fire safety measures followed the same pattern. When outside fire escapes became required in some contexts, other measures that provided greater fire safety (e.g., fireproof stairs and corridors) were considered but rejected as too costly: "In dropping the requirement for fireproof stairs [per the 1871 revision of the 1867 NYC building law] and making fire escapes the all-purpose solution for emergency egress, lawmakers most likely accommodated the preferences of landlords for a cheap solution."[16] The costs and benefits of sprinklers versus passive systems (like fireproof stairs and corridors) are still being argued. New building codes have radically reduced the requirements for passive protection in cases where sprinkler systems are used:

In fact, there are literally hundreds of code-approved provisions to eliminate or reduce fire and smoke control features in the IBC [International Building Code] when sprinklers are installed. This trend to reduce or eliminate passive features while installing more sprinklers flies in the face of traditional views on fire safety as espoused by generations of fire scientists, fire protection engineers, and published experts.[17]

Even after the collapse of the World Trade Center buildings in 2001 as a result of internal fires (where both passive and sprinkler systems proved ineffective), recommendations to strengthen building code requirements for fire safety have been only partially implemented, based on the cold calculation of costs and benefits. National Institute for Standards and Technology (NIST) recommendations for improved fire safety standards have been criticized on the basis of an implicit cost–benefit criterion:

From a theoretical standpoint, a requirement for redundant water supplies for a sprinkler installation seems logical in order to reduce the required fire ratings of the structural frame of a building. Again, our real world experience over the past 25 years indicates that providing a redundant water supply is unnecessary. A single tragic event, where providing a redundant water supply wouldn't have made any difference anyway, shouldn't change what our real world experience tells us.[18]

The function of making buildings safe from fire is routinely undermined by both building users—who prop open doors that are part of fire barriers separating offices from corridors, or corridors from exit stairs, and so on—and building owners, who have locked exits to keep workers from leaving (most infamously at the 1911 Triangle Shirtwaist Factory fire in New York City, where 146 garment workers died), or who have locked exits to keep customers from entering without paying (492 people were killed in the Cocoanut Grove nightclub fire in Boston in 1942 and 194 people were killed in the Cromañón Republic nightclub fire in Buenos Aires in 2004).

Instances of owners or builders lobbying against, or circumventing, fire safety regulations are a consistent thread within the historical evolution of fire protection. Even well into the second decade of the 21st century,

U.S. requirements for fire sprinklers in one- and two-family homes—included in model building codes since 2006—are not required in most states at the time of this writing, as lobbyists have successfully argued for legislation specifically prohibiting implementation of this particular code provision: "U.S. homebuilders and realtors unleashed an unprecedented campaign to fend off the change, which they argued would not improve safety enough to justify the added cost."[19]

In other words, by this logic, the added "benefit" of extra safety needs to somehow justify the added cost of residential sprinklers. But how are such calculations actually made? The first part of the equation—the added cost for residential sprinkler systems—is fairly easy to determine, being approximately one percent of the total construction cost in the U.S. (i.e., about $1.50 per square foot), or about $2,000 for a home otherwise costing $200,000. In contrast, the second part of the equation—accounting for "added safety" brought about by this fire safety measure—is harder to quantify, as it includes not only the cost of property damage due to fire, but also, somehow, the "costs" of death and injury. Based on 2016 U.S. data alone, 257,000 residential fires occurred in one- and two-family homes, accounting for 2,410 deaths (representing 81 percent of all civilian fire deaths), 7,375 injuries, and $4.9 billion in property loss.[20] The average cost per residential fire, not including the cost of death and injury, is therefore about $19,000. On the other hand, prorating this property damage over all 75 million owner-occupied homes in the U.S., the yearly average property loss would be only about $65 per home.[21]

But what about the risk of death and injury in such fires? Assuming 2.53 people per household and 2,410 deaths per year out of the 190 million people living in 75 million one- and two-family houses, the chance of dying in such a fire in any given year is about one thousandth of one percent. Looked at over an 80-year lifetime, the chance of any given individual dying in a one- or two-family house is closer to one tenth of one percent, or about 1 out of 1,000. But can the "costs" of those lost lives really be determined? It turns out that there is a considerable academic literature that purports to calculate the "value of life," all of it testifying to the insanity of an economic system in which the need for safety measures is determined by assigning a dollar value to each human life. Yet it is only by using such values (e.g., "estimates of the value of life in the U.S. are clustered in the $4 million to $10 million range, with an average value of life in the vicinity of $7 million"[22]) that such cost–benefit decisions can be made. Following the same logic used in the calculation of property loss, the average value of $7 million per fire death is multiplied by 2,410 deaths (in 2016) for a total loss of $16.87 billion. Divided by all 75 million owner-occupied homes, the yearly average loss of life becomes about $225 per home. The average cost of a fire injury is about one thirtieth that of a fire death,[23] or $7 million divided by 30, which equals $233,333 per fire injury. Multiplied by the 7,375 injuries and then divided by all 75 million owner-occupied homes, the yearly average cost of fire injury becomes about $23 per home. Thus, the average total cost associated with maintaining the status quo—that is, eliminating requirements for sprinklers in one- and two-family homes, while assuming that such sprinklers would dramatically reduce the incidence of residential fire damage, death, and injury—is about $313 per home, per year, while the average cost of installing sprinklers is about $2,000.[24]

Even using these extremely rough calculations, it is easy to see why model code agencies have included requirements for such residential sprinklers in their model codes: a one-time "annuity" of $2,000 for sprinkler installation compares favorably with an annual stream of $313 to cover the prorated costs of fire damage, death, and injury, at least when the assumed discount rate does not exceed approximately 14 percent. However, it is also easy to see why opponents of sprinkler mandates have been successful in counteracting these model code provisions in many states. First, homeowners are not actively organizing to demand sprinklers in their homes, in large part because there is an extremely low probability of dying in a residential fire; second, for any politician voting on such measures, the cost–benefit calculation is not really that compelling, with the outcome hinging upon exactly which discount rate is chosen, and the difference between computed costs and benefits not really being that great; and third, for home builders (and realtors) working in a competitive market that includes existing homes—for which retroactive sprinkler installation is not required—an additional cost of $2,000 either makes their product more expensive (and therefore harder to sell) or reduces their profit, giving them an incentive to advocate strongly against such provisions.

The idea that cost may motivate architects, builders, or building owners to reduce levels of fire safety is central to many of the examples already given: the refusal of property owners after the Great Fire of London (1666) to agree to any reconfiguration of London's street plan that would negatively affect the value of their own property; the use of fire escapes instead of (more expensive and safer) interior fireproof stairways; the painfully slow implementation of automatic sprinkler requirements, even after their effectiveness had been demonstrated; state legislation that actually prohibits model code requirements for residential sprinklers in one- and two-family homes from being implemented—all of these examples demonstrate that reducing cost can be an important motivation for lowering fire safety standards. The negative impacts of such cost-saving measures cannot be precisely determined for any individual building but only in the aggregate, since the probability of any given building being damaged is certainly low and, in any case, unknown. It is usually only when individual buildings are actually damaged by fire, and especially in those disasters where many deaths occur, that criticism of cost-saving measures enters the public discourse. This occurred, for example, in the aftermath of the Grenfell Tower apartment fire in London in 2017:

> Promising to cut 'red tape,' business-friendly politicians evidently judged that *cost concerns outweighed the risks* of allowing flammable materials to be used in facades. Builders in Britain were allowed to wrap residential apartment towers—perhaps several hundred of them—from top to bottom in highly flammable materials, a practice forbidden in the United States and many European countries. And companies did not hesitate to supply the British market.[25]

While cutting costs that reduce fire safety in buildings is widely criticized, at least *after* fire calamities occur, such practices are entirely consistent with the competitive, profit-seeking ethos of capitalism and are only effectively curtailed by governmental regulation and enforcement.

4
ACCESSIBILITY

The idea that accessibility is a function of buildings—that handicaps or disabilities should not impose needless barriers to access—has a relatively short history, although specific attitudes toward the disabled, ranging from the patronizing to the scornful, can be found over a much larger timeframe.[1] In the U.S., early attitudes were characterized by a kind of moralistic benevolence in which "persons with disabilities were often viewed as part of the 'deserving poor,'" but by the 19th century, attitudes had changed in response to "industrial and market revolutions and the growth of a liberal individualistic culture" in which "persons with disabilities, increasingly deemed unable to compete in America's industrial economy, were spurned by society."[2]

While various particular conditions of the disabled provided fertile grounds for both moralizing attitudes as well as misguided fear-mongering, the creation of huge numbers of disabled citizens in the 20th century as a result of both war and industrial injuries changed the underlying logic of remediation. Early organizations of disabled persons (e.g., the Disabled Veterans of America, founded in 1920) and early examples of governmental intervention (e.g., the Veterans' Rehabilitation Act of 1918) specifically addressed the consequences of war injuries. Yet at the same time, the state's interest in *appearing* to take care of its wounded soldiers—derived at least in part from the need to attract future enlistees—is invariably matched by a reluctance to actually expend resources on citizens no longer useful in its war efforts.[3]

The specific history of accessibility legislation in the U.S. begins with the Civil Rights Act of 1964, not because it extended access to disabled persons (it did not), but because it established the "principle [that] discrimination according to characteristics irrelevant to job performance and the denial of access to public accommodations and public services was, simply, against the law."[4] Prior to the passage of this legislation, in 1961, the American National Standards Institute issued its *Specifications for Making Buildings and Facilities Accessible to, and Usable by, the Physically Handicapped* (ANSI A117.1) as a voluntary consensus standard. This voluntary standard contained specifications for virtually all of the elements now explicitly required in both federal legislation and building codes: ramps or elevators to provide access to floors above or below grade; minimum dimensions for hallways and doors; minimum maneuvering space for wheelchairs within all rooms (typically implemented by requiring an unencumbered space in each room defined by a circle with a 5-foot, or 1.5-meter, diameter); curb ramps at street intersections; accessible ("handicapped") parking spaces; and the avoidance of physical elements that project ("protrude") more than four inches (102 mm) into circulation paths, unless they can be readily detected by those with vision impairments, that is, they are within so-called cane-sweep.[5]

Seven years after ANSI A117.1, the first piece of legislation was passed in the U.S. that actually mandated accessibility in buildings. However, the Architectural Barriers Act of 1968 applied only to buildings financed with federal money, leaving business interests unfettered by such requirements. Up until this point, voluntary compliance with the ANSI Specifications was virtually non-existent.

The next important piece of disability legislation, the Rehabilitation Act of 1973 (specifically Section 504 of that Act), framed disability as a civil right rather than as a welfare issue, requiring that: "No otherwise qualified handicapped individual in the United States . . . shall, solely by reason of his handicap, be excluded from the participation in, be denied the benefits of, or be subjected to discrimination under any program or activity receiving Federal financial assistance."[6] As might be expected, the controversy surrounding passage of this legislation, beginning in the Nixon administration, centered around cost. Nixon, in vetoing the initial legislation in 1972, "claimed that the bill was 'fiscally irresponsible' and represented a 'Congressional spending spree.' He urged: 'We should not dilute the resources of [the Vocational Rehabilitation] program by turning it toward welfare or medical goals.'"[7] Regulations to implement the legislation that ultimately passed in 1973 were postponed during the Carter administration, also due to concerns about cost. The Rehabilitation Act of 1973 introduced an exemption provision based on the concept of "undue hardship" that reappears in later legislation.

Both the Architectural Barriers Act of 1968 and the Rehabilitation Act of 1973 applied only to federally financed buildings. The Americans with

Disabilities Act (ADA) of 1990 extended such requirements to much of the private sector. While it is, and was, publicly lauded in idealistic and moralistic terms, the actual "back-room" political debates leading to its passage reveal a close attention to cost–benefit analysis, and the particular details of the legislation ensure that private interests are not damaged. In fact, politicians' speeches in favor of the ADA often demonstrate a combination of moral fervor along with a sensitivity to costs and benefits. Congressman Steny H. Hoyer's comments are typical:

> We are sent here by our constituents to change the world for the better. And today we have the opportunity to do that. . . . Many have asked: 'Why are we doing this for the disabled?' My answer is twofold. As Americans, our inherent belief is that there is a place for everyone in our society, and that place is as a full participant, not a bystander. The second answer is less lofty. It is steeped in the reality of the world as we know it today. If, as we all suspect, the next great world competition will be in the marketplace rather than the battlefield, we need the help of every American. . . . We cannot afford to ignore millions of Americans who want to contribute.[8]

Congressman Steve Bartlett is even more direct: "ADA will empower people to control their own lives. It will result in a cost savings to the Federal Government. As we empower people to be independent, to control their own lives, to gain their own employment, their own income, their own housing, their own transportation, taxpayers will save substantial sums from the alternatives."[9]

To spare business the costs of actual remediation of existing structures under the ADA, the "undue burden" clause of the Rehabilitation Act of 1973 reappears: "Title III provides that 'no individual shall be discriminated against on the basis of disability' unless providing such aids would 'fundamentally alter' the nature of the goods and services or result in an 'undue burden.'"[10] This "undue burden" clause, together with a compromise agreed to by the bill's primary sponsor, make the ADA's accessibility provisions much less effective than the self-congratulatory speeches by its political supporters might lead one to believe. The so-called "fragile compromise" supported by Senator Tom Harkin altered the enforcement scheme in Title III of the ADA so that only injunctive relief was permitted, thereby providing "little incentive for plaintiffs and their lawyers to seek legal remedies." In other words, because no monetary compensation was included as part of a remedy, low-income individuals with handicaps would not have the means, and lawyers would not have the incentive, to seek such relief. Moreover, in the years since its passage, "the courts and Congress have actually taken steps that have worsened the problem."[11] Such legislative and judicial maneuvering is hardly accidental, but rather reflects an explicit interest in limiting governmental intervention according to its impact on economic growth. As Senator Dale Bumpers explained in 1989: "We are obligated here to weigh the interest of the rights of the handicapped, which ought to be total, against what is obviously going to be quite a burden for a lot of small business people."[12]

As in the historical evolution of fire safety measures, moral sentiments are often expressed when social or environmental "problems" (i.e., damage to human or natural elements) are noticed. Such sentiments, which tend to frame as ideals the actions required for remediation, always differ from the actual responses to these problems in the following way: actual responses seek, not to solve problems per se, but to manage them in such a way that business interests are not threatened. It is not arguments about morality or safety—whether evaluating the case for accessible buildings or assessing the risk of fire—but rather calculations based on cost and benefit that tend to prevail. As Susan Mezey writes: "Reflecting its concern for the cost to business owners, Congress limited the ADA's mandate on accessibility of existing structures. . . . Owners of existing structures are only obligated to remove structural and communication barriers when 'such removal is readily achievable,' meaning 'easily accomplishable and able to be carried out without much difficulty or expense.'"[13]

Specifically, governmental intervention occurs only when, and to the extent, necessary; that is, only when private interests cannot themselves create the preconditions for continued, or optimal, economic growth. In the case of accessible building, private interests, on their own and in competition with each other, are generally unwilling to make their facilities accessible. Action is taken only based on government mandates that apply equally to all competitors. The availability of ANSI Specifications as a voluntary standard had virtually no effect on building access until it was effectively incorporated into law, first through individual legislative action in various states (e.g., Michigan, California, and North Carolina in the early 1980s) and then through federal passage of the ADA (1990).

Thus, accessibility has become a building function not because building owners or architects independently determined that such access was useful, but because governmental entities mandated conformance with accessibility requirements that had originally been developed as voluntary standards. The heart of these standards comprises two chapters, one dealing with so-called building blocks and the other defining accessible routes. Building blocks include guidance on such things as the configuration of floor surfaces, with or without changes in level; clearances for toes and knees; constraints on protruding objects; and standards for reach ranges (i.e., locations on a vertical surface that can be reached by someone in a wheelchair). Accessible routes consist of things like walking surfaces, doors and doorways, ramps, curb ramps, elevators, and platform lifts. Many of these elements have entered into the design vocabulary of contemporary architects, so that new buildings generally do not have issues with the provision of elevators or ramps or required turning spaces in accessible bathrooms.

However, one element in the standards—created to accommodate people with vision disabilities—remains widely misunderstood and ignored: constraints placed on protruding objects, that is, objects that extend ("protrude") into circulation paths in such a way that they cannot be detected by people with vision disabilities and thus present a hazard (Fig.4.1). This issue has become increasingly important as works of architecture manifest non-orthogonal geometries in which elements, designed to challenge the orthodoxy of traditional vertical or horizontal surfaces, extend into circulation paths above the cane-sweep zone used by vision-impaired individuals to maneuver safely through the built environment. And non-conformance with this particular standard, as with all other access standards, is a problem not just for people with permanent disabilities, but for all people. Most individuals will experience at least temporary disabilities for which elevators or ramps, for example, will prove useful—even wheeling a piece of luggage, or a bicycle or baby carriage, in and out of buildings is facilitated by such mandates—and many humans experience temporary moments of distraction where rules constraining protruding objects may well prevent nasty collisions with building elements or surfaces.

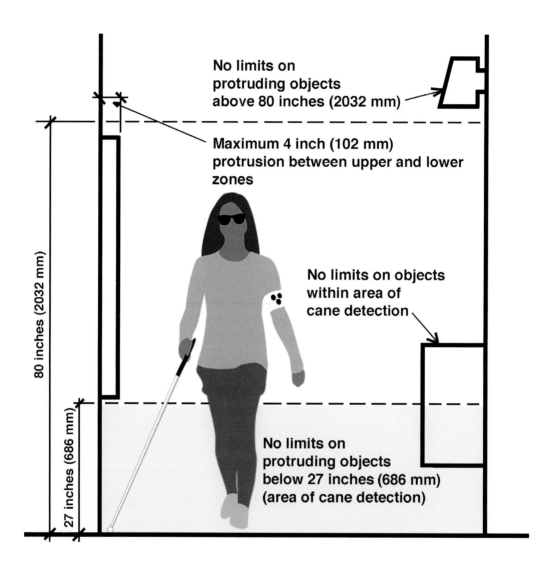

4.1   Limits of protruding objects.

Milstein Hall—the architecture facility at Cornell University designed by Rem Koolhaas and OMA—will serve as a case study illustrating how architectural design concepts may come into conflict with accessibility rules, in particular, those that determine how far protruding objects can extend into circulation paths in buildings. The architects' own description of their intentions is revealing. Rather than being defined by mere walls or floors, the building is conceptualized as consisting of "plates" "punctured" by "the bulging ceiling," a "bump" that "continues to slope downwards on both sides," and so on.[14] These bumps and collisions of sloping planes with floor and ceiling surfaces result in a sculptural composition that provides enticing views for photographers, but produces a dangerous landscape for humans moving through the spaces.

None of the protruding objects in Milstein Hall have a utilitarian (functional) basis. In the case of the sloping curtain wall that bounds an auditorium and a lobby (Fig.4.2, *left*), the angled surface is entirely expressive, intended perhaps to represent the type of design freedom that was first articulated by early modernist architects (the idea of *freedom* as an expressive function is discussed in Chapter 14). Le Corbusier, for example, famously extolled the potential "freedom" of the ground plan: "The interior walls may be placed wherever required ... There are no longer any supporting walls but only membranes of any thickness required. The result of this is absolute freedom in designing the ground-plan ..."[15] Where freedom for Le Corbusier is tethered, however tenuously, to some ideal of utility—note how the word "required" appears twice in this short quote, suggesting that the ability to adjust and position the "membranes" separating inside from outside has some rational ("required") basis—the freedom represented by the sloped wall in OMA's Milstein Hall composition is purely expressive and is not linked to any type of programmatic or utilitarian rationale.

This becomes even more clear when we examine another protruding object in the building, a sloping reinforced concrete column in the below-ground Critique Room (Fig.4.2, *right*). The hazard of this sloping object for those with vision disabilities is self-evident, but perhaps there is a structural rationale: the doubly curved surface of the "dome," whose shape was modeled by the architects without recourse to any structural form-finding methodology, may have required some extra support at this point. In this case, perhaps the sloping column was suggested by the structural engineers to counteract the downward thrust of the heavy

4.2   Protruding objects in Milstein Hall,
Cornell University, Ithaca, NY.

ceiling. As it turns out, the design of the sloping column, just like the shape of the reinforced concrete "dome," was not determined by structural necessity or structural efficiency, but rather by the architects, acting on their own. Apparently, they thought that a sloping column was somehow interesting, or appropriate, in that context, and incorporated it into their schematic design drawings before a structural model even existed. The structural engineers, eventually establishing a "dome" thickness of 12 inches (305 mm) and a dense pattern of steel reinforcement, had no need for the sloping column, but went along with the architect's aesthetic sensibilities and incorporated it into their structural model.[16] Eventually,

4.3   Cane-detection devices installed at Milstein Hall after the building
was occupied, Cornell University, Ithaca, NY.

cane-detecting bars were added at the sloping curtain wall and below
the sloping column (Fig.4.3), providing some warning to people with
vision disabilities.

In fact, there are 20 instances where cane-detection devices were
installed around sloping objects in Milstein Hall (Fig.4.4), and several other
instances where such devices should have been installed but were not.
While these devices have some utility in providing warning of protruding
objects to people with vision disabilities (or to distracted faculty, staff, or
students), their utility is the result of an entirely dysfunctional set of design
strategies which create such dangerous conditions in the first place.

4.4   All 20 cane-detection devices installed at Milstein Hall,
Cornell University, Ithaca, NY.

5
SUSTAINABILITY

The very idea that a building can be "green" is, on the face of it, problematic. For one thing, as pointed out by Pat Murphy, the term is so imprecise that its use in any particular instance cannot be validated:

> Green has become a word that can be applied to almost anything e.g., a green lifestyle. Its widespread use makes it very difficult to come up with measurements that are vital to determining the energy inputs and the waste products of buildings . . . It is unfortunate that green became the word of choice for buildings, since there is terminology available that does a better job of communicating the environmental and energy considerations with which we are concerned—energy-efficient, high-performance, energy rating, low-energy, energy savers, super-insulated, etc. Of great importance is that these are measurable and comparable.[1]

In other words, "green" is, *prima facie*, a meaningless description of a building because there are no metrics attached to the term that would establish some sort of testable (falsifiable) criteria. But there is a larger problem with the idea of a green, or sustainable, building. Sustainability only makes sense in relation to *an entire society* (or humanity as a whole), that is, with respect to a society's ability to reproduce itself more or less indefinitely by managing natural and human resources in a manner consistent with human survival. But to view human survival (reproduction) as the sole criterion for sustainability is setting the bar a bit low: such a standard is consistent with a global history of destructive wars, widespread human despondency, along with low life expectancy and grinding poverty for the majority of the species. Natural resources are exploited by competing private entities, each seeking to profit by such exploitation, and, at the same time, each driven by the fear of being overtaken by more successful competitors. This competition puts pressure on individuals, corporations, local jurisdictions, states, and nations to "balance" issues of environmental and human well-being against their own self-interest (i.e., in terms of economic and military power). Within that context, some agreements are reached between competing political entities (whether at the local, national, or international level) to allow for continued exploitation of resources by organizing their extraction according to scientific management principles. Yet this ad hoc management of resources does not preclude massive species extinction, despoliation of the environment, or the continued misery and impoverishment of large segments of the population. It simply establishes a minimum floor for sustainable exploitation, without abolishing poverty or environmental damage.

It is this observation that has led some scholars—like biologist E.O. Wilson—to propose a radical vision of "non-use" in which half the planet is excluded from direct anthropocentric activity: "The Half-Earth solution does not mean dividing the planet into hemispheric halves or any other large pieces the size of continents or nation-states. Nor does it require changing ownership of any of the pieces, but instead only the stipulation that they be allowed to exist unharmed. It does, on the other hand, mean setting aside the largest reserves possible for nature, hence for the millions of other species still alive."[2] The idea that "ownership" need not change hands would be, of course, small consolation to those owners whose property rights have been so radically constrained; Wilson admits that such a virtual taking of property would need to be accompanied by a "major shift in moral reasoning."[3] Yet the sort of reasoning that accepts the continued division of planetary resources into privately owned parcels of property while simultaneously agreeing to relinquish the use-function of that property has yet to be adequately explained.

Jan Laitos, a Professor of Environmental and Natural Resources Law, attempts to establish a legal framework for a similar objective, proposing to somehow establish for property a *right of non-use*. For Laitos, "the environmental and resource-protective fixes that humans have added to their laws, rules, and legal requirements do not seem to be working . . . Despite a promiscuous array of both proposed and adopted government standards for saving the planet, there has been a continuous deterioration of nature, natural resources, and environmental goods."[4] He explains the inability of current laws to adequately protect environmental resources by critiquing the *use*-function of property—a function that historically has been enshrined in law and ideology as the absolute right of property owners to exploit their property according to their own self-interest—and then proposing a more contentious *non-use* function for property—a function that historically "was grounds to divest the owner of a property interest"[5] but, according to Laitos, has become necessary to protect both humans as well as "nature" from damage, depletion, or extinction. Like Wilson, Laitos has no apparent interest in challenging property itself; rather, he wants to provide nature, *as property*, with an independent right of non-use—that is, the right to be left alone. Such a right has already been implemented in several constitutions (e.g., Ecuador) and even in U.S. law (e.g., Endangered Species Act). But like all other rights granted to citizens within capitalist democracies, any right of non-use does not challenge, and only reinforces, the freedom to accumulate wealth on the basis of property and competition. In any case, sustainable buildings, in this context, are part of the problem, and do not, by themselves, seriously address the function of non-use that is inherent in any rational and truly sustainable organization of the planet.

But whereas the exploitation of natural resources in the past has been destructive, both to environments and humans, the damage itself could often be managed and compartmentalized so that those with wealth and power were insulated from its worst effects. Many urban reforms at the beginning of the 20th century that established standards for light and air, or provided public parks, for example, have this character. The more recent concern with global warming (climate change) adds a new dimension to this old story, since its impact cannot be compartmentalized in quite the same way: sea-level rise threatens not only small Pacific islands, but also the wealth and productive capacities of coastal cities in industrialized countries. Worsening environmental conditions in poor third-world countries threaten the security of wealthy nation-states as drought and famine trigger large-scale migrations. And changing climate patterns threaten to disrupt both natural ecologies and agriculture.

Since managing the emission of greenhouse gases or the use of finite resources (such as fossil fuels or even uranium) can only be accomplished on a global scale, the term "sustainability" simply does not, and cannot, describe the qualities of a single building—except perhaps in reference to Robinson Crusoe or other survivalist fantasies. Rather, human needs are satisfied within a web of social production. And whether or not that web collapses due to some combination of "environmental damage, climate change, hostile neighbors . . . [lack of] friendly trade partners . . . [or] the society's responses to its environmental problems"—a framework suggested by Jared Diamond[6]—any number of platinum-rated green building designations for individual structures has no useful meaning if the sustainability of that society remains at risk.

The term itself was popularized in a 1987 report prepared by the United Nation's World Commission on Environment and Development ("Our Common Future," or the Brundtland Report) that defined *sustainability* and provided its rationale: "Humanity has the ability to make development sustainable to ensure that it meets the needs of the present without compromising the ability of future generations to meet their own needs."[7] Current interest in sustainability as an architectural function builds upon prior movements with different names but similar motives: that is, to live in harmony with the natural world or, putting it more bluntly, to live without destroying the conditions necessary for continued survival.[8]

Clearly, two factors have "energized" and validated current initiatives in this area: high fuel costs and global warming. But whereas the motivation to invest in "sustainable" building practices triggered by the energy crisis of 1973 dissipated to a great extent with the return of cheap oil in the 1980s (although the legacy of increased governmental intervention to reduce the use of energy persisted), the global warming crisis appears to have successfully disengaged itself from the price of fossil fuels. For example, even as oil prices have generally trended lower in the decade since the financial crisis of 2008 (with the price of a barrel of crude oil reaching $157.73 in June 2008, $48.74 in January 2009, $29.64 in January 2016, and even falling below zero during the coronavirus pandemic in April 2020), the interest of architects in reducing the "carbon footprint" of buildings, and the interest of (some) governments in mandating reductions in the use of fossil fuels—since those fuels, even when relatively cheap, still contribute to global warming—have not appeared to subside.

The list of "problems" related to sustainability also includes other sources of human and environmental damage (e.g., poor indoor air quality, threats to endangered species, loss of natural areas such as wetlands, pollution of the air, water, and ground, and so on). As is typical when such problems are discussed, two arguments are made: first, that individuals, corporations, or governments can be convinced to take action through moral exhortation; and second, that market forces, driven by competition, render state intervention unnecessary. Two books dealing with sustainability will be examined in this light. Both arguments are represented in each book, although the emphasis in each book is markedly different. *The Hannover Principles* provides only a brief summary of practical strategies and only occasional hints about markets and governmental intervention, but contains a large dose of advice from idealist, moral, and even mystical standpoints. It will be discussed in Chapter 13, in the context of expression. The *LEED Reference Guide*, on the other hand, is mainly a practical manual with specific advice on the utilitarian functions of sustainable buildings within a market-driven context—although there is also some interest in moral principles, particularly in the discussion of "community"—and will be discussed in this chapter.

LEED, standing for "Leadership in Energy and Environmental Design," is the name of the "Green Building Rating System" developed by the U.S. Green Building Council (USGBC) and first released in 1998. There are numerous LEED guides planned for different development needs ("Existing Construction," "Core & Shell," etc.) and the volumes themselves are constantly being revised, with new editions issued periodically. The discussion that follows refers primarily to the Version 4 *Reference Guide for Building Design and Construction* (LEED v4) and the older Version 2.2 *New Construction Reference Guide* (LEED v2.2), covering commercial and institutional buildings, as well as high-rise—that is, more than three stories—residential or hotel occupancies.

The preface to LEED v4 cites evidence that humans use resources, and generate waste, at a rate that would be only sustainable if the planet had 50 percent more capacity than it actually has. What are the "forces driving this situation"? According to LEED, a global capitalist economy—in which growth, accumulation, and profitability force corporate entities to damage human and environmental resources in order to compete and survive—has nothing to do with it. Rather, three "problems" are cited: the growth of population, the "linear use of resources, treating outputs as waste," and the forecast that populations in developing nations will eventually increase their standards of living.[9]

These forces create major global issues that, according to LEED, consist of pollution ("toxins that are accumulating in the atmosphere, in water, and on the ground"[10]), the depletion of finite resources, and climate change. Climate change is considered by LEED to be the biggest threat; energy, per se, is not even mentioned except as one of many finite resources threatened with depletion. LEED then makes the connection between the issues it has identified and the rationale for its green building standard: first, that "in the U.S., buildings are associated with 38% of all emissions of carbon dioxide" and, second, that human survival is at stake.[11]

These facts, however, are misleading. U.S. buildings actually produce relatively little CO_2, mainly by burning oil or gas directly for heating, cooking, and hot water; and indirectly by using electricity for lighting and cooling. The big generators of global warming gases are not buildings, but rather coal- and gas-burning electric utilities. By including the CO_2 emissions from electric power plants in the category of "buildings," LEED essentially lets the electric utilities off the hook—their contribution to global warming is barely mentioned in the Reference Guide. The reason for this is clear: LEED has no interest in threatening the infrastructural basis of corporate profitability by challenging the cheap supply of energy. Yet there is another flaw in the statistics showing how much electricity is used by buildings. A significant percentage of fossil fuel use *in* buildings is not used by the "building" itself. Some primary fossil fuel use is for cooking and clothes dryers, or to heat water; and much secondary fossil fuel use (secondary because it is used to generate electricity which then enters into buildings) is in the form of so-called plug loads, drawn by appliances, computers, printers, televisions, and other items that are "plugged" into outlets. These types of fossil fuel uses have absolutely no relationship to the question of whether a building itself is energy-efficient, or how much the building itself contributes to CO_2 emissions and global warming.

Not all building types have the same ratio of "building" vs. non-building utilization of fossil fuels, and it is difficult to find reliable statistics that itemize exactly how energy—derived from various sources and used in various building types—is actually consumed. However, an estimate can be obtained by cobbling together data compiled for, on the one hand, energy consumption by source and sector and, on the other hand, residential and commercial energy use. We find, first, that a total of 81.1 quadrillion BTU (81.1 quad, 85.56 exajoules, or 85.56 EJ) of energy—used both directly and indirectly in the generation of electricity—is consumed annually in the U.S. by burning fossil fuels, primarily petroleum, natural gas, and coal. Of this amount, buildings in the residential and commercial sectors consume 40.18 quad (42.39 EJ), or close to 50 percent of all fossil fuel energy in the U.S.[12] Industrial buildings are excluded from this calculation since their use of fossil fuels is almost entirely for industrial "processes" that occur *within* the buildings; HVAC and lighting in such buildings consume only about 1.5 quad (1.6 EJ) annually.[13]

Second, we find that the percentage of fossil fuels consumed directly or indirectly for heating, cooling, and lighting in the residential and commercial sectors is far less than 50 percent. In fact, the residential sector consumes only 5.25 quad (5.54 EJ)[14] and the commercial sector consumes only 7.97 quad (8.41 EJ)[15] for heating, cooling, and lighting so that the percentage of fossil fuels actually used by the buildings themselves (i.e., excluding the consumption of fossil fuels for process activities *inside* the buildings) is only about 16 percent. If water heating is added to the building's energy consumption, the residential contribution rises to 8.14 quad (8.59 EJ), the commercial contribution rises to 8.52 quad (8.99 EJ), and the percentage of fossil fuels actually used by the buildings themselves rises from about 16 percent to 20 percent. A disclaimer is needed, however: these percentages derive from several sources, compiled by different agencies in different years for different purposes, since it is virtually impossible to find a single statistical breakdown of energy use that addresses this question directly. Nevertheless, it seems clear that the oft-cited figure of 38 percent or 40 percent for the contribution of *buildings* to fossil fuel use is more than twice the actual percentage of primary and secondary fossil fuel use for heating, cooling, lighting, and heating water in the buildings themselves.

LEED is not interested in any form of regional, national, or global planning that might actually address the questions it raises. Rather, its ideology is consistent with that of the corporate entities it serves so well, providing as it does a branding tool to validate their "sustainable" and "green" efforts. According to LEED, one must tap into the corporate desire for profitability, and put into motion the miracle of "markets" to solve all problems, one building at a time. In spite of LEED's claim that the non-residential (i.e., corporate) "green building portion of the construction market" has achieved a 35 percent market share in 2010,[16] the planet continues to lurch closer and closer to some sort of disastrous climate crisis, global poverty persists, and most workers still lead lives—as Henry David Thoreau wrote in 1854—of quiet desperation. But as long as the LEED brand grows, these contraindications will not dampen the spirits of the pragmatists in the USGBC or call into question their vision of a voluntary, consensus-based, market-driven program.

The LEED Reference Guide is divided into six main chapters in order to deal separately with issues of location/transportation, site, water, energy/atmosphere, materials, and indoor environmental quality. Each chapter contains specific guidelines for improving a building's sustainable characteristics; a seventh chapter accounts for innovation. LEED certification is based on accumulating a stipulated number of points derived from meeting criteria for credits enumerated in these chapters, as well as by satisfying minimum standards ("prerequisites") in several categories, for which no points are given. Recognition beyond mere certification, metaphorically linked to the value of precious metals (silver, gold, and platinum) can be obtained by accumulating additional points.

While it is possible to criticize particular procedures enumerated in these chapters, or to find contradictions in what they separately stipulate, it is the general attitude towards profitability, articulated in virtually every section of the Guide, that is the most striking aspect of the LEED system.

The notion of measuring the usefulness of any given sustainable practice by checking its "rate of return" appears in virtually every section of the Version 2.2 Reference Guide as an "economic issue." The obvious problem is that this benchmark for implementation of sustainable practices—profitability—is precisely the criterion that has resulted in the very damage to natural and human resources that the Guide purports to address. Even the commentary within the LEED Reference Guide itself admits this contradiction. For example, LEED concedes that environmental degradation caused by dumping wastes in landfill is a natural consequence of business decisions made on the basis of profitability: "In the past, when landfill capacity was readily available and disposal fees were low, recycling or reuse of construction waste was *not economically feasible*. Construction materials were inexpensive compared to the cost of labor; thus, construction jobsite managers focused on worker productivity rather than on materials conservation."[17] Where particular "sustainable" practices, specifically those seeking more efficient utilization of resources, coincide with the drive towards increased productivity characteristic of normal business practice, the Reference Guide becomes, to that extent, irrelevant.

The most important LEED credit, as might be expected, is found within the chapter dealing with "Energy & Atmosphere." Within the "Optimize Energy Performance" credit, worth up to 20 points in Version 4, energy cost savings are computed by comparing baseline energy costs (for a default code-compliant building design) with simulations of projected energy costs (for the proposed design). In prior versions of the LEED Reference Guide, cost was explicitly made the basis of the design's sustainable value, as if cost and sustainability were somehow inversely proportional. "The intent is to encourage simulations that provide owners value, and help them minimize their energy costs."[18] Yet the history of energy use and consequent environmental damage—whether the fuel of choice was timber, coal or oil—is set in motion by the same calculation of cost and profitability advocated here. President Reagan's dismantling of President Carter's White House solar panels illustrates precisely this tendency: "Reagan's actions were more of a response to a series of events than a catalytic action meant to trigger them. America had turned its attention away from the promise of solar power simply because it could afford to."[19]

Where profitability might be threatened by implementing sustainable practices listed in the Reference Guide, warnings are posted. For example, in the chapter on "Water Efficiency," building owners are told that reusing graywater might not be a realistic strategy. Alternatively, where sustainable practices recommended by the Reference Guide do not necessarily correspond to profitable strategies for businesses, specious arguments are often employed to argue the case anyway. For example, in the chapter called "Sustainable Sites," it is suggested that development in "downtown"-type urban areas improves worker productivity and occupant health: productivity because workers spend less time driving (as if workers somehow automatically live near their places of employment simply because residential areas exist within a specified radius; and as if workers with shorter commute times spend the "extra" minutes thereby obtained by arriving early at work and donating free labor to their employers); and health because of increased physical activity as people walk to the neighborhood grocery store (as if this small-town model of local grocery stores and daily walks to shop for fresh vegetables corresponds to typical patterns of life).

This LEED section also defends urban development by criticizing "sprawl," using two familiar arguments: first, that suburban commuters spend more time commuting (in cars), and may require additional cars to support their suburban lifestyles; second, that by developing projects in urban areas, cities are restored and invigorated, creating "a more stable and interactive community."[20] Both arguments, however, lack historical perspective. It is precisely the congestion of urban areas that leads to the development of interstate highways and the redefinition of growth centered on the nodes created at the intersections of such highways.[21] The ideal of living one-half mile (0.8 km) both from one's workplace as well as from "basic services" abstracts from the reality of work under capitalism: the city is useful to particular businesses precisely to the extent that their physical proximity to a range of services and labor pays off. The attraction of such places to those who need to find work has a well-documented trajectory, but one that is entirely contingent upon the presence of businesses whose decisions to locate in a particular place have to do only with calculations concerning profitability. Whether workers move to follow jobs, or businesses move to reduce their costs, has nothing to do with supporting a more stable community. Community is a historically bounded and often unintended consequence of urbanization, neither its driving force nor its inevitable result.

For many of its credits, LEED establishes "baseline" points of comparison so that compliance can be measured. This strategy has several problems (or advantages, depending on one's point of view). First, the value of an improvement compared to a baseline value depends on how the baseline is defined. For example, the baseline standards for indoor air quality are set relatively low, so that an improvement may not constitute a healthy indoor environment (although it could generate a LEED point). In fact, the Reference Guide describes its criterion for "increased ventilation" as being significantly lower than what would be required to achieve optimal air quality, justifying it "as a compromise between indoor air quality and energy efficiency."[22]

Second, relative improvements over baseline conditions indicate neither the extent of environmental problems, nor the steps actually needed to remediate those problems. For example, increasing the energy efficiency of individual buildings is completely consistent with an increased overall use of energy in buildings (perhaps because more buildings are being built). This discontinuity between so-called sustainable actions and global impacts has been noticed by numerous commentators: "For every BTU of energy saved through better insulation and proper solar orientation," argues Richard Ingersoll, "the same amount has been squandered in other forms of consumption, mostly related to the Western way of life."[23] In the same vein, Alex Williams writes that "it's as though the millions of people whom environmentalists have successfully prodded to be concerned about climate change are experiencing a SnackWell's moment: confronted with a box of fat-free devil's food chocolate cookies, which seem deliciously guilt-free, they consume the entire box, avoiding any fats but loading up on calories."[24] Andrew Revkin adds, in relation to carbon-offset programs: "The average American, by several estimates, generates more than 20 tons of carbon dioxide or related gases a year; the average resident of the planet about 4.5 tons. . . . 'Instead of reducing their carbon footprints, people take private jets and stretch limos, and then think they can buy an indulgence to forgive their sins' [quoting Denis Hayes, president of the Bullitt Foundation, an environmental grant-making group.]"[25] The point is not whether things would have been even worse were it not for programs such as LEED, but the fundamental lack of interest in actual global environmental outcomes built into the design of the guidelines themselves. LEED has no mechanism for considering or evaluating alternate courses of action. Any building can potentially gain certification, even if a far more rational scheme was never considered or was considered and rejected.

Third, isolated comparisons (e.g., this building uses 10 percent less energy; air quality in this building is 10 percent better) have no bearing on the reasons that businesses choose to implement various "sustainable" practices, nor on the actual ramifications of such practices. In fact, by asking the same question over and over again ("Does this building, in comparison with some arbitrary baseline, perform a bit better?"), LEED guarantees that an examination and explanation of ongoing environmental and human damage will not emerge. Buildings that support the long-term destruction of both environmental and human factors can achieve certification, since no questions are asked about what actually takes place either in these buildings, or out in the world as a result of plans hatched in these buildings.

In this regard, it is hardly surprising that Walmart feels quite comfortable in the role of exemplary "green" retailer. Using less energy, urging its workers to take responsibility for their own well-being by sponsoring various self-improvement initiatives (the "personal sustainability project"[26]), or pressuring suppliers to reduce packaging (and packaging costs), all are designed to increase efficiency, productivity, and profits. That such efficiency also makes efficient use of resources is not the point: Walmart would be engaging in such efforts whether or not the word "sustainability" even existed. This can be seen by comparing their "default" Supercenter designs with two experimental stores built in 2005 to find out "how to achieve sustainability improvements," among other things. Subsequent testing showed that, in many respects, the default stores out-performed the experimental prototypes, proving not that the experimental designs were necessarily flawed, but that the drive for profitability already has led to relatively energy-efficient store designs.[27]

That the drive to reduce costs can sometimes lead to reductions in energy, materials, and resources does not mean that this competitive drive for profitability is consistent with human and environmental well-being. On the contrary, reduced corporate costs often mask low wages that damage workers as well as externalized costs of pollution (including global warming gases) that damage the environment without showing up on the corporate balance sheet. Nor do they account for global growth—more buildings, more cars, more factories, more people—that puts additional strain on environmental systems even when *individual* buildings and vehicles become more energy-efficient.

Comparisons are not only used as a basis for misrepresenting sustainability, but also as a general tactic to disarm any criticism of corporate or governmental practices. For this purpose, it is most often argued that the history of any particular "problem" reveals a trajectory towards improved conditions: after all, look at all the cell phones and refrigerators in use now, compared with some other epoch (pick your century) or some other culture (pick some third-world destination). What such progress-centric attitudes overlook is the fact that human misery cannot be measured quantitatively on the basis of material objects; that extreme global poverty is rampant and, by some measures, increasing;[28] and that using "absolute" metrics (e.g., defining the threshold for extreme poverty at $1.02 vs. $1.08 per day) obscures the ever-widening gulf between the *potential* for human well-being—arising out of enormous gains in agricultural and industrial productivity—and the *reality* of human exploitation and poverty within a global "market" (aka capitalist) economy.

LEED's Reference Guide provides actual standards for building design similar in form to what one finds in building codes and zoning ordinances. It is therefore not surprising that the cost–benefit basis of such government-imposed mandates also constrains the Reference Guide, even if the specific economic rationale presented in the commentary accompanying each LEED credit is often illogical or implausible. To the extent that the LEED credits make economic sense to business, they are implemented without consideration of their status as "sustainable" design objectives; to the extent that they make sense for overall economic growth, but where competition among businesses prevents their implementation through individual initiative, governmental intervention increasingly makes such practices mandatory. Where there is still uncertainty about the economic impact of sustainable practices (whether from the standpoint of an individual business or of economic growth as a whole), one finds large quantities of moral posturing, but only tentative, exploratory steps to test the waters.

Non-sustainable building practices—using up finite resources while polluting the ground, the oceans, and the atmosphere—are not aberrations in an otherwise idyllic world populated by "responsible" business owners; rather, they are logical outcomes in the actual world where competition for profitability underlies every business decision. LEED, as we have seen, prefers to sell its product on the basis of an economic argument rather than a moral one. And if its economic argument made any sense, we would already be living in a world consisting of pedestrian-friendly communities, working within healthy indoor environments, and congratulating ourselves on having successfully averted global warming, the greatest environmental threat to our anthropocentric lifestyles in the past 10,000 years. Yet arguing for green buildings on the basis of moral, rather than economic, principles is equally pointless. Such an exercise is either naive, to the extent that it implicitly presumes that business, compelled by the laws of competition to consider nothing other than profitability, might be influenced by such moral niceties; or else cynical, where such moral principles are knowingly used to sugar-coat the practice of "business as usual"—what has come to be known as greenwashing. Only governmental intervention, by enforcing standards applicable equally to all competitors, can overcome the inability of property owners to transcend their competitive drive for profit; but only comprehensive *global* agreements can induce nations to seriously intervene and address the problem in the first place. Yet such agreements are problematic, in particular for those nations that not only benefit from the status quo—because of their access to cheap sources of energy—but would lose a competitive advantage under a low-carbon regime.

To what extent, then, is sustainability a function of buildings? On the one hand, a sustainable building is an oxymoron, since sustainability— essentially a code word for reducing CO_2 emissions, mitigating global warming, and managing both finite and renewable resources—cannot, by definition, be addressed by any single building, any more than a forest fire can be controlled by protecting a single tree. On the other hand, from the standpoint of USGBC and the LEED Reference Guides, sustainability can most effectively be addressed by individual property owners, collecting their points and certifications one building at a time. Their counter-argument— that buildings "use" 40 percent of the electricity generated in the U.S. and that, well, you have to start somewhere—is both pure cynicism and self-delusion. Constructing another corporate office building with "sustainable" features merely adds *more* CO_2 to the atmosphere and uses up *more* resources, since these new buildings almost always add to, rather than replace, an equivalent amount of "non-sustainable" office space. A 10 percent increase in energy efficiency combined with a 10 percent increase in building area does nothing to mitigate climate change or promote "sustainability."

Capitalist businesses *require* growth; that is their essential nature. Moreover, this growth must take place on the basis of minimum cost— including the cost of energy—because businesses are competing in an unforgiving "marketplace" where success requires lowering costs of production. So, the wiggly black lines in those ubiquitous graphs depicting the amount of CO_2 in the atmosphere keep going up (Fig.5.1), albeit with some temporary reprieves during economic crises when industrial production slows down. And the relentless burning of fossil fuels within this competitive environment, to the extent that these fuels combine higher energy density, greater ease of transport and storage, and lower cost, will prevail.

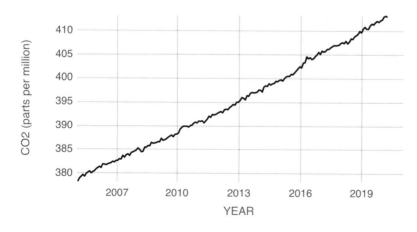

5.1 In spite of the hype generated by green-building rating systems like LEED, the amount of CO_2 in the atmosphere keeps increasing.

6
LIGHT AND AIR

The LEED Reference Guides gives buildings points for providing outside air (ventilation) and daylight, in spite of the fact that the relationship between light and air, on the one hand, and sustainability, on the other hand, is hardly self-evident. Let's look at these items separately before examining them together.

The need for bringing outdoor air into buildings arises from the pollution of indoor air, not only from building products and processes (e.g., incomplete combustion from stoves, radioactive radon from the ground, lead from old paints, asbestos from various old finishes and insulation, mold growth associated with excess humidity, and volatile organic compounds—VOCs—from paints, preservatives, aerosol sprays, cleansers, air fresheners, dry-cleaned clothing, certain building materials and furnishings, photocopiers and printers, glues, and permanent markers), but also from people themselves (e.g., increased concentrations of CO_2 due to ongoing respiration, as well as all the nasty artifacts associated with scents—perfumes—and deodorants). Assuming that outdoor air is not, itself, polluted, it makes sense to dilute the polluted indoor air with fresh air from outdoors, thereby improving the indoor air quality. Doing so is therefore a function of buildings, and has been considered to be one since the acceptance of "germ theory" in the late 19th century and the subsequent codification of air quality provisions, initially in "hygiene" regulations promulgated by Boards of Health, then in various ad hoc housing laws, and ultimately in building codes.[1]

Providing fresh air is, in fact, a requirement in modern building codes and a required "prerequisite" in the LEED Reference Guide, but this requirement is fraught with contradictions and difficulties. The most fundamental contradiction is between, on the one hand, the desire for fresh (outdoor) air and, on the other hand, the desire to reduce building energy consumption. This conflict is most acute in air-conditioned buildings during hot, humid weather: compared with recirculating "stale"—but relatively cool and dry—*indoor* air, dehumidifying and cooling *outside* air is quite energy-intensive. From this standpoint, the drive to lower energy use is therefore in direct conflict with the desire to improve indoor air quality. This has led to more sophisticated strategies for bringing in fresh air, not on a continuous basis according to flat rates tabulated in building codes, but rather only to the extent that it is actually needed. To determine when a room needs more fresh air, it is theoretically possible to continuously measure levels of likely pollutants in the room, including carbon monoxide, particulate matter, VOCs, and so forth. This being quite costly, the more common approach is to place CO_2 sensors in individual rooms, where the level of CO_2 is assumed to be an adequate stand-in for the whole array of possible pollutants. Such sensors, if calibrated correctly—something far from certain[2]—activate mechanical ventilation systems bringing in outdoor air only when a predetermined threshold ("setpoint") is reached; the name of this system, *demand-controlled ventilation*, reflects this energy-saving strategy.

Legislating increased outdoor air by upwardly revising tabulated ventilation rates (or recommending such increased ventilation rates for LEED points) may also be problematic, paradoxically leading in some cases to more—not less— indoor air quality problems. Joseph Lstiburek makes the case as follows: "Overventilation in hot, humid climates has led to more indoor air problems due to mold resulting from part-load issues than underventilation anywhere else ... In my not-so-humble opinion, all of the [Code-based prescriptive ventilation] rates have been just wild guesses without a sound epidemiological basis. But, the resulting mold from overventilation is real and demonstrable."[3]

A discussion of mold growth due to increased ventilation rates would not be complete without at least briefly mentioning a 2015 study that attributed ghost sightings in "haunted" houses to toxic mold growth. Professor Shane Rogers of Clarkson University argues that "human experiences reported in many hauntings are similar to mental or neurological symptoms reported by some individuals exposed to toxic molds. It is known that some fungi, such as rye ergot fungus, may cause severe psychosis in humans. ... Hauntings," he continues, "are very widely reported phenomena that are not well-researched. They are often reported in older-built structures that may also suffer poor air quality."[4] While Sigmund Freud argued in 1919 that "many people experience the feeling [of the uncanny] in the highest degree in relation to death and dead bodies, to the return of the dead, and to spirits and ghosts"[5] and Anthony Vidler in 1992 added that "the uncanny has, not unnaturally, found its metaphorical home in architecture: first in the house, haunted or not, that pretends to afford the utmost security,"[6] Rogers's research calls into question the notion that "haunting" is a condition of psychological, economic, or political alienation or estrangement. Instead, we can invest the "ghost in the machine"—a phrase introduced by Gilbert Ryle in 1949—with an entirely new meaning: more than 70 years after Ryle, the questionable recommendations of ventilation enthusiasts may well have surrounded the entirely rational fear of global warming and sea-level rise with an extra dose of psychotic paranoia.

Just as fresh air ventilation can be provided either naturally or mechanically, light can be provided either naturally (daylight) or electrically. The *International Building Code* calls electric light "artificial light," which is a bit strange, since electric light is still light and not a "copy" of light. And just as the provision of fresh air is not necessarily compatible with maximum energy efficiency, the provision of natural daylight may also, in some cases, be in conflict with energy efficiency. This is because glass, through which daylight enters buildings, is not only less thermally resistive than typical opaque walls, but also permits high-frequency radiant energy to pass through, while trapping the lower-frequency energy re-emitted: welcome to the greenhouse effect. While such greenhouse behavior is often idealized as a method to use solar energy passively to heat buildings, the reality is that many commercial buildings are challenged by significant *cooling* loads, so that the addition of the solar heat gain that inevitably accompanies daylight may be counterproductive from the standpoint of energy efficiency. This potential conflict can be measured by modeling energy loads associated with heating, cooling, and lighting for different window–wall ratios in different climate zones. Making some assumptions about climate, location, orientation, and window–wall ratio, such models have indeed been made, for example, as illustrated in case 1 of Figure 6.1, based on a study of office buildings in Italian cities.[7]

What case 1 in this diagram shows schematically is that total energy consumption (demand) in a typical office building using fluorescent lighting—represented by the solid line at the top of the graph—depends on the ratio of window to exterior wall area (WWR) and that, furthermore, there is an optimal WWR at which this total energy demand is at its minimum value (labeled "MIN" in the figure). That this optimal average ratio ranges from 23.5 percent to 32 percent—depending on whether the building walls are relatively uninsulated, or whether the best spectrally selective glazing is used—is the conclusion drawn in this particular study. The long-dashed line in Figure 6.1, representing energy used by *lighting*, falls dramatically as the WWR increases, corresponding to the need for less electric lighting as daylighting is increased. On the other hand, heating and cooling loads, represented by the shorter dashed lines, increase in a modest way as the WWR increases, since more power for heating and cooling is required when there is more glazing. Adding together these three sources of energy demand—with heating and cooling demand *increasing*, but lighting *decreasing*, as WWR increases—creates the low-point in the total energy curve, and therefore the minimum (optimal) value for WWR.

The idea that there is an optimal ratio of window to wall area has stimulated all sorts of research into strategies for using daylighting to reduce overall energy consumption since, at least in the past, electric lighting was a large contributor to overall energy use in buildings. And when energy models assume fluorescent fixtures with a lighting density (the amount of power needed per unit area) of $20W/m^2$, as is assumed in case 1 of Figure 6.1, the logic of capturing daylight to reduce electric light consumption makes sense when the percentage of window area is relatively modest. The problem is that fluorescent fixtures are rapidly being superseded by LED fixtures that use far less electricity. And when the energy consumed by lighting goes down sufficiently, the *total* energy used in buildings no longer validates even the relatively modest areas of glass deemed optimal for energy savings with fluorescent lighting. It is now feasible, using LEDs, to design buildings with a lighting density as low as $5.0 \ W/m^2$, according to California's *Codes and Standards Enhancement (CASE) Initiative* for 2019.[8] And with the lighting density thereby reduced from $20W/m^2$ to $5.0W/m^2$ (case 2 in Figure 6.1), the WWR that optimizes the energy costs of heating, cooling, and lighting occurs when the amount of glazing is reduced to about 15 percent of the total exterior wall area. The surprising result of incorporating more and more efficient LED lighting in buildings is that energy demand is actually optimized when *almost no glass* is placed in exterior walls; in other words, the "MIN" or optimum WWR approaches zero.

The increasing efficiency of LED lighting has also rendered the distinction between shallow and deep floor plates moot, at least from the

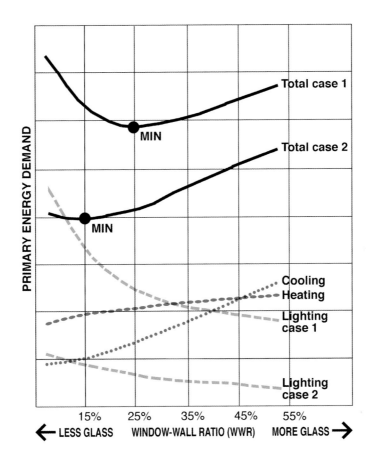

6.1   Primary energy demand vs. window–wall ratio in a typical
office building comparing two lighting scenarios: a lighting density
of 20 W/m² (case 1) corresponding to fluorescent light fixtures and a
lighting density of 5 W/m² (case 2) with highly efficient LED lighting.
Comparing case 1 with case 2, the optimal window–wall ratio goes
down from about 25 percent to about 15 percent.

standpoint of energy use, since "advancements in lighting have reduced the sensitivity of the ratio of interior to exterior office spaces and, as a result, limited differences are seen."[9]

Some disclaimers are in order. First, optimal values for window–wall ratios depend on many variables, including the climate zone, the occupancy type (e.g., office vs. residential), the quality (energy efficiency) of the glazing and the solid portions of the exterior wall, and the building geometry. Second, strategies involving things such as light shelves (horizontal surfaces that bounce daylighting further into deep floor plans) can be deployed to improve the viability of daylighting strategies. Third, there may be other reasons for using glass that have nothing to do with energy efficiency—mainly that humans often like to look outside when they're inside buildings. Nevertheless, simply assuming that daylight saves energy, even with energy and daylight modeling, is no longer self-evident.

So much for fresh air and daylight considered independently. It turns out that reform movements in the late 19th and early 20th centuries—motivated by mid-19th-century studies that "began to indicate a correlation between the lack of light and air, and spread of disease"[10]—considered the functions of providing light, from the sun, and fresh air, from the outside, to be inseparable. In tenement housing, with mechanical ventilation non-existent and electric (or coal, oil, natural gas) lighting, where present, providing only a minimal level of illumination, the exterior window seemed like the perfect remedy, since it let in both light (when open or closed) and air (and not only when open; leaky construction practices insured that at least some outside air would enter buildings even with windows closed in the winter months). Yet windows were not always provided for all rooms in low-end housing: the prevailing pattern of speculative tenement construction in places such as New York City took maximum advantage of available property by constructing buildings with up to 90 percent lot coverage. Windows facing the street were effective, but many interior rooms had no connection to the outdoors. Sometimes, but not always, interior rooms would have nominal access to light and air via small air shafts, but in a context where the smells of cooking—on stoves with no mechanical exhaust systems—or of excrement—from outhouses or water closets placed in side or back yards—could be overwhelming, access to fresh air and daylight required legislation that addressed conditions on both the exterior and the interior of buildings.

In terms of the building exterior, minimum dimensions of courts and yards between buildings on adjacent lots in New York City were established, first, by the Tenement House Act of 1879 (creating "dumbbell" or "old law" tenements) and, 22 years later, by the Tenement House Act of 1901 (creating "T-shaped" or "new law" tenements). The latter act mandated larger air shafts and stipulated a maximum lot coverage of 70 percent. To improve conditions on the building interior, operable windows were required in all rooms. Since conventional double-hung windows, with upper and lower operable sashes, provide twice as much daylighting area (transmitted through the glass in *both* sashes) as ventilation area (since only *one* sash can be fully opened; or both sashes only half-opened), building codes beginning in the 1940s conveniently stipulated that windows in each habitable room must be at least half openable, perfectly consistent with the prevailing window technology of the time. Minimum window sizes (areas) were established based on some fraction of the room's floor area, this fraction getting smaller and smaller as modern model building codes evolved. In the U.S., the "Uniform Building Code" (UBC) required overall window areas to be at least *12.5 percent* of each habitable room's floor area in 1937, with a stipulation that the area be at least 12 square feet (1.1 m²) added in 1946; this was reduced to *10 percent* of the room's floor area in 1970, with the minimum window area also reduced from 12 to 10 square feet (0.9 m²) in 1973; and this was further reduced to *8 percent* of the room's floor area with the introduction of the *International Building Code* (IBC) in 2000.

Through these incremental revisions, buildings codes permitted the area of windows required for light and air to be reduced, yet an even more radical vision began to be implemented that implicitly questioned the functional status of windows as elements necessary to promote human health through the provision of light and air. Certainly, the development of air-conditioning systems and mechanical ventilation in sealed commercial buildings provided evidence that the function of providing light and air was not intrinsically dependent on having operable windows that provided "natural" light and ventilation. Natural ventilation was the first casualty. Beginning in 1970, the UBC no longer required windows to be *openable* in habitable rooms as long as some fresh air was delivered by other means: "In lieu of openable windows for natural ventilation, a mechanical ventilation system may be provided. Such system shall be capable of providing two air changes per hour in all guest rooms, dormitories, habitable rooms, and in public corridors. One-fifth of the air supply shall be taken from the outside."[11] Ironically, the *option* of mechanical ventilation is now—for most new residences—a *requirement*, since it is no longer rational to assume that outside air will infiltrate through leaky windows and doors and, in doing so, provide sufficient fresh air to dilute indoor pollutants when those windows and doors are closed. And in parts of the world where outdoor air is too polluted to provide any consistent relief from indoor air pollution, it makes some sense to completely invert the assumptions made by those late 19th-century reformers—that the function of windows was to introduce natural light and air into buildings—and instead *prohibit* operable windows in such locations, relying instead on mechanical ventilation with effective filters.

Perhaps more surprising than the negation of natural ventilation is the gradual elimination of requirements for windows to provide natural light. Beginning with the 1970 UBC, skylights were allowed to provide natural light instead of windows; in the 1994 UBC, artificial (i.e., electric) light was permitted to replace daylight in kitchens only, with natural light still required in other habitable rooms; and finally, with the inauguration of the 2000 IBC, *all* spaces were given the option of using artificial light instead of natural light, with a minimum illumination requirement of only 10 footcandles (108 lux). Thus, 99 years after New York City's Tenement House Act of 1901 required operable windows in all rooms, a point was reached in the U.S. where—at least outside of New York City[12]—neither natural lighting nor natural ventilation was deemed necessary in any occupied room.

A discussion of light and air as functions of buildings would not be complete without placing such functionality in a political context. While modern building codes may have eliminated requirements for natural ventilation and daylight, requirements for the provision of *some sort* of light and air are unlikely to be challenged, since they can easily be justified on the basis of health and safety considerations. Yet such considerations are not absolute, and the boundary between health and safety, on the one hand (e.g., through the provision of light and air), and the freedom to use one's property as one sees fit, on the other hand, has often been contested.

This can be seen in the "Matter of Application of Jacobs," where the New York State Court of Appeals ruled in 1885 that an 1884 New York State Law entitled "An act to improve the public health by prohibiting the manufacture of cigars and preparation of tobacco in any form in tenement-houses in certain cases, and regulating the use of tenement-houses in certain cases" was unconstitutional.[13] What is most interesting about this case is not that the court attacked the "well-established health-related rationale for exercise of a state's police powers,"[14] but rather that it used rather extreme language in making a case for property and freedom. In other words, the opinion did not actually deny the right of governments to pass legislation designed to protect public health, but insisted on a clear and consistent rationale:

> When a health law is challenged in the courts as unconstitutional on the ground that it arbitrarily interferes with personal liberty and private property without due process of law, the courts must be able to see that it has at least in fact some relation to the public health, that the public health is the end actually aimed at, and that it is appropriate and adapted to that end. This we have not been able to see in this law, and we must, therefore, pronounce it unconstitutional and void.[15]

Yet the court's underlying bias in favor of property rights clearly shows up when it argues that *any* legislation curtailing property rights potentially leads us down a slippery slope towards autocratic government, thereby threatening our birthright of freedom:

> Such legislation may invade one class of rights to-day and another to-morrow, and if it can be sanctioned under the Constitution, while far removed in time we will not be far away in practical statesmanship from those ages when governmental prefects supervised the building of houses, the rearing of cattle, the sowing of seed and the reaping of grain, and governmental ordinances regulated the movements and labor of artisans, the rate of wages, the price of food, the diet and clothing of the people, and a large range of other affairs long since in all civilized lands regarded as outside of governmental functions. Such governmental interferences disturb the normal adjustments of the social fabric, and usually derange the delicate and complicated machinery of industry and cause a score of ills while attempting the removal of one.[16]

This notion of a slippery slope—with any governmental intervention posing a threat to property rights and freedom—is hardly an anachronism of 19th-century jurisprudence, but is alive and well in the modern Supreme

Court, supported by the Fifth and Fourteenth Amendments to the U.S. Constitution, the former preventing governmental "taking" of private property except for the public good and when compensated; and the latter prohibiting the state from depriving "any person of life, liberty, or property, without due process of law." For example, Supreme Court Justice Antonin Scalia, writing in *Lucas v. South Carolina Coastal Council* in 1992, was more than willing to cite Justice Oliver Wendell Holmes's opinion in *Pennsylvania Coal Co. v. Mahon et al.* (1922) which reprised the "slippery slope" argument made in the 1885 case. Georgetown Law Professor J. Peter Byrne, quoting Scalia quoting Holmes, concludes that Scalia's "assessment of property use regulations was warped by his fear that if 'the uses of private property were subject to unbridled, uncompensated qualification under the police power, "the natural tendency of human nature [would be] to extend the qualification more and more until at last private property disappear[ed]."'"[17]

Thus, the apparently self-evident functional requirements for light and air in buildings are regulated by governments through building codes that prescribe minimum window areas (or minimum levels of "artificial light" and/or mechanical ventilation) and, more indirectly, through zoning ordinances that regulate the massing or bulk of buildings (in part to ensure that light and air reach buildings and public rights-of-way). Yet the functional provision of minimum standards for public health and safety is constantly threatened by claims for the freedom to dispose of one's property without constraint. And while the trajectory of court opinions in the U.S.—at least since the 1926 validation of zoning in "Euclid v. Ambler"—seems to point in the direction of increasing governmental intervention on behalf of public health and safety, the advocates for freedom and the unbridled exercise of property rights have hardly conceded defeat: "Liberals might root against the government . . . But they should be careful what they wish for. The conservative majority can, and most likely will, rule against the government using broad theories that would also eat away at the constitutional foundations of the New Deal system, which is essential for protecting health and safety, the environment and much else."[18]

7
SECURITY

Functional requirements for building security address such things as the need to control entry (e.g., in stadiums, museums, homes, etc.; in short, in pretty much all building occupancies) and the prevention of damage from explosive devices. In the first case—to prevent or control entry—physical, electronic, and human means can be deployed (walls, gates, locks; motion sensors, alarms, video cameras; and guards, gatekeepers, bouncers). So much is self-evident and need not be belabored.

What is more interesting is the way in which both physical and psychological ("sociophysical") elements interact to create both the reality and the appearance of security. Creating a *real* barrier that is designed to prevent unauthorized access to a building (or to a city) is a never-ending contest between the technology of control and the technology of transgression. On the one hand, barrier design is intended to forestall access by unauthorized agents—mainly human—who might attempt to overcome or overwhelm the barrier's physical form by going over, under, or around it, or by penetrating through it. Medieval cities were therefore surrounded by thick and high walls; castles were surrounded by moats; and so on. Surfaces were constructed of materials that were hard enough, high enough, and continuous enough to repulse conventional would-be invaders. As a further disincentive to those who might challenge the integrity of such barriers, weapons could be deployed against invaders from the relatively protected and strategically advantageous sites created for that purpose within or behind the various barriers.

On the other hand, potential invaders might still succeed in breaching defensive barriers by being deceptive (Trojan Horse), technologically more sophisticated (battering ram, catapults, siege towers), or by using any number of alternate strategies that have evolved over time.

In contemporary society, the functional basis of building security presupposes not only the ownership of real property (enforced by state power) that divides a society's geographic surface area into individual parcels from which the owner may lawfully exclude everyone else; but also a pervasive antagonism among the various individuals and classes within that society that makes literal barriers to entry (reinforced by the threat of injury, death, or incarceration faced by would-be intruders) necessary.

As the technology of surveillance becomes more sophisticated and ubiquitous, the requirement for *physical* barriers that prevent access on the basis of strength, size, and continuity decreases, but is hardly eliminated. Closed-circuit television (CCTV) and other forms of electronic surveillance—including motion- or heat-sensing devices—can trigger alarms or provide identifying information; these act both as disincentive and, for those who nevertheless break through security barriers, as a means of identification and apprehension. The use and potential of surveillance as a deterrent to transgression, admittedly reaching new heights in the 21st century, was nevertheless understood long before the ubiquitous presence of cameras and other electronic devices. Thus, even in the 18th century, "the old simple schema of confinement and enclosure—thick walls, a heavy gate that prevents entering or leaving— began to be replaced by the calculation of openings, of filled and empty spaces, passages and transparencies."[1] The classic architectural manifestation of this notion is the so-called Panopticon developed by Jeremy Bentham (1748–1832) in which an observer, the agent of control, could surveille the building's inmates who were arranged in wings radiating from a central tower in which the control agent was situated (Fig.7.1). That these inmates—whether hospital patients, school children, or prisoners—*would not know* if they were being watched at any given time was the key insight. It was the mere potential of being watched that sufficed to keep them well behaved.

Yet, even modern surveillance devices can be overcome; the contest between control and transgression is hardly over. CCTV cameras can be disconnected or blocked; digital or physical surveillance records can be destroyed; masks can cover faces, increasing the difficulty of identification; gloves can prevent fingerprints (or DNA) from adhering to surfaces; innocent bystanders can be turned into hostages; security personnel, police, and judges can be bribed or otherwise coerced into complicity with criminal acts; and physical force—including bullets and bombs—can be used to confront and contest any power deployed in defense of property.

More importantly, modern interconnected digital networks can be breached, not merely to penetrate a physical space, but to disrupt architectural functions controlled through these networks, or to access

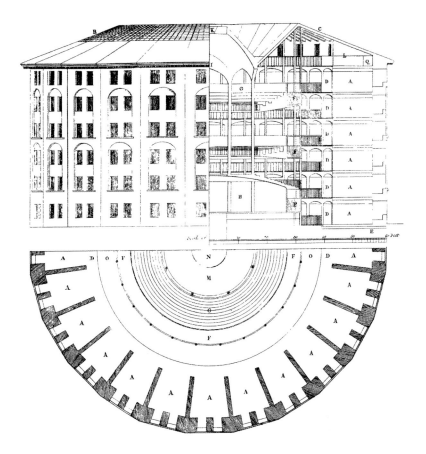

data contained on the networks. The infamous theft of 40 million credit
and debit card accounts at the American retail giant, Target, is an example
of data systems being breached, not to enter buildings or disrupt their
functionality, but for their own sake.[2] On the other hand, disruption of
building functionality can also be the desired outcome. For example,
"residents of two apartment buildings in Lappeenranta, a city of around
60,000 people in eastern Finland, were literally left in the cold [when]
environmental control systems in their buildings stopped working
[because of] a DDoS attack that took them down"[3] in 2016, where DDoS
stands for "distributed denial-of-service," that is, the deliberate assault
on a computer network with so many unwanted messages that normal
operation of the system becomes impossible. In fact, environmental

control (HVAC) systems are increasingly coordinated through building automation systems, such as BACnet ("Building Automation and Control Networks") in the U.S., a protocol first published by ANSI/ASHRAE in 1995. Such systems are often implemented through the internet so that heating, ventilation, and cooling devices can be controlled or monitored from remote locations. A paper published in 2014 discussing the threats to such systems concluded that "even if security features are available in standards they are commonly not integrated in devices or used in practice."[4] Aside from the confusion resulting from multiple protocols, the major issue to overcome, according to Justin Clacherty, is a lack of expertise: "When these systems are installed, the people involved in the deployment are typically electricians whose expertise centres on wiring and physical installation. Integration is often done by electricians who have moved on to different roles. However, security is rarely a discipline that these parties have great expertise in."[5]

In this context, the U.S. General Services Administration (GSA) has developed strategies to prevent security breaches, especially damage from bombs, by identifying zones within and outside any given building. Various mitigating measures can then be applied to the different zones, depending on the risk (Fig.7.2). For federal buildings, as an example, the "risk assessment [is] based upon the actual or perceived threat to the building (the events that must be defended against), the vulnerability of that building (the susceptibility to the threat), the consequences if an event should occur, and the probability of that event based upon a variety of factors."[6]

In the case of the building enclosure ("Zone 5"), the following possible actions are listed by the GSA: prevent access to vents/air intakes, design emergency egress to allow easy evacuation from a facility, place cameras and light fixtures to maximize visibility, harden the building structure and envelope, and design orientation and massing of building to lessen impact of explosion.[7]

All of these functional requirements for security are portrayed as a rational response to what is typically mischaracterized as human nature, but in reality derive from the economic compulsion to compete on the basis of one's property. The GSA, in formulating its security guidelines for buildings, puts an almost comical spin on how the unpleasant consequences of capitalism can be turned into something useful for its citizens:

7.2 The U.S. General Services Administration (GSA) identifies six site security zones in and around buildings.

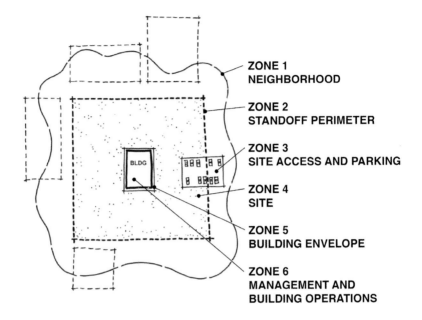

ZONE 1
NEIGHBORHOOD

ZONE 2
STANDOFF PERIMETER

ZONE 3
SITE ACCESS AND PARKING

ZONE 4
SITE

ZONE 5
BUILDING ENVELOPE

ZONE 6
MANAGEMENT AND
BUILDING OPERATIONS

The U.S. General Services Administration (GSA) sees the evolving need for security as an opportunity—to achieve the best design, contribute to the sustainability of the environment, create a portfolio of buildings that will endure into the future, provide safe and productive federal workplaces, and improve the communities in which we work.

In meeting these responsibilities, we demonstrate how thoughtful security design can represent permanence and encourage citizen participation. Increased setbacks can become active public spaces, physical restraints can serve as seating areas or landscape features, and new amenities can both increase the safety of federal employees and integrate our public buildings into their neighborhoods.[8]

There are also "sociophysical" aspects of building security that have been identified by proponents of *defensible space* to enable natural surveillance by residents, and to establish both legal and psychological territorial zones.[9] Such empirically derived wisdom about safety has two primary flaws. The first flaw is actually inherent in all empirically derived social science. By looking only at what exists, not only are the *reasons* for such patterns of behavior ignored, but—more fundamentally, and abstracting from such reasons—these prevailing conditions are often considered to be inevitable and unchangeable: a function of human nature. Yet even the empirical basis for such claims—that territoriality explains the form of traditional or primitive settlements—has been challenged. Bill Hillier, in his critique of Oscar Newman's influential book on *Defensible Space*, argues that this explanation, more often than not, "has failed miserably." He quotes the archaeologist Ruth Tringham, who "concluded that the territoriality/aggression argument 'would seem to have no support in either archaeological or ethnographic evidence: it is rather the simplistic ethnocentric concept of sophisticated guilt-ridden western investigators.' She added: 'The defense and physical demarcation of territory is by no means universal and is dependent on a large number of interrelated factors.'"[10]

Second, especially with respect to the "natural surveillance" of streets and yards by residents, there is both a sexist and racist undercurrent to the recommendations. The sexist component is the implicit idea that "eyes on the street" are provided mainly by women who stay at home while men are at work. This was undoubtedly true when Jane Jacobs wrote her landmark book with its famous discussion of sidewalk safety in the 1950s (*The Death and Life of Great American Cities* was published in 1961) and demonstrates the limitations of empirical observations. Thus, in the New Urbanism influenced town of Seaside, Florida, porches facing the street are rarely used and therefore "the social function for which they were designed (that is, to keep eyes on the street and as a place from which to greet passers-by) has not really been realized."[11]

The racist component is rarely explicit in such studies; rather, the preferred vocabulary involves "strangers," some of whom pose threats.[12] The relationship between abstract notions of "territoriality" and racism can be seen in historic segregation and redlining practices that created and preserved ethnically pure neighborhoods. "Redlining," writes Emily Badger, is not just "a practice that exists only in history and our re-tellings of it. . . . Neighborhoods were ranked and color-coded, and the D-rated ones—shunned for their 'inharmonious' racial groups—were typically outlined in red. . . . But black communities have warned that it still exists in subtler and changed forms, in bank tactics that have targeted these same neighborhoods for predatory lending, or in new patterns like 'retail redlining.' Some of the persistent redlining, though, still looks an awful lot like the original."[13]

This relationship can also be seen in the unspoken terror that enforces a de facto segregation in many American neighborhoods. Ta-Nehisi Coates, in *Between the World and Me*, writes to his son about their prior visits, first to Harlem, and then to Jane Jacobs's idyllic West Village in New York City:

> They [white folks] were utterly fearless. I did not understand it until I looked out on the street. That was where I saw white parents pushing double-wide strollers down *gentrifying Harlem boulevards* in T-shirts and jogging shorts. Or I saw them in conversation with each other, mother and father, while their sons commanded entire sidewalks with their tricycles. The galaxy belonged to them, and as terror was communicated to our children, I saw mastery communicated to theirs. And so when I remember pushing you in your stroller to other parts of the city, *the West Village for instance*, almost instinctively believing that you should see more, I remember feeling ill at ease, like I had borrowed someone else's heirloom, like I was traveling under an assumed name.[14]

And this relationship can be seen in the application of "neighborhood watch" strategies within certain neighborhoods; the case of Trayvon Martin is only one of many such instances: "On the night of February 26, 2012, in Sanford, Florida, United States, George Zimmerman fatally shot Trayvon Martin, a 17-year-old African American high school student. Zimmerman, a 28-year-old mixed-race Hispanic man, was the neighborhood watch coordinator for the gated community where Martin was temporarily living and where the shooting took place."[15] The ideological justification of cultural separation and "community" comes up again in Chapter 8; and the ideal of community along with the exclusionary concept of a "people" is discussed again in Chapter 14.

8
FUNCTION AS PATTERN

To propose a theory of architectural functionality in a comprehensive manner is, indeed, a daunting task, and I know of only one such attempt in modern times—Christopher Alexander's systematic investigation and compilation of "patterns" that address specific functional issues and interrelationships.[1] The idea of *patterns* as the basis of an all-encompassing functionality was not invented by Alexander; Frank Lloyd Wright used the term decades earlier to evoke a type of organization in which "purpose" (function) aligned with the sense of being "alive." Alexander's patterns respond explicitly to functional utilitarian considerations and are also intended to be "alive," echoing Wright's definition of "organic" as something that "applies to 'living' structure—a structure or concept wherein features or parts are so organized in form and substance as to be, applied to purpose, *integral*. Everything that 'lives' is therefore organic. The inorganic—the 'unorganized'—cannot *live*."[2]

Although Wright was far less precise and comprehensive than Alexander, his increasing reliance on the word "pattern" to describe his architectural intentions is striking. In his 1939 *Sir George Watson Lectures* in London, Wright asked rhetorically why civilization "is everywhere so jittery and miserable" and responded that—with the exception of his own vision of an organic architecture that acts as "a *pattern* for a free communal life"—"there has been no great vision, no real thought, which wisely accepted the law of change and went along with it, making *patterns for life* so free that to the life concerned the law of change need not mean unhappiness and torture."[3]

Wright had already written about patterns in the first edition of his *Autobiography*, published in 1932, but radically extended the scope of the term in the second edition, published in 1943; "pattern" now applied to everything from the smallest house (which "must be a pattern for more simplified and, at the same time, more gracious living"[4]) to the entire culture ("Civilization is this affair of Pattern"[5]). In fact, at least one passage from the first edition was consciously edited in the second edition, not only to replace an ellipsis with an em dash, but to clarify that the *pattern* of reality ("And—after all you will see that the pattern of reality *is* supergeometric"[6]), and not merely reality itself ("And . . . after all, reality *is* supergeometric"[7]), could cast "a spell or a charm over any geometry, and is such a spell in itself."[8]

Alexander, too, wrote about patterns years before formalizing his "pattern language," beginning with *Community and Privacy* (co-authored with Serge Chermayeff) in 1963: "Forces have a characteristic pattern, and the good form is in equilibrium with the pattern, almost as though it were lying at the neutral point of a vector field of forces . . . The first step in the process of design, therefore, involves an explicit statement of the forces at work and the pressure pattern the form is to reflect."[9] In *Notes on the Synthesis of Form* (1964), Alexander argued that mathematics "can become a very powerful tool indeed if it is used to explore the conceptual order and *pattern* which a problem presents to its designer."[10] Alexander's patterns, in their mature form, emerged out of the diagrams he created in this earlier book: "These diagrams, which, in my more recent work, I have been calling *patterns*," he wrote in the preface to the 1973 edition of *Notes*, "are the key to the process of creating form."[11]

But whereas Wright refused to speculate about how such patterns might evolve in the future ("As for the definite future pattern of the community life in such circumstances, who knows just what any community life of the future is going to be like? The old relationships are bound to change"[12]) and never systematically articulated an inventory of functional patterns for contemporary life, Alexander tackled the problem of functionality head-on:

Each pattern is a three-part rule, which expresses a relation between a certain context, a problem, and a solution. As an element of language, a pattern is an instruction, which shows how this spatial configuration can be used, over and over again, to resolve the given system of forces, wherever the context makes it relevant. The pattern is, in short, at the same time a thing, which happens in the world, and the rule which tells us how to create that thing, and when we must create it. It is both a process and a thing; both a description of a thing which is alive, and a description of the process which will generate that thing.[13]

According to Edward De Zurko, this strategy of isolating and logically compiling problems and solutions has its roots in the "rational mathematico-syllogistic method recommended by Leibniz and applied

. . . to architecture among other disciplines"[14] by the 18th-century German philosopher Christian Wolff, whose eighth theorem in his book, *Elements of Architecture*, states:

> A window must be wide enough to allow two persons to place themselves conveniently at it. . . . It is a common custom to place one's-self at a window, and look from it in company with another person. As now it is the duty of the architect to consult in all respects the intentions of the builder . . . he will necessarily make the window wide enough to allow two persons to place themselves at it—q.e.d.[15]

A comparison with Alexander's Pattern No. 180 for a window place is instructive, not because Alexander's recommendation is the same as Wolff's, but because both Alexander and Wolff first identify a functional window "problem" and then propose a logical solution to that problem, based on empirical observation. Alexander writes: "These kinds of windows which create 'places' next to them are not simply luxuries; they are *necessary*. A room which does not have a place like this seldom allows you to feel fully comfortable or perfectly at ease. Indeed, a room without a window place may keep you in a state of perpetual unresolved conflict and tension—slight, perhaps, but definite."[16]

Functional problems emerge where patterns are not followed, for example in seminar rooms at University of California Berkeley's College of Environmental Design that, according to Alexander, are

> functionally defective in a number of ways. First of all, a long narrow table, and the long narrow group of people which form around it, are not suitable for intense discussion; this is a seminar room—it should be more nearly square. Second, the position of the blackboard with respect to the window means that half of the people in the room see the window reflected on the blackboard, and can't read what is written there—the blackboard should be opposite the window. Third, because the window is so large, and so low, people who sit near it appear silhouetted to those who are sitting further away. It is extremely difficult to talk properly with someone seen in silhouette—too many of the subtle expressions of the face get lost. Seminar communication suffers. The windows should be above the height of a sitting person's head.[17]

While Alexander's compilation has ambitious and somewhat mystical goals—to describe a "quality without a name" that *provides a subtle kind of freedom from inner contradictions*"[18]—and while his thorough and nuanced examination contains much useful guidance, it also has two major flaws. First, his recommendations rely on "feelings," based on the experience of what currently exists, to justify certain patterns. Yet such a "truth" is inherently limited. Alexander's contention that "people who come from the same culture do to a remarkable extent agree about the way that different patterns make them feel"[19] not only abstracts from the diversity of "cultures" in increasingly heterogeneous contemporary societies, but also from well-known variations in how humans—even from within the same cultural group—actually experience form and space. For example, people with phobias (e.g., acrophobia, agoraphobia, claustrophobia) or with conflicting tolerances for noise vs. quiet, or light vs. dark, or day vs. night, may well have specific and contradictory spatial preferences.[20]

It is true that some of these conflicts might be resolved precisely through the kind of methodology developed by Alexander, but the enormous variation in human responses to environmental conditions makes it likely that at least some individual preferences may fall through the cracks in someone else's pattern language. For example, compare Alexander's claim that "high buildings make people crazy"[21] with Louis Sullivan's counter-claim that "loftiness is to the artist-nature its thrilling aspect" and constitutes "the very open organ-tone in its appeal."[22] Of course, Sullivan's defense of tallness is not a scientific refutation of Alexander's claim, but it does point out the difficulty of creating functional patterns intended to be applied more or less universally (or even within a single subculture).

Moreover, as Herbert Marcuse writes in *Reason and Revolution: Hegel and the Rise of Social Theory*, truth is never merely about facts (that exist in the present), but about human potential and the freedom to reach that potential: "Man alone has the power of self-realization, the power to be a self-determining subject in all processes of becoming, for he alone has an understanding of potentialities and a knowledge of 'notions.' His very existence is the process of actualizing his potentialities, of molding his life according to the notions of reason."[23] Hegel, according to Marcuse, thought of truth as being something "not only attached to propositions and judgments . . . but of reality in process. Something is true if it is what it can be, fulfilling all its objective possibilities. In Hegel's language, it is then identical with its 'notion.'"[24] Alexander's patterns, in opposition to this view, are rooted in what currently exists rather than in what could or should exist. In fact, Alexander considers it futile or non-productive to say, "It should be otherwise." Instead, "the fact that [one of his patterns] is capable of making us feel at one with ourselves is based on thoroughgoing *acceptance of these forces as they really are*."[25]

Second, Alexander's focus on spatial or formal relations alternately relies upon, and abstracts from, destructive and exploitative social relations. On the one hand, and as an example of the former, Alexander justifies racial and cultural separation by arguing that

> when subcultures are separated from one another by communal land, each one can grow in its own way . . . this certainly comes from the fact that we feel good in places where this pattern does exist. In places like the Chinatown of San Francisco, or in Sausalito, which are vivid with their own life because they are a little separate from the nearby communities, we feel good.[26]

This justification of racial or cultural separation on the basis of "feeling good" with one's "own kind" is an argument shared by both white separatists (such as Iraq war veteran Kynan Dutton, who explains to a *New York Times* journalist that "they're a normal family who just want to live with their own kind—in this case, other white people"[27]) and Black separatists (such as Malcolm X, who, before leaving the Nation of Islam in 1964 and renouncing such views, spoke of "complete separation or some land of our own in a country of our own"[28]).

Alexander specifically denies that *his* attitude is racist, arguing that "a great variety of subcultures in a city is not a racist pattern which forms ghettos, but a pattern of opportunity which allows a city to contain a multitude of different ways of life with the greatest possible intensity."[29] And it is true that enthusiasm about cultural identity—a position consistent with spatially distinct ethnic or racial neighborhoods—is hardly a deviant position within U.S. political discourse:

> Nobody finds it objectionable when politicians on the campaign trail seek the 'Latino vote' or the 'African-American vote,' i.e., address people as members of an ethnically defined 'community' to whose

particular interests they vow to give priority attention as office holders. Regarding and treating people in terms of their race like this is seen to have nothing to do with racism, as if ethnic characteristics could be appropriately taken into account without there being such a thing as unequal treatment. For all sides, ethnic distinction is fully consistent with America's highest principles of all citizens being free and equal.[30]

On the other hand, and as an example of how Alexander's "patterns" *abstract from* social relations, consider how he understands "stress" as the outcome of bad spaces, ignoring other societal sources. For example, he writes that "the 'bad' patterns—the window which does not work, the dead courtyard, the badly located workplace—these stress us, undermine us, affect us continuously. Indeed, in this fashion, each bad pattern in our environment constantly reduces us, cuts us down, reduces our own ability to meet new challenges, reduces our capacity to live, and helps to make us dead . . ."[31] Later, Alexander describes the "morphological feeling" underlying all pattern generation:

> A pulsating fluid, but nonetheless definite entity swims in your mind's eye. It is a geometrical image, it is far more than the knowledge of the problem; it is the knowledge of the problem, coupled with the knowledge of the kinds of geometries which will solve the problem, and coupled with the feeling which is created by that kind of geometry solving that problem. It is above all a feeling—a morphological feeling. This morphological feeling, which cannot be exactly stated, but can only be crudely hinted at by any one precise formulation, is the heart of every pattern.[32]

And how does anyone know if a pattern works? "To do this, we must rely on feelings more than intellect . . . The fact is that we feel good in the presence of a pattern which resolves its forces."[33] In other words, Alexander sees societal "stress" as fundamentally formal and spatial, rather than having anything to do with property, competition, capitalist relations of production, and the entire range of destructive outcomes that come about on this basis.

Alexander's use of the generic pronouns "we," "us," "our," and "your" is symptomatic of his abstraction from the class society where such all-inclusive pronouns mask essential divisions between those that own and control necessary social resources, and those forced to sell their labor-power in order to survive. Furthermore, he insists that creating harmony and making people feel good—rather than creating disharmony and inducing people to feel strange ("making strange," the concept of defamiliarization, is discussed in Chapter 9)—are essential functions of architecture. On the one hand, this attitude abstracts from social conditions that have produced an epidemic of anxiety and depression within contemporary society,[34] by arguing that harmonious *formal or spatial* qualities are the necessary and sufficient conditions such that "urban man may once more find his life in equilibrium."[35] On the other hand, Alexander acknowledges the ubiquity of anxiety in contemporary society, but evinces neither interest in its sources nor sympathy for its aesthetic manifestations. "Don't you think there is enough anxiety at present?" he asks fellow architect Peter Eisenman. "Do you really think we need to manufacture more anxiety in the forms of buildings?"[36] Alexander thus not only conflates dissonant aesthetic expression—in some cases reflecting an anxiety-producing culture—with the anxiety itself, but also abstracts from the competitive forces which both trigger anxiety and marginalize his own architectural ideas.[37] We revisit this conversation in Chapter 9.

PART II

THE FUNCTION OF EXPRESSION

9
INTRODUCTORY CONCEPTS

There is a tension between the art and science of architecture originating in the suspicion that focusing too intently on practical and utilitarian considerations could overwhelm the conceptual and abstract fantasies that increasingly characterize architectural style.[1] The Roman architect, Vitruvius, would not have understood the basis for such a fear, as he considered the formal or abstract qualities of architecture (manifested in *venustas*, or beauty) to be a complementary function of architecture, along with *utilitas* and *firmitas* (utility and strength). From his standpoint, there was no conflict between the expressive and utilitarian functions—the art and science—of architecture. So why is there one now? The short answer is that architects, and their clients, are driven by competition to exploit the inexhaustibly mutable expressive potential of buildings. Modernist abstraction, discussed in Chapter 11, has become increasingly disengaged not just from conventional elements of construction, for example, columns, walls, windows, roofs, and so on, but more importantly from an appreciation of structural and control layer theories, to the extent that these building science principles may appear to threaten the hegemony of unfettered architectural expression.

It is this implicit threat that drives a wedge between the rigors of building technology and the freedom of design, affecting not only speculative or "theoretical" unbuilt projects, but also the production of real buildings. At the extreme, the result—for both architecture students and practitioners who have internalized a design method almost completely disengaged from conventional building science principles (aka "reality")—may be a palpable antipathy toward the disciplines of structure, control layer theory, and even the rudiments of what might be called sustainable design.

To dig deeper into this conundrum, one must examine the nature of *venustas*, the most subjective and contentious element within Vitruvius's functional triad. The first thing one uncovers is the difficulty in pinning down its relation to functionality. This is because the word "function" is used in two ways. First, function is used to identify purely utilitarian qualities. For example, the function of a chair, in this sense, would be to provide a structurally and ergonomically adequate surface for sitting. Second, function is used in a broader sense, to include not only utilitarian aspects, but also subjective and expressive qualities. For example, the chair might also function as an article of conspicuous consumption, or as a means of aligning its owner with a particular stylistic tendency, and so on. Denise Scott Brown has fashioned a similar argument using a table, rather than a chair: "It seems that the functions of so simple and general an object as a table may be many and various, related at one end to the most prosaic of activities and at the other to the unmeasurable, symbolic and religious needs of man."[2]

Difficulties and confusion emerge when these two meanings of function are not made clear. For example, if "functional" architecture is defined as something, per Hermann Muthesius, without "superficial forms of decoration, a design strictly following the purpose that the work should serve,"[3] one can always argue that precisely those things excluded—decoration, ornament, or any other "superficial" elements or strategies—are also part of "the purpose that the work should serve." But this apparent paradox is just an artifact of the alternative meanings of function, nothing more. One must be careful when arguing that the utilitarian meaning of function excludes both gratuitous *and* symbolic elements. More precisely—since one can neither exclude "symbolism" nor, in general, prescribe what subjective responses will arise in the presence of a work of architecture—this first, utilitarian, meaning of functionality excludes only those elements considered "decorative" or gratuitous and therefore non-utilitarian.

A decorative element embedded in an architectural facade *really* is an element of the building—it is actually present, can be seen, and consists of tangible material like brick or stone or paint—whereas a so-called symbolic element is little more than a theoretical sleight-of-hand in which a subjective interpretation of a building is given a tangible basis, as if it is actually present (as an "element") *in* the materials of the building itself. We tend to say: "This food *is* delicious," as if being delicious is an absolute quality of the food, rather than saying: "*I* find this food delicious," thereby acknowledging the subjectivity of taste.

Physical or formal aspects of a building may well trigger various subjective responses in individual beholders. And just as a chef cannot create a dish that is objectively delicious, it is the beholders of architecture, rather than the building's designers, who "construct" its meaning. This does not preclude a special role for critics and connoisseurs, but, on the other hand, neither does it give their (often contradictory) opinions an objective status. And designers, working within a subculture in which particular formal strategies are recognized and valued, may well provide precisely the types of coded forms of expression that are recognized as such within those architectural subcultures. However, even in such cases, the formal codes to which they subscribe are external to the forms themselves and must be internalized by the beholder if the intended expression is to be "properly" understood. Those without knowledge of, or interest in, such codes will interpret the same forms through a different lens.

That symbolic expression cannot be found in the physical materials of art or architecture does not mean that such expression does not exist and has no function within artistic production. It is possible to admit some common understandings of symbolic expression within subcultures or even entire cultures, always, however, with the disclaimer that such subjective interpretations can be fractured, revised, or otherwise transformed by individuals or by entire groups. Tracing such movements of subjective phenomena is at best a speculative task, and probably hopeless, given the idiosyncratic psychological content that directs any individual perception towards some subjective interpretation. The Rorschach test, to cite but one example, exploits precisely this indeterminacy in attempting to draw psychological conclusions from the multiplicity of subjective interpretations that can be made from the same formal design.

Commentators on fashion and taste also challenge the idea that it is possible to "design" symbolic content. Joshua Rothman, discussing the "vision" of J. Crew, suggests that the *meaning* of certain clothing items during "the Obama years" changed when Donald Trump became president: "During the Obama years, nostalgia might have seemed harmless, even admirable, but today it feels like a troubled and doubtful impulse. Does it make sense for young, urban men to dress up like Rust Belt factory workers, or for women to embrace the style of Hyannis Port in the nineteen-sixties? The answers to those questions have changed over the past six months."[4] One year later, analysts concerned with the symbolic content of fashion had an even more explicit conundrum: what meaning to attribute to the

"I Really Don't Care" jacket worn by Melania Trump, the First Lady, on her way to a children's shelter in Texas. Was it "insensitive," "heartless," and "unthinking"; or was it just a jacket with "no hidden message"? The divergent theories that emerged in the aftermath of "Jacket-gate" reinforce the notion that it is the "beholders" that assign meaning to an object, even one—in this case—where the *apparent* meaning is literally written on the back of the jacket. Clearly, then, the artists themselves (or the clients who display the "artwork") also have no magic power to embed meaning in the object. Even when an intention may be present in the artist's (or client's) mind, there is no way to guarantee that the intended meaning will be properly understood. In the case of Ms. Trump, "between intention and analysis an enormous gulf can exist" and whatever she may have been thinking, "this time it may have backfired."[5] Even the meaning of a plain white coat—the type often worn by doctors and other health care workers—is subject to evolving and diverging symbolic interpretations. While some doctors continue to think of the white coat in positive terms "as a defining symbol of the profession," others—influenced by studies showing that these garments "are frequently contaminated with strains of harmful and sometimes drug-resistant bacteria associated with hospital-acquired infections"—find the meaning far more ominous.[6]

There is, nevertheless, a tendency to think of aesthetic objects (buildings, paintings, songs, etc.) either as potentially expressive, solely on the basis of their form, or as communicative devices, analogous to language. In the first case, we could cite the mythology propounded by architects like Le Corbusier that Platonic solids are intrinsically beautiful. In the second case, Charles Osgood and his co-authors make the "communication" argument explicitly in their seminal book from 1957, *The Measurement of Meaning*:

> Like ordinary linguistic messages, the aesthetic product is a Janus-faced affair; it has the dual character of being at once the result of responses encoded by one participant in the communicative act (the creator) and the stimulus to be decoded by the other participants (the appreciators). Aesthetic products differ, perhaps, from linguistic messages by being more continuously than discretely coded (e.g., colors and forms in a painting can be varied continuously whereas the phonemes that discriminate among word-forms vary by all-or-nothing quanta called

distinctive features). They also differ, perhaps, in being associated more with connotative, emotional responses in sources and receivers than with denotative reactions. ... But nevertheless, to the extent that the creators of aesthetic products are able to influence the meanings and emotions experienced by their audiences by manipulations in the media of their talent, we are dealing with communications.[7]

Yet this notion that a work of architecture—or any aesthetic object—can have a particular meaning embedded in it—meaning which, by analogy to language, is both *intended* by the architect and able to be *decoded* by the beholder (or "appreciator," using Osgood's term)—is flawed. Mark Gelernter traces the origin of the idea that material objects do not actually contain "secondary" qualities of beauty or expression to Galileo (1564–1642) who wrote that "tastes, odors, colors and so forth are no more than mere names . . . and that they have their habitation only in the sensorium." John Locke (1632–1704) borrowed Galileo's distinction between such primary and secondary (subjective) qualities; and the Scottish philosophers Francis Hutcheson (1694–1746) and David Hume (1711–1776) continued this line of reasoning, the former concluding that "were there no mind with a sense of beauty to contemplate objects, I see not how they could be called beautiful," and the latter writing that "it is almost impossible not to feel a predilection for that which suits our particular turn and disposition. Such preferences are innocent and unavoidable, and can never reasonably be the object of dispute, because there is no standard by which they can be decided."[8]

Even the premise that artists *have* "intentions"—that they "know" what they intend to communicate—and that decoded responses of beholders are somehow reliable cannot be substantiated. Unlike the denotative function of language where, for example, the sentence "That is a cat" has no likely ambiguity in its intention (as a description) or in its decoding by a beholder, *architecture has no denotative function*, except in the trivial sense that gas stations, elementary schools, office buildings, and so on communicate their utilitarian functions through their form (see Chapter 10). Architecture as an *expressive* art, however, is analogous to the *connotative* use of language, which proves, not that architecture communicates like language, but rather that *language can also be employed aesthetically*, like architecture.

But in this latter case, neither language nor architecture is being created with explicit and objective intentions and neither language nor architecture can be decoded with any sense of objective certainty. This is because it is impossible to ascertain the motivations of architects that inform their creative process, and it is equally impossible to validate the process of decoding through which beholders assign meaning to works of architecture. Without being certain about the architect's and beholder's motivation in creating particular expressive forms or assigning meaning to a work of architecture, the whole project of intentionality crashes to the ground. According to Erich Fromm:

> Courageous behavior may be motivated by ambition so that a person will risk his life in certain situations in order to satisfy his craving for being admired; it may be motivated by suicidal impulses which drive a person to seek danger because, consciously or unconsciously, he does not value his life and wants to destroy himself; it may be motivated by a sheer lack of imagination so that a person acts courageously because he is not aware of the danger awaiting him; finally, it may be determined by genuine devotion to the idea or aim for which a person acts, a motivation which is conventionally assumed to be the basis of courage. Superficially the behavior in all these instances is the same in spite of the different motivations.[9]

Just as it is hardly clear whether courageous people are aware of their own (true) motivations, or whether beholders of courageous acts can properly decode the true intentions underlying such acts, it is similarly unwise to draw any conclusions about the intention—the meaning—underlying works of architecture. Nor is it necessary to invoke an "unconscious" source for this uncertainty as does Fromm, following Freud. The false consciousness of both architects (with respect to their creative processes) and beholders of architecture (with respect to their conclusions about architecture's meaning) is sufficient to explain both intentions and judgments about architectural meaning without recourse to unconscious motives: "When people put their definitely *free will* into practice on the basis of false consciousness, they are doing nothing other than making their individuality *obedient* to the dictates of capital and state in any number of different ways."[10] It is within this larger context that the underlying meaning of architecture—building made fashionable for competition—will be discussed in Chapter 15.

E.H. Gombrich refers to a "function of art" in explaining the radical transformation within Greek art between the 6th and 4th centuries B.C.: "Surely," he writes, "only a change in the whole function of art can explain such a revolution."[11] That such artistic functionality carries over to works of architecture is a commonplace in architectural writing, although confusion in the use of the term "function" is equally common. For example, Christian Norberg-Schulz, in discussing three functions (he calls them "purposes") of architecture, lists "the functional-practical, the milieu-creating and the symbolizing aspects"—in other words, he considers being "functional" as but one of three functions of architecture. The two other functions of architecture are, in this formulation, not "functional."[12]

Other writers on architecture insist that being "functional" is not even architecture's primary function. Sigfried Giedion, according to Karsten Harries, "reaffirmed what he took to be the main task [i.e., the main *function*] facing contemporary architecture, 'the interpretation of a way of life valid for our period.'"[13] Along these same lines, Harries proposes to extend to architecture Paul Valéry's claim that the function of poetry is "to create an artificial and ideal order of a material of vulgar origin." Harries writes that the theorists Tzonis and Lafaivre "proclaim that 'the poetic identity of a building depends not on its stability, or its function, or on the efficiency of the means of its production, but on the way in which all the above have been limited, bent, and subordinated by purely formal requirements.'"[14] In other words, according to Tzonis and Lafaivre, the function of a building (to create a "poetic identity") comes about by *subordinating its utilitarian function* to formal concerns.

Aside from assigning architecture the non-utilitarian function of expressing the idealized zeitgeist of the period or, perhaps, the tortured soul (poetic identity) of the individual artist, the early 20th-century concept of "defamiliarization" is also often invoked; here, the function of architectural expression is to "make strange" what otherwise might be taken for granted and therefore not really noticed. At the extreme, we enter into territory typically broached by charlatans, comedians, or logicians who gleefully relate linguistic paradoxes such as that of the Cretan who claims that all Cretans are liars (and so must be telling the truth). In the realm of architecture, the analogous condition is a building with the anti-heroic function of being *dysfunctional*. Alison and Peter Smithson, for example, proposed in 1957 that "the word 'functional' must now include so-called irrational and symbolic values."[15] This sentiment gets echoed and even amplified by some contemporary architects and engineers: Rem Koolhaas writes that the work of engineer Cecil Balmond expresses "doubt, arbitrariness, mystery and even mysticism."[16] A more conventional spin on the function of defamiliarization is attributed to the architect Le Corbusier, who is said to have "defined architecture as having to do with a window which is either too large or too small, but never the right size. Once it was the right size it was no longer functioning."[17]

This idea of defamiliarization would have been anathema to 19th-century theorists like John Ruskin, or his contemporary Edward Lacy Garbett; the latter would have seen only ugliness in buildings with such "immoral" qualities: "I cannot but regard the perfection of domestic architecture as an embodied courtesy," wrote Garbett in 1850. "And will any one dare to say that this courtesy is useless?"[18] Well, yes: many architects—and not only in and after the 20th century—celebrated precisely this lack of courtesy, although their stance was contested. A classic confrontation over this issue occurred in a 1982 debate between Peter Eisenman and Christopher Alexander. In the following excerpt, the two architect-theorists discuss the Town Hall at Logroño (Fig.9.1) designed by Rafael Moneo in 1973–1974:

CA: The thing that strikes me about your friend's building—if I understood you correctly—is that somehow in some intentional way it is not harmonious. That is, Moneo intentionally wants to produce an effect of disharmony. Maybe even of incongruity.

PE: That is correct.

CA: I find that incomprehensible. I find it very irresponsible. I find it nutty. I feel sorry for the man. I also feel incredibly angry because he is fucking up the world. . . . Don't you think there is enough anxiety at present? Do you really think we need to manufacture more anxiety in the form of buildings?

PE: . . . What I'm suggesting is that if we make people so comfortable in these nice little structures of yours, that we might lull them into thinking that everything's all right, Jack, which it isn't. And so the role [function] of art or architecture might be just to remind people that everything wasn't all right.[19]

9.1   Rafael Moneo's
Town Hall at Logroño.

Alexander, representing the forces of politeness and comfort, asks Eisenman: "Don't you think there is enough anxiety at present? Do you really think we need to manufacture more anxiety in the form of buildings?" Eisenman's response, justifying the disorienting or upsetting qualities of some avant-garde architecture, is that people are thereby reminded "that everything wasn't all right." A similar argument is made by Herbert Marcuse, the German-American philosopher and political theorist, who writes that

> a work of art can be called revolutionary if, by virtue of the aesthetic transformation, it represents, in the exemplary fate of individuals, the prevailing unfreedom and the rebelling forces, thus breaking through the mystified (and petrified) social reality, and opening the horizon of change (liberation) . . . The aesthetic transformation becomes a vehicle of recognition and indictment. *But this achievement presupposes a degree of autonomy which withdraws art from the mystifying power of the given and frees it for the expression of its own truth.* Inasmuch as man and nature are constituted by an unfree society, their repressed and distorted potentialities can be represented only in an estranging form.[20]

But it is hardly clear that architecture has the necessary "autonomy" that Marcuse suggests it must have as a revolutionary medium. Unlike the production of literature—the art form that Marcuse is primarily interested in—the *appearance* of architecture (where appearance is used in the double sense of what it looks like, *and* its coming into existence) is contingent upon, first, a patron whose interests the architecture serves; and, second, the literal deployment of wealth and power in order to create (bring into existence) the physical elements of architecture. It is true that this first condition could elicit "revolutionary" form, where such formal qualities might serve the patron (client); but that alone cannot overcome the second criterion. It may well be that in literature the revolutionary thing is its printing and distribution as much as the aesthetics of the work itself. The relative ease of printing and distribution, compared to the creation of construction documents and then the actual construction of a building, is, at least in this respect, what separates literature from architecture.

Even if a "disturbing" work of architecture somehow comes into being, its power to "open up the horizon of change (liberation)," being based on the feelings it elicits rather than on conclusions drawn from a logical explanation, puts it immediately into competition with other emotion-based content supplied in much greater quantities by the ideologically driven representatives and apologists of wealth and power. Neil Leach describes how Walter Benjamin, for example, "explored the problem of how Fascism used aesthetics to celebrate war" and how "it could be extrapolated from Benjamin's argument that aesthetics," rather than opening up revolutionary horizons, "brings about an anaesthetization of the political."[21]

That symbolic content can and should be expressed by a building's outward form is nevertheless taken as self-evident in much architectural theorizing. Christian Norberg-Schulz, for example, writes: "During the great epochs of the past certain forms had always been reserved for certain tasks. The classical orders were used with caution outside churches and palaces, and the dome, for instance, had a very particular function as a symbol of heaven."[22] He goes on to argue that not only did such forms correspond to particular social functions, but that there is a physiological (emotional) basis for assigning particular forms to these functions:

> The psychologist Arnheim discusses this problem [i.e., the structural similarity between content and form] in detail and maintains that we have the best reasons to assume that particular arrangements of lines and shapes correspond to particular emotional states. Or rather we should say that particular structures have certain limited possibilities for receiving contents. We do not play a Viennese waltz at a funeral.[23]

Actually, we may well play up-beat music at funerals, for example, as part of the jazz funeral tradition in New Orleans. In other words, there is no intrinsic correspondence between functional activities and the manner in which they are expressed. Some people fear tight spaces; others open spaces. How could one possibly assign some singular meaning to space given the divergent ways in which the same space is experienced? Norberg-Schulz adds that the perception requires "training and instruction ... A *common order* is called *culture*. In order that culture may become common, it has to be taught and learned. It therefore depends upon common symbol-systems, or rather, it corresponds to these symbol-systems and their behavioral effects."[24] Well, of course, if one is *told* how to interpret a form, the connections can be memorized and regurgitated. Aside from internalizing the meaning of specific symbols, the mere suggestion of an expressive theory, however arbitrary and subjective, might well affect one's subsequent experience. For example, after reading historian Heinrich Wölfflin's argument that "we judge every object by analogy with our own bodies," and that therefore any "object—even if completely dissimilar to ourselves—will ... transform itself immediately into a creature, with head and foot, back and front,"[25] it is quite possible to start imagining such zoomorphic qualities in buildings or other objects.

Similarly, certain forms—by virtue of being uniquely congruent with the activities they support *and, therefore, express*—have a relatively stable and widely shared symbolic content. And it is also true that, within a given time and place, the expression of poverty, wealth, and other more subtle distinguishing marks of a class society may well be manifested by formal means. Cole Roskam, for example, makes the case that the characteristic constructional elements of traditional Chinese buildings "over time ... took on greater representational significance. Clear hierarchical rankings of buildings determined the particular proportions used, which in turn informed column height, beam span, and the number of bracket sets."[26]

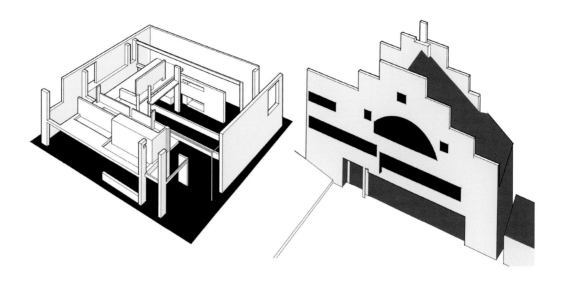

But this is an inadequate model for understanding contemporary societies, which are characterized by multiple and shifting subcultures. What, for example, would constitute the "common symbol-systems" of Peter Eisenman's House I and Venturi and Rauch's D'Agostino House (Fig.9.2), both projects conceived in 1968? Any answer, in my view, must distinguish between formal modes of expression ("symbol-systems"), which are evidently quite diverse, and the overarching *function* of such expression, which—consistent with the competition that drives the multiplicity of formal outcomes—always serves to reinforce and validate the various ideologies associated with capitalist freedom: on one side of the coin, democracy and community; on the other side, wealth and power (more on this in Chapter 14). Yet the expression of freedom, triggered by the functional necessity to serve as a mode of competition, may well result in dysfunctional buildings (as argued in Chapter 15).

In that sense, and in spite of differences in their formal attributes, the architecture of Eisenman and Venturi (and everyone else) has the same overarching cultural function. It is precisely in supporting that function that the task of reconciling the increasingly deviant manifestations of *venustas* with building science principles (*utilitas* and *firmitas*) grinds to a halt. Having reached this impasse, the struggle with reality experienced by both students and practitioners of architecture—struggling to become accomplices within this maladaptive mode of production—will not soon be assuaged.

9.2   Peter Eisenman's House I (*left*) and Venturi and Rauch's D'Agostino House (*right*), both projects conceived in 1968, provide some evidence that no single zeitgeist can be identified within contemporary societies.

10
EXPRESSION OF UTILITY

Most of what counts as the expression of *utilitas*—that is, the expression of those utilitarian functions or activities that a building is intended to support—has developed incrementally, over time, within particular cultures. This happens to the extent that the forms associated with particular activities became familiar and recognizable as such: gas stations look a certain way (like gas stations), and so the form becomes an expression of—a symbol of—"gas station." Elementary schools look a certain way (like elementary schools), and so the form becomes an expression of—a symbol of—"elementary school." Office buildings look a certain way (like office buildings), and so the form becomes an expression of—a symbol of—"office building"; and so on. If this appears tautological, it is because this type of expression is nothing more than the equation of the appearance of a building type with the *symbolic expression* corresponding to that building type's appearance. This type of self-evident expression permits humans within a given time and place to read (understand) the utilitarian functions assigned to much of the built environment.

To the extent that utility fosters expression through this simple process of association, such expression simply communicates a self-evident purpose or function. A more radical tradition in architectural theory goes further, equating utility with *venustas*, or fitness with beauty, mostly through an analogy to natural form. The idea is that when something is designed, or evolves to fit its purpose precisely, it then requires no further ornamentation or elaboration: it will be beautiful *because* it is functional. Joseph Gwilt, to cite but one example of the articulation of this principle, writes in the 1867 edition of his *Encyclopedia of Architecture*:

> Throughout nature beauty seems to follow the adoption of forms suitable to the expression of the end. In the human form, there is no part, considered in respect to the end for which it was formed by the great Creator, that in the eye of the artist, or rather, in this case the

better judge, the anatomist, is not admirably calculated for the function it has to discharge; and without the accurate representation of those parts in discharge of their several functions, no artist by means of mere expression, in the ordinary meaning of that word, can hope for celebrity.[1]

By the early 20th century, this type of form, created in a manner analogous to natural processes, was given the name "organic," as described in 1907 by Samuel Taylor Coleridge in his *Essays and Lectures on Shakespeare*:

> The form is mechanic, when on any given material we impress a predetermined form, not necessarily arising out of the properties of the material; as when to a mass of wet clay we give whatever shape we wish it to retain when hardened. The organic form, on the other hand, is innate; it shapes, as it develops, itself from within, and the fulness of its development is one and the same with the perfection of its outer form. Such as the life is, such is the form.[2]

Several years later, in 1914, Frank Lloyd Wright adopted the word "organic" to describe his own architecture ("By organic architecture I mean an architecture that *develops* from within outward in harmony with the conditions of its being as distinguished from one that is *applied* from without."[3]), and, 25 years later, in his George Watson Lectures delivered in London, Wright fleshed out the idea that beautiful (organic) form was the "common-sense" outcome of function and materials:

> So here I stand before you preaching organic architecture: declaring organic architecture to be the modern ideal and the teaching so much needed if we are to see the whole of life, and to now serve the whole of life, holding no 'traditions' essential to the great TRADITION. Nor cherishing any preconceived form fixing upon us either past super-sense if you prefer, present or future, but—instead—exalting the simple laws of common sense—or of—determining form by way of the nature of materials, the nature of purpose so well understood that a bank will not look like a Greek temple, a university will not look like a cathedral, nor a fire-engine house resemble a French château, or what have you? Form follows Function? Yes, but more important now *Form and Function are One*.[4]

The idea that a logical and precise attention to functionality will inevitably lead to beauty can be seen as a middle ground between two extreme positions. At one extreme is the idea of "mechanic" form articulated by Coleridge, implying an independence between utilitarian function and beauty. This idea can be traced all the way back to Vitruvius, who argued that "if we do not gratify [the eye's] desire for pleasure," then the outcome will be "clumsy and awkward." A building's form ought to be tweaked, according to Vitruvius, not to more precisely meet some utilitarian objective, but simply to make it more beautiful, for example, to "counteract the ocular deception [corresponding to the observation of corner columns] by an adjustment of proportions."[5]

At the other extreme is the "functionalist" view that beauty is not even a relevant criterion for designing buildings. Such a view—that not only is beauty *not* an inevitable outcome of a logical and utilitarian design process, but that beauty is not even a relevant criterion for architectural design—turns out to be more of a straw man in the history of architectural theory than a serious protagonist. Adrian Forty makes this point, writing that

> while some of the views about function expressed by German-speakers in the late 1920s might seem straightforwardly mechanistic—for example Hannes Meyer's often-quoted article 'Building' that begins 'All things in this world are a product of the formula: function [funktion] times economy'—the foregoing discussion makes it clear that . . . this was by no means a generally held point of view, and was no more than an extremist's polemic within the context of a larger debate about the extended meaning of 'function.'[6]

Forty criticizes Henry-Russell Hitchcock and Philip Johnson, authors of the influential book, *The International Style*, arguing that "in order to present modern architecture as a purely stylistic phenomenon, they had to invent a fictitious category of 'functionalist' architecture to which they consigned all work with reformist or communist tendencies. In fact," Forty continues, "their categorization of the 'functionalists' as those to whom 'all aesthetic principles of style are . . . meaningless and unreal' bore so little relation to what had been happening in Europe that they succeeded in finding only one architect, Hannes Meyer, who fitted their description."[7]

Yet Meyer, though certainly in the minority, was not entirely wrong about the possibility of *designing* buildings on the basis of function and economy alone. In fact, buildings are often designed and constructed in this way; the presupposition of "socially necessary" normative form—buildings designed and intended to satisfy merely utilitarian requirements, at least as understood within a given culture—is taken, by analogy, from Marx's concept of "socially necessary labor," allowing us to be precise about varying and unstable social conditions that otherwise would be impossible to pin down.[8] Whether or not designers or beholders attribute non-utilitarian qualities to such normative utilitarian buildings does not invalidate the premise; they are simply attaching a "utility *equals* beauty" disclaimer to the "functionalist" bugbear. This elaboration of Meyer's argument shows up whenever "primitive," "indigenous," "vernacular," or "engineering" works are cited as sources of inspiration, for example, in Bernard Rudofsky's celebration of *Architecture Without Architects* or in Le Corbusier's invocation of utilitarian grain elevators in *Vers une architecture*, notwithstanding the fact that Le Corbusier painted over—retouched—the images to remove decorative embellishments: "Each of the borrowed grain elevator pictures was painted with a mixture of pigment, natural gum, and water known as gouache. The gouache allowed Le Corbusier to remove imperfections, reshape buildings, and produce a cleaner, less-granulated photograph than either Gropius or the Atlas Portland Cement Company had been able to achieve."[9]

Aside from the trivial type of expression that simply becomes associated with utilitarian forms through repeated exposure, it is also possible that building designers intend the buildings' functions or activities to be expressed (symbolized) with more nuance or subtlety, or that beholders attribute to the buildings' functions or activities something symbolically more nuanced or subtle. In that case, we enter into a different, contentious, and *subjective* territory whose gatekeepers are the critics and connoisseurs seeking to establish new, often arcane, and typically class-based frameworks within which architecture can be analyzed and judged.

One persistent trope is the idea that formal qualities of enclosure systems provide information about, or evidence of, the structural or constructional characteristics of interior spaces. For example, the 19th-century German architectural theorist Karl Bötticher, eager to explain (justify) the mimicking of wooden joints on the surface of Greek temples constructed of stone, proposed a theoretical scheme in which a superficial or decorative "art-form" represents or expresses a necessary and internal "core-form." The art-form, according to Harry Mallgrave, "came to be seen as the artistic dressing applied to the core-form, symbolizing in effect its mechanical or structural function."[10]

This metaphorical notion of transparency is hardly unique to the 19th century but emerged in the Middle Ages and continued into 20th-century modernism. The historian Erwin Panofsky argues that

> as High Scholasticism was governed by the principle of *manifestatio*, so was High Gothic architecture dominated—as already observed by Suger—by what may be called the 'principle of transparency.' . . . And so did High Gothic architecture delimit interior volume from exterior space yet insist that it project itself, as it were, through the encompassing structure; so that, for example, the cross section of the nave can be read off from the façade.[11]

That the spatial logic of interior spaces should be "transparently" revealed (expressed) on a building's exterior surfaces was also a tenet of 20th-century modernism. This can be seen, for example, in the argument made by Alan Chimacoff and Klaus Herdeg in their scathing criticism of I.M. Pei's Johnson Museum of Art at Cornell University, published in Cornell's student-run newspaper in 1973 (and, in slightly revised form, in Herdeg's *The Decorated Diagram: Harvard Architecture and the Failure of the Bauhaus Legacy*, ten years later):

> Hypothetically, meaning could exist in two spheres. First, the physical expression of the building's functional organization (the famous shibboleth of Modern Architecture); second, the manifestation of an aesthetic and intellectual argument addressing itself to a range of historical and cultural issues which attach themselves to the project at hand. The Johnson Museum addresses itself to neither. With respect to the first sphere of meaning, it presents schizophrenic inconsistencies, the most blatant of which is the disposition of the gallery spaces themselves. The form of the building would suggest that the 'great north slab' contained spaces of similar and perhaps repetitive use, while

the spaces assembled to the south of 'the slab' connote a contrasting, perhaps unique, set of uses. It appears contradictory that the gallery boxes are buried in 'the north slab' and sculpturally expressed within 'the great void.'[12]

In other words, the museum's great crime was to have been *designed from the outside*, on the one hand, so that its "great north slab" would, through its massing, align with historic academic buildings on the north side of Cornell's arts quad, and, on the other hand, *designed from the inside* so that its complex, and somewhat contradictory, programmatic requirements could be met. Since there were not enough administrative spaces to fill the "great north slab"—which would have, per Chimacoff and Herdeg's logic, given it conceptual consistency by reconciling internal programming with external form—and since the form of the "great north slab" was nevertheless desired because its external massing was considered of paramount importance, per the architect's logic, in relation to spatial patterns prevailing on Cornell's historic arts quad, I.M. Pei employed a design strategy which allowed the exterior form to "respond" to exterior conditions while allowing the interior spaces to independently "respond" to programmatic requirements (Fig.10.1). Of course, it is possible that both criteria could have been met in a manner that reconciled the two imperatives. But, even so, the stipulation for such metaphorical "transparency" is quite arbitrary; one could just as easily *praise* the museum's design for eschewing such facile expression and, instead, embracing the contradictions of its site and program. In the final analysis, the contentiousness of arguments about the appropriateness— some might say the *truthfulness*—of such subjective determinations of expression is inversely proportional to the objective basis underlying the claims: nothing elicits more passionate and cut-throat criticism than arbitrary, subjective, and fleeting expressions of taste.

In fact, Herdeg was quite willing to make an exception for such "schizophrenic inconsistencies" if he could identify an acceptably ironic attitude at work. For example, in approving Le Corbusier's house at Vaucresson, he admits that

all this posturing on the front facade makes it actually too large and apparently massive compared to the few rooms inside, its outside having little correspondence with what lies behind it in total opposition

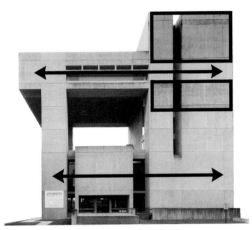

10.1   Viewed from the exterior, I.M. Pei's Johnson Museum of Art at Cornell University is articulated into what Chimacoff and Herdeg call a "great north slab," shown (*left*) with a black outline that appears to contain "spaces of similar and perhaps repetitive use," in contrast to gallery spaces in the rest of the composition. Understood from the interior (*right*), it turns out that "gallery boxes are buried in 'the north slab' and sculpturally expressed within 'the great void,'" with only two floors of repetitive office and conference rooms, shown with black outlines, actually within the "great north slab."

to the modern movement belief that the exterior of a building should reflect its interior, or that 'the plan should generate the facade,' as Le Corbusier was fond of saying.[13]

In instances like this, where *irony* trumps the literal or expressive correspondence between inside and outside, we discover the perfect non-falsifiable refuge of the connoisseur!

This type of expression is, by definition and design, subjective and obscure. Only critics, connoisseurs, and their initiates can read such designs "properly," although this does not prevent such designs from taking on any number of (unintended) symbolic/expressive values. Consider the CCTV tower in Beijing, designed by Rem Koolhaas, as one example among many. In an interview with *Spiegel*, Koolhaas argued that the intended expression of the building's function was, naturally, quite nuanced and sophisticated: "Now that it's almost complete, *the way it functions becomes clear*. It looks

different from every angle, no matter where you stand. . . . That was what we wanted: To create ambiguity and complexity, so as to escape the constraints of the explicit."[14] Yet this type of expressive framework is not easily internalized by the uninitiated masses, at least at first: "Mocking monuments, a form of architectural appropriation, is common to the Chinese construction culture, but the most recent invention—referring to CCTV as the 'Big Underpants' Building'—has caused a stir and a laugh on several websites"[15] (Fig.10.2).

Of course, initial popular reception does not necessarily persist over time. Before its unveiling at the 1889 Exposition Universelle in Paris, the Eiffel Tower was famously scorned by "forty-seven of France's most famous and powerful artists and intellectuals [who] signed their names to an angry protest letter," calling it a "dizzily ridiculous tower dominating Paris like a black and gigantic factory chimney, crushing [all] beneath its barbarous mass . . . which even commercial America would not have."[16] Yet it has turned into a symbol of "enduring glamour and popularity" and is ubiquitous "as a globalized image" of Paris and France.[17] The point is not

10.2 The intended expression of Koolhaas's CCTV headquarters in Beijing was nuanced and sophisticated (*left*), yet the expression of "Big Underpants" prevailed within the popular imagination (*right*).

that OMA's CCTV building, by analogy to Eiffel's Tower, will also come to be embraced as a glamorous symbol of Chinese modernity; rather, the point is that symbolic expression—except for the trivial case of conventional building form symbolically representing functions that have come to be associated with such forms—is neither determined by the designer of the form nor intrinsically related to the form itself.

While this might seem non-controversial, there are still theorists and social scientists who are eager to prove the opposite: that, in fact, certain forms are *inherently* expressive or symbolic to all humans, irrespective of time, place, or culture. This idea, promoted by Charles Osgood and his collaborators in 1975, was discussed in Chapter 9. Yet even Osgood implicitly admits that, when it comes to artistic expression, it is the cultural framework one inherits that determines the meaning, rather than some innate quality in the work itself. After finding "that artists have highly polarized and emotional reactions to abstract paintings," Osgood turns his attention to ordinary non-artists evaluating the same works and finds that "semantic chaos results. . . . When non-artists judge a set of abstract paintings, there is very little structuring of the judgments—as if they had no frame of reference for the task."[18]

Whatever frame of reference underlies the evaluation of a painting's artistic expression, no threat is posed to the painting itself or the functionality of the physical space it occupies. The painting remains safely confined within its literal frame. Yet the expression of architectural utility is hardly confined in the same way and, in some cases, such expression may actually compromise the building's functionality. An example can be seen in the "looped" circulation system within Koolhaas's CCTV Tower in Beijing. From a purely utilitarian standpoint, circulation systems are needed to facilitate interrelationships among activities associated with various internal rooms and spaces, whether at a residential scale (hallways connecting bedrooms, bathrooms, kitchen, living areas) or at a commercial/institutional scale (corridors connecting offices, meeting rooms, elevators, egress stairs; or vestibules, lobbies, and waiting rooms providing transitional spaces in service of other rooms or areas). In some cases, they can be so complex that movement and orientation require a comprehensive system of signs. A building like Grand Central Terminal in New York City, for example, could not function without utilitarian signs pointing users to subways, food courts, trains, restrooms, ticket

counters, and so on (Fig.10.3). Such "signed" circulation systems function adequately to the extent that movement between any two given points is not needlessly constrained. To get from the upper to the lower level, one just goes down one level, rather than being forced to first go up one level and then down two levels.

Yet Koolhaas argues that precisely such dysfunctional circulation—going up in order to go down, or vice versa—is a feature rather than a flaw in the CCTV Building: "The interesting thing to us is that all these entities at CCTV [referring to production, scriptwriting, business, etc.] are in one single structure and that they can be organized in a loop, so that every part is connected to another."[19] First, it is not clear why a "loop" is beneficial in connecting the various parts of the CCTV organization. In his humorous series of "patent" drawings, the intention of CCTV's circulation system is said to avoid "the isolation of the traditional high-rise by turning four segments into a loop," because "a loop of building can be generated that unites and confronts its population in a single whole and cements a coherence of elements, isolating and separating them."[20]

10.3   Without signs literally painted on the stone arches at Grand Central Terminal in New York City, orientation and circulation would become impossible.

Aside from the incoherence of this explanation (how is "isolating and separating them" consistent with "a single whole [that] cements a coherence of elements"?), it can be easily shown that this loop is relatively dysfunctional, and not only because it requires duplication of vertical circulation systems (elevators and egress stairs). This duplication is necessary since there are, in fact, two disconnected floor plates at most levels. Yet in spite of this duplication, it is still quite difficult for people in different offices to find each other. To get from floor 30 in Tower 1 to floor 30 in Tower 2, one must go down from the 30th floor of Tower 1 to the lobby level, walk across from the Tower 1 to the Tower 2 elevator banks, and take another elevator up to the 30th floor of Tower 2 (Fig.10.4). This is no different from organizing the CCTV offices in two separate towers, connected only at the ground level, and much less efficient than organizing the entire program in a single tower.

Remarkably, Koolhaas thinks that this expression of circulation is a logical outgrowth of a functional analysis—a "serious effort"—and resents any comparison of his looped tower with buildings, such as Frank Gehry's Guggenheim Museum in Bilbao, that he characterizes as mere "architectural spectacles."[21] In fact, this insistence that the spectacular architecture

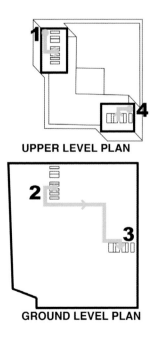

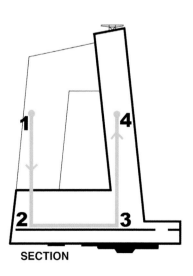

UPPER LEVEL PLAN

GROUND LEVEL PLAN

SECTION

10.4   To get from point 1 to point 4, two offices on the same level in OMA's CCTV Tower in Beijing, it is necessary to first go to the lobby level (point 2), walk across to the elevator bank for the other tower (point 3) and then take another elevator up to point 4.

routinely created by his office is somehow different from—more serious than—that produced by his peers is a current that runs through much of his commentary: Peter Eisenman is similarly dismissed as someone whose "subversive" work is really just "another fiction or fairytale," that is, "a style and nothing more."[22]

The expression of utilitarian function has one more variation, in which utility is expressed with such exuberance that its underlying functionality is obscured. Under this category are things like trim and molding, whose utilitarian function is simply to mediate between two surfaces that are, on their own, incapable of being easily, or cleanly, joined together. This often occurs, for example, when doors or windows are inserted into so-called rough openings, leaving a space for leveling and shimming that must be covered up somehow (Fig.10.5). It also often occurs at the intersection of perpendicular surfaces like walls and ceilings or walls and floors, where

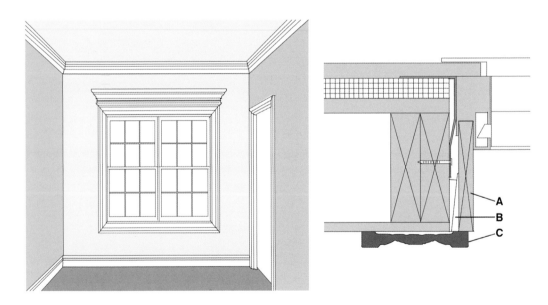

10.5   The expressive quality of molding and trim evolved from the utilitarian need to cover shimmed spaces or awkward intersections of perpendicular surfaces. This can be seen in the perspective sketch showing window and door trim, as well as baseboard and ceiling moldings (*left*). The detail of an ordinary window (*right*) shows the window's jamb extension (A), the open, shimmed space between the finished window frame and the rough opening behind it (B), and the molding or trim (C) whose underlying utilitarian function is to cover the otherwise open, shimmed space.

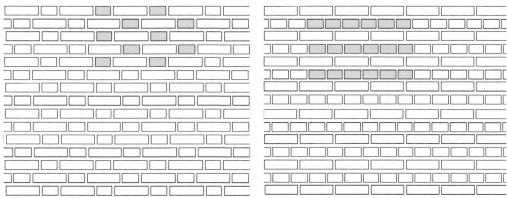

Flemish Bond　　　　　　**English Bond**

10.6 The utilitarian function of bonding multiple layers (wythes) of a loadbearing brick wall using header bricks—shown shaded—has evolved into an expressive function with variations corresponding to different national brick-laying cultures.

baseboard or ceiling molding is sometimes employed to finesse what otherwise might be an awkward intersection. The awkwardness comes about for different reasons: sometimes two surfaces are difficult to join together because they need room to expand and contract; sometimes because their surface textures (rough vs. smooth) are not compatible; or sometimes because the tolerances commonly accepted in construction leave gaps between them. Sometimes baseboards are desired, irrespective of these compatibility issues, simply to protect wall surfaces from floor cleaning protocols involving brushes, brooms, vacuum cleaners, and mops that might otherwise damage an unprotected wall surface. Over time, such utilitarian "sliding joints" have evolved into formal devices that are commonly used, or sometimes eschewed, on the basis of their stylistic or aesthetic meaning, irrespective of their underlying utility.

Another example of the elaboration of utilitarian functions into expressive systems occurs in traditional loadbearing brick walls, where multiple layers (wythes) of brick must be physically tied together, or bonded, so that the multi-wythe walls behave structurally as single, monolithic units (strong) rather than as multiple independent and disconnected units (weak). To tie a multi-wythe wall together, some bricks are turned perpendicular to the wall surface, so that they span between two wythes and in that way bond the wythes together. These perpendicular "header" bricks may well form a repeating pattern, and various nations have lent their names to the distinctive designs that have evolved as expressive bonding strategies within their own brick-laying cultures (Fig.10.6). Needless to say, one can also find such patterns employed in contemporary single-wythe brick cladding, where the traditional bonding function from which these patterns emerged no longer exists.

10.7   The top image shows a house on which both exterior trim and roof elements have been applied to the exterior surface as elements of symbolic expression; the bottom image shows the same house—identical in form and utilitarian function—but with all gratuitous elements digitally removed.

These examples, in which utilitarian functional elements have evolved into an independent expressive system, thus serve as a transition to the *entirely* gratuitous use of superimposed symbols in what Venturi, Scott Brown, and Izenour call decorated sheds.[23] Both in the ordinary house shown in Figure 10.7 and in the Palazzo Farnese in Rome—a canonical example of the "decorated shed" provided by Venturi et al. and shown in Figure 10.8—various exterior elements have become literally detached from functional necessity and are applied to the surface of the facade as pure symbolic expression. In both the modest and monumental versions, the principle is the same.

Expressing utility in the manner illustrated in these examples was anathema to most of the heroic modernists at the beginning of the

10.8   The top image shows the Palazzo Farnese, a High Renaissance palace in Rome designed by Antonio da Sangallo the Younger beginning in 1515 (with Michelangelo redesigning the third story and cornice later in the 16th century); the bottom image shows the same facade, digitally stripped of its decorative elements.

20th century, since elaboration of moldings and decorative treatment of brick bonding were inconsistent with the ethos of geometric abstraction that formed the basis of their architecture. This ideological aversion to building elements like trim or copings—elements that were understood as traditional building elements rather than being subsumed within abstract systems of surface and void—is one of several factors that have led to a virtual epidemic of non-structural building failure. This phenomenon is further discussed in the following chapters.

11
MODERNIST ABSTRACTION AND DYSFUNCTION

Architecture cannot be understood without reference to the notion of abstraction.[1] We discuss buildings in terms of form, space, geometry, context, color, meaning, or anything else only to the extent that we abstract from the infinite qualities that are actually present in its material. Tabulating or adding up the infinite objective qualities of building elements does not get you any closer to an understanding of architecture, so abstraction is a fundamental necessity in both critiquing and producing architecture. Understanding architecture as having a conceptual basis is the same as understanding architecture as an abstraction: a concept describes what the architecture is by abstracting from what it is not. As an example: if the concept of the Pantheon in Rome is of a sphere within a cube, such a description simultaneously abstracts from all that is not relevant to this concept—the particular qualities of each brick, stone, and concrete element from which it is constructed, the ornamentation of the exterior and interior surfaces, and so on. If a designer is unable to abstract from these useful and specific material qualities, a design concept will never emerge.

That architecture has a conceptual basis does not mean that prosaic material properties and material relationships are not important. It only means that, to the extent that architecture is understood conceptually, such information is placed in a different file folder. If it is accepted that abstraction is a requirement for the appreciation, understanding, and creation of architecture, the question remains as to how all the elements abstracted from—those things placed in our metaphorical file folder—become part of the building, as they must: for one cannot build an abstraction.[2]

Up until the end of the 19th and the start of the 20th centuries, the type of abstraction underlying architectural design was generally built upon—paradoxically—an acceptance of conventional building elements, building materials, and building construction techniques. Windows remained windows, doors remained doors, walls remained walls, and roofs remained roofs. In general, structural forces were resolved in conventional ways, construction proceeded along conventional lines, and environmental constraints on site planning, building orientation, and so forth were respected.

The conceptual basis of such architecture neither challenged, nor threatened, these prosaic elements and conventions, but was rather developed with these elements in mind. Window openings may have been elaborated or framed with Ionic columns and decorated with various ornamental forms, and the geometric organization of the facade may have abstracted from the material or constructional logic of brick, stone, or plaster surfaces from which its expression emerged, but the window was still understood as a window, and the wall was still understood as a wall. That architecture took as its point of departure walls, columns, windows, and roofs was rarely questioned; Alberti and other 15th- to 19th-century architects and writers maintained a conventional and uncontroversial attitude towards such building elements even as they explored issues of architectural design and abstraction.

The origins of a more radically abstract way of understanding architecture were already present but were not recognized as serious alternative strategies for designing buildings. Rather, examples of conceptually pure forms devoid of references to conventional building elements appear almost exclusively in works of monumental scale, expressing the most unfathomable and sublime concept of all: death. The Great Pyramid of Giza, completed in 2560 BCE, and the Cenotaph for Newton designed—but never built—by Étienne-Louis Boullée in the late 18th century, can be cited as precursors to the radically abstract forms characteristic of later works of architecture. However, such precedents were not considered, at the time, to be legitimate role models for non-funerary building types.

Architectural abstraction as a mere elaboration, or ordering, of conventional building elements began to be challenged in the late 19th century, and especially in the early 20th century. While the canonical houses of 20th-century modernism were hardly representative of domestic building, then or now, they were extraordinarily influential in creating a kind of beachhead from which radical attitudes towards abstraction could take root and ultimately become major factors in both the pedagogy and practice of architecture. This new form of abstraction differed markedly from traditional forms of abstraction. Le Corbusier's five points of architecture describe the potential of new technologies—in particular, the replacement of loadbearing walls by a structural framework—to overcome what were considered insufferable constraints of traditional construction. In many of his buildings, windows are abstracted as rectangular openings, or voids. Other conventional building elements are defamiliarized or eliminated entirely: stucco replaces clapboards as it betrays no material origin and can be more easily understood as abstract surface. Roof shingles, along with sloped roofs of any sort, are simply eliminated, as they contain such strong references to the traditional tectonic geometry of attics and gables. Brick chimneys are replaced with painted metal cylindrical pipes. And all traditional ornamental or decorative embellishments are banished. The point here is not to criticize any particular aesthetic outcome, or to propose a return to any particular stylistic tendency. The key change, from the standpoint of building failure and building function, is that—for the first time—architectural abstraction was made independent of building construction and building conventions.

Many advances in building technology can be cited to explain the motivation, as well as the potential, for changes in architectural form and construction associated with modernism. Perhaps the most obvious were major improvements in the production of ferrous metals used to create structural frameworks, leading to the widespread use of standard I-beams and, later, wide-flange sections made from rolled steel. At about the same time, near the turn of the 19th (into the 20th) century, reinforced concrete also became, for the first time, a viable structural material. It is hardly accidental that the formal inventions of modern architecture drew upon the structural potential of these new materials.

Other materials used in modern buildings were not particularly new, but—at least in some cases—were becoming available as mass-produced commodities. However, unlike structural frameworks that used steel or reinforced concrete to create formal typologies associated with modernism, it is not as easy to make explicit connections between these other building materials and this type of formal abstraction. Even glass, which served as a necessary bridge between the spatial ideals of modernism and the realities of enclosure, was not exactly a new material at the beginning of the 20th century, although incremental improvements in its manufacture did permit greater experimentation with formal compositions that relied on large "voids."

If structure were abstract grid (or abstract plane, in the case of loadbearing walls), and if glass were abstract void, other constructional elements or materials required to complete the desired abstract compositions of modern design were harder to find. The neutral solid surface had to consist of something, but nothing new was available, except perhaps the mottled gray surface of reinforced concrete. More often, such surfaces were created as they had been for thousands of years—by applying a layer of stucco to an underlying substrate of brick or, later, concrete block.

The important point is this: in spite of an abstract conception of buildings which eschewed conventional building elements and conventional material expression, modern buildings still needed to be actually and physically constructed. Moreover, modern architects had hardly given up, or gone beyond, a traditional understanding of building construction as consisting fundamentally of physical things whose value was measured as it had always been measured: by their strength, by their resistance to movement, and by their durability. Expressing such characteristics of building materials—as heroic elements that were both visible and tangible—may not always have been a *formal* preoccupation of modern architects, but the heroic quality of constructional elements remained for modern architects an unchallenged model for putting together, for building, their abstract concepts.

The belief that traditional (heroic) materials constituted the basis of building construction, if not always the conceptual basis of the architecture, became increasingly untenable in the 20th century because the underlying basis of architectural technology underwent a radical transformation. The reasons for, and results of, this transformation can be summarized as follows:

- Steel and reinforced concrete frameworks, together with newly invented elevators, made it possible to develop tall commercial and residential buildings.
- The obsolescence of loadbearing masonry walls in this context created both the possibility, and the incentive, for reducing the thickness and weight of cladding systems. Air-conditioning as part of mechanical ventilation systems—and therefore the ability to eliminate natural ventilation—made it possible to think of the building enclosure as "skin" or "envelope" rather than as wall and window, while the elimination of the requirement for natural ventilation also permitted deep floor plates and formal geometries that were no longer constrained by the need to create "rooms" with "windows."

- The relatively high cost of mechanical air-conditioning provided an incentive to develop and deploy thermal control layers (insulation) at the building perimeter.
- Problems with failed sealant joints, condensation, polluted outside air, increasing energy costs, and water intrusion led to the conceptualization and deployment of rigorous control layers for vapor, rainwater, and air, in addition to the thermal control layer.[3]

It is important to emphasize the fact that what had previously controlled rainwater, vapor, air, and heat loss—the thick and more-or-less monolithic masonry walls of traditional construction—were the same elements that largely defined the "architectural expression" of traditional buildings. That is, architecture grew out of, and supported, this underlying technology, just as the technology supported the architectural expression. However, while the technology of control layers has migrated from the "heroic" materials of traditional architecture to the separate, optimized, and non-heroic membranes and insulative materials characteristic of contemporary construction, formal architectural design in the 20th and early 21st centuries remains stuck in the paradigm of traditional and heroic material expression, not only ignoring this profound technological shift, but actually moving in directions that exacerbate problems of vapor, air, and rainwater intrusion, as well as energy efficiency.

In the new paradigm for architectural technology, four control layers need to occur consistently at the boundary between inside and outside space in order to control these four environmental factors: rainwater, vapor, air, and heat. Wherever a control layer's integrity is violated along that boundary, the potential for problems increases, in the following ways:

- Thermal bridges (i.e., discontinuities in the thermal control layer) not only may lead to unintended heat loss or heat gain but may also alter the temperature gradient between the outside and inside surfaces of the enclosure system, leading potentially to condensation, whether on interior surfaces, exterior surfaces, or interstitially. Such condensation may lead to structural damage, non-structural damage, and to the growth of mold.
- Holes or gaps in the rainwater control layer obviously increase the potential for water to enter the building in unintended ways. Water

is probably the single most damaging element in buildings when not properly controlled: in its presence, wood may rot or decay, ferrous metals may rust, dissimilar metals in contact with each other may undergo galvanic corrosion, gypsum board may be damaged, mold (mildew) may grow, and so on.

- Holes or gaps in the air control layer can increase the probability that air will move through the enclosure wall, or within the enclosure wall, in unintended ways. All sorts of negative consequences may result: in particular, energy may be lost in much greater quantities than from discontinuities in the thermal control layer, since pressure differentials between outside and inside areas can drive large amounts of unconditioned air into the building (while driving large amounts of conditioned air out of the building). Such unintended patterns of air intrusion can also wreak havoc on HVAC systems, and create unexpected condensation within enclosure walls as conditioned or unconditioned humid air finds its way onto cold surfaces outside or inside the thermal control layer.
- Where a vapor control layer is not properly configured, or where an unintended vapor control layer is created by the inappropriate use of low-permeance materials (e.g., vinyl wall coverings in air-conditioned spaces), water vapor can migrate through enclosure wall assemblies, whether originating on the outside or inside of buildings, and condense on cool surfaces.

Assuming that the various control layers are properly configured with respect to each other—so that, for example, an air barrier is not positioned within the enclosure wall assembly in such a way that it prevents water or vapor from draining or drying out—the primary task is to make these control layers continuous. This is not particularly easy to do; because control layers are most efficiently deployed outside the building's structural frame (so that they are not constantly interrupted by interior partitions and floor–ceiling assemblies and so that the building's structure is protected from thermal changes and other environmental damage), they must be supported by, or connected to, the building's structure in some way. Unless they are adhered to the building's structure (or to some sort of back-up surface or substrate supported by the building's structure), then their means of support (clip angles, bolts, screws, nails, etc.) invariably penetrate not only the control layer being supported, but also any control layers positioned between the control layer being supported and the structural substrate. And even if all the control layers are light enough so that they may be adhered without the use of penetrating fasteners, the outer "rain screen" cladding material—needed not only to establish some sort of architectural presence for the building, but also to protect relatively delicate control layers from various forms of damage and, in some cases, to create an air cavity or pressure-equalization chamber—still requires some sort of fastening system that invariably must penetrate the control layers it covers and protects.

Roof systems require the same control layers, but have different problems to reconcile—in particular, problems with penetrations for mechanical equipment or skylights, and transitions between vertical, sloping, or horizontal surfaces.

This illustrates a fundamental contradiction in the theory of control layers, but it is a contradiction that can be largely overcome both by minimizing these inevitable penetrations, and by detailing them explicitly where they occur (e.g., at windows or other openings, penetrations, and at the fasteners themselves) to maintain the continuity of the various control layers that would otherwise be interrupted. This strategy, however, is compromised when the architectural design itself—not just the inevitable encounters with windows, penetrations, and fasteners for cladding support—has a conceptual basis rooted in the expression of discontinuity.

Such discontinuity takes many forms, and it is not my purpose to document them all, or to suggest that all contemporary architectural expression is aligned with this tendency. The important point is this: where conceptual or schematic design is understood as a process of abstraction in which formal ideas can be developed without any consideration of control layer continuity, where contemporary modes of representation can capture virtually any formal geometry, where structural and energy analysis software can provide numerical validation for the most complex and indeterminate geometric models imaginable, and where architectural culture in general, and generative design methods in particular, encourage a disjunction between formal conceits and constructional logic, the probability of encountering problems with control layer discontinuities dramatically increases.

The logic of control layer design in modern construction cannot simply be ignored. Describing the Wexner Center for the Arts at Ohio

State University, designed by Peter Eisenman in 1989 (Fig.11.1, *left*), Robin Pogrebin wrote that

> it would seem embarrassing for any architect, let alone one as prominent as Peter Eisenman. You design a museum—your first large-scale work, a breakout project whose exterior scaffolding design, a virtual celebration of impermanence, sets the architecture world buzzing. Within just a few years, however, cracks start to show. Quite literally: the skylight leaks. The glass curtain wall lets in too much light, threatening to damage delicate artwork. The interior temperature swings by as much 40 degrees some days.[4]

Different control layer problems plagued the Stata Center at M.I.T., designed by Frank Gehry in 2004 (Fig.11.1, *right*):

> MIT has settled its 2007 lawsuit against the architects and builders of the Ray and Maria Stata Center. . . . MIT's lawsuit cited design and construction failures in the building. These included masonry cracking

11.1 Problems with abstraction: the Wexner Center for the Arts at Ohio State University (*left*, opened 1989), designed by Peter Eisenman; and the Ray and Maria Stata Center at M.I.T. (*right*, opened 2004), designed by Frank Gehry.

and poor drainage in the amphitheater; 'mold growth at various locations on the brick exterior vertical elevations'; 'persistent leaks' throughout the building; and sliding ice and snow.[5]

Paradoxically, not only the expression of discontinuity, but also the expression of a kind of hyper-continuity can lead to control layer problems—this may occur when walls and roofs become indistinguishable from each other as morphed and flowing building enclosure surfaces turn the conventional understanding of "facade" or "roof" into quaint anachronisms. Potential problems with such hyper-continuity come about because necessary connections at vertical walls are different from those at steep-slope or low-slope roofs. Control layer penetrations that are required for fastening cladding panels may be tolerable in the vertical surface of a metal rain screen wall, for example, but may well become increasingly risky as the enclosure surface bends or curves from a vertical to a more horizontal position. The orientation of enclosure surfaces with respect to the force of gravity matters, and it is dangerous to confuse the abstract formal desire for "continuity" with the practical requirement for control layer continuity derived from building science principles.

Some would argue that it's no big deal if a few buildings leak—better to live in a world with formal design freedom (even if accompanied by various forms of building failure) than in a dull, repetitive world where everything functions properly. There is some truth, and a number of fallacies, in the argument that accepting and applying principles of building science within the design process prevents a designer from heroically pursuing an avant-garde agenda. The truth is that such considerations *do* constrain design freedom. A "paper" architecture conceived without gravity, for example, will surely be frustrated when confronted with the reality of, and requirements for, vertical equilibrium.

Yet it is equally true that the constraints brought about by what might be termed "reality"—not only gravity, but also the necessary control of air, vapor, rainwater, and heat at the building's perimeter—can be reconciled with a desire to create new architectural forms of expression. Yes, freedom is constrained, but it is not entirely destroyed. The problem is that in a world of architectural production driven by competition, any logical constraint on a designer's freedom of expression leads the designer— perversely but inevitably—to explore precisely those forbidden places outlawed by prevailing conventions. In defying such logic, the designer seeks to defamiliarize what has become so commonplace that it is no longer capable of eliciting an aesthetic response and, therefore, serving as a useful mode of competition. This is the heroic conceit of the contemporary avant-garde: to confront "danger" in whichever of its manifestations appears as an appropriate target at any given point in time.

Joseph Campbell abstracts from the culture of competition that motivates artists to embark on such counterproductive hero's journeys, seeing only the mythical and idealized shell of heroism in such attempts:

> Artists are magical helpers. Evoking symbols and motifs that connect us to our deeper selves, they can help us along the heroic journey of our own lives. . . . Over and over again, you are called to the realm of adventure, you are called to new horizons. Each time, there is the same problem: do I dare? And then if you do dare, the dangers are there, and the help also, and the fulfillment or the fiasco. There's always the possibility of a fiasco. But there's also the possibility of bliss.[6]

Ironically, an inattention to building science is—precisely—what this version of heroism entails. Architects (*qua* artists) are not so much "help[ing] us along the heroic journey of our own lives" but rather creating, out of thin air, a heroic journey for themselves: leaving the world of safe, predictable constructions; proposing buildings that have both the appearance and the reality of danger (where danger comes from challenging conventional notions of aesthetic, and sometimes literal, comfort; challenging class-based conventions regarding economy of means; and especially, challenging forces of nature such as gravity, or rain, or snow); and returning in glory after having confronted the agents of conformity (whether owners, users, public officials, etc.). For such heroes, having proposed, or built, such a brave thing with all the attendant risks of failure is a badge of honor. Peter Eisenman, in his interview with Robin Pogrebin, boasts that "there's not an architect I know that doesn't have problems with important buildings."[7]

Abstraction, in and of itself, is not directly the cause of non-structural building failure. Rather, problems emerge due to the interaction of several factors, outlined below, that relate to the use of abstraction in modern architecture—not all of which are necessarily present in any given instance.

ABSTRACTION PRECEDES FUNCTION

Abstract ideas tend to precede, rather than evolve from, considerations of a technical or functional nature. This is partly a result of a misplaced confidence in the power of science to compensate for any a priori design decisions, and partly a result of an education in construction derived from empirically based rules that provide neither the theory to grasp, nor even the vocabulary to define, the issues that have become relevant in the design of enclosure systems. As a result, abstract "volumes brought together in light," Le Corbusier's idealized definition of architecture first published in 1920 ("volumes assemblés sous la lumière"[8]), often experience problems when they are also, invariably, brought together in rain, wind, and snow, and subject to unanticipated environmental pressures.

ENCLOSURE IS ARCHITECTURE

Whereas a steel or concrete structural framework (or an environmental control system) can be conceptually and physically separated from the rest of the building, permitting a specialized process of engineering design that supports the architectural concept, it is difficult to see how the enclosure of a building can be dealt with in an analogous manner without reducing the architect's role to a purely schematic one. From the standpoint of both traditional and modern architecture, the enclosure, to a great extent, *is* the architecture. Delegating the detailed design of enclosure to others (aside from loss of prestige and remuneration) opens up the risk of compromising the abstract basis of the design. Vertical surfaces may terminate in unwanted copings; what was conceived as abstract void may appear as conventional window; and the precise articulation of formal elements, based on subtleties of alignment and proportion, may suffer.

TECHNOLOGY AS THREAT TO FREEDOM

The architect, while maintaining control over the building's external surfaces, tends to resist serious application of "engineering" criteria to the design of building envelopes. Within the academic design studio as well as in practice, such criteria are perceived as threats to the freedom of formal invention that are characteristic of modernist abstraction. In the words of the Dutch painter and theoretician Piet Mondrian: "If one takes technique, utilitarian requirements, etc., as the point of departure, there is a risk of losing every chance of success, for intuition is then troubled by intelligence."[9]

RISK OF FAILURE NOT APPRECIATED

The risk of enclosure failure is neither as obvious, immediate, nor usually as catastrophic, as is the case with structural failure, so there is less pressure to develop the necessary theoretical or empirical basis. Details often seem reasonable when initially conceived and executed, as their intrinsic defects may be far from obvious. In fact, "obvious" or "common-sense" solutions are sometimes problematic. For example, the popularity of non-redundant barrier walls "may result from a common-sense approach to the problem of rain exclusion—when it is raining, we wear a mackintosh, so why not treat our buildings likewise?"[10] Additionally, many non-structural failures take years to manifest themselves. Even "short-term or accelerated tests may give misleading indications. A tentative judgment only may be possible, based on technical knowledge and subject to confirmation in due course by observation."[11] Cracking and bowing of marble cladding panels on the Standard Oil Company Headquarters in Chicago were first noticed almost seven years after initial construction, became increasingly prevalent only within 13 years of construction, and finally led to complete replacement after 19 years.[12] Such non-structural failures are often costly, inconvenient, and dangerous, but they are rarely catastrophic.

WE DON'T KNOW WHAT WE DON'T KNOW

Because the traditional means of dealing with enclosure is primarily based on empirical rather than on scientific knowledge, modern architects do not necessarily know what they don't know about the subject, and are thus more inclined to either extrapolate inappropriately from prior experience, or simply invent constructional details based on a superficial understanding (i.e., a misunderstanding) of the complex forces at work. In other words, the empirical basis for much prior construction success, having little basis in a theory of building science, is discarded without the modern architect knowing exactly (or even approximately) what is being lost. If a 24-inch-thick (600 mm) loadbearing masonry wall seems to work well at keeping water out, it may not be clear why 8-inch-thick (200 mm) cladding supported on a structural frame wouldn't keep water out just as well. The process of abstraction, unmediated by any serious building science, reduces the complex behavior of specific wall-types to formal ideas: the "wall" becomes a "plane," a "surface," or a constituent part of a "volume" or "mass." Even the origin and purpose of the pitched roof, understood traditionally as a culturally specific response to environmental conditions, is dismissed by R.S. Yorke, architect and author of *The Modern House*, as a structural anachronism made obsolete by the employment of "frame construction and concrete slabs."[13]

HEROIC STATUS OF STRUCTURE AND CLADDING

In the modern conception of construction, visible and "heroic" elements of building are seen either as purely formal elements (enclosure) or as abstract manifestations of "structure," while the subtle realities of material behavior and their relationship to the construction of buildings are often ignored. As a more rigorous building science develops, these attitudes become increasingly untenable.

INVENTIONS BASED ON WISHFUL THINKING

With neither a working knowledge of building science, nor empirically based standards for reliable detailing, it is not surprising that the modern architect may be incapable of inventing reliable strategies for enclosing buildings. Yet it is still common for architects to creatively "invent" construction details. Some of the reasons for this have already been given: the risk of failure is not fully appreciated. The lack of theory associated with an empirically based construction practice makes it difficult to know what one does not know. And the state of building science itself may be relatively undeveloped. Additionally, an attitude of heroic contempt for the conventional may be present. *The Architects' Journal* wondered in 1975 whether the cause of misguided architectural invention lay "in a disdain for the 'standard solution' or the principle, perhaps, that any designer worth his salt should be able to work everything out from first principles?"[14]

DURABILITY, MAINTENANCE, AND GREED

There is also a tendency to overestimate the durability of many modern systems and materials; as "modern" becomes identified in popular culture with overcoming traditional labor-intensive practices, habits of maintenance characteristic of traditional building practice (continual repair, replacement, pointing, painting, etc.) are loosened from their bearings. While expectations of permanence, toughness, and resiliency become part of the culture, if not the reality, of modern materials, two other factors make decisions regarding durability more difficult for the architect. First, it is not easy to obtain definitive information on the performance characteristics of complex components, equipment, and systems. Knowledge is limited because those who have it tend to view it in a proprietary manner and are reluctant to share it. Competing manufacturers vying for market share may not always be inclined to objectively compare their products with others. Second, the desire to extract the maximum profit from investments in commercial building tends to encourage both marginal construction practices and deferred maintenance.

GRAPHIC STANDARDS

Many 20th-century texts on construction practice lack both a coherent theory of building science as well as a base of empirical knowledge corresponding to the new architectural forms, materials, and systems that are emerging. Charles Ramsey and Harold Sleeper describe a situation in which "facts are so deeply buried in the body of technical literature that they only come to light in the course of research." Their *Architectural Graphic Standards*, first published in 1932, is intended to overcome the "pressure of time [that] often forces the making of assumptions and trusting to luck."[15] But there are at least two problems with these assertions. First, it is not clear that the "research" referred to is yet capable of dealing with the complexity of modern materials and systems. For example, effective utilization of insulating material, vapor retarders, and air barriers was still, after more than 80 years of discussion and research, subject to uncertainty and inconsistent practice.[16] Second, it is not clear that available "state-of-the-art" research is being incorporated consistently into the graphic details. Research into the relationships among insulation, vapor migration, and condensation, already available in 1923, does not begin to appear in *Architectural Graphic Standards* until 1951.[17] Even when such research conclusions finally appear, they are not consistently applied to the details; for example, generic advice on condensation does not prevent the continued reprinting of numerous details that contradict the theory.

Publishing graphically oriented material with little explicit theoretical grounding also makes the underlying premise—that of providing a "core of skeleton data useful for further development, design, or improvement"[18]—a dangerous proposition. For how can one modify or extrapolate from a detailed drawing if the underlying logic is not known? Details supplied by manufacturers of specific systems are also often difficult to incorporate properly into an overall building design, but for a different reason. Perhaps to avoid liability for providing information about elements over which they have no control, many manufacturers avoid showing precisely how their systems connect to adjacent construction.

UNTESTED COMBINATIONS

Even where familiar materials are used, many problems in modern construction arise from the untested interactions among those materials. Viollet-le-Duc, in his *Lectures on Architecture* (Lecture XI), refers to this potential, already manifested in 19th-century construction, as being proportional to the variation in component materials. Contemporary practice, with its proliferation of new materials, makes the problem worse. Even familiar materials may cause problems when used in new contexts. Not only individual materials may interact to cause failure, but individual factors, each by itself perhaps acting below the threshold of damage, can combine to trigger failure.

REJECTION OF CONVENTIONAL TECHNOLOGY

A disdain for conventional applications of technology may seem somewhat paradoxical, in light of modernism's invocation of precisely this technology in its manifestos opposing traditional modes of building, but several factors are at play. There is, first, a distrust of, and backlash against, technical solutions within *postmodern* culture, and this phenomenon lends support to architectural forms that express these feelings by literally distorting that which appears as logical within modernist practice. Second, with the victory of modernism over traditional construction practices, what was "heroic" and "radical" in the deployment of steel and reinforced concrete frames becomes conventional. Given the cyclic movement of fashion, it is inevitable that an avant-garde style, once integrated and accepted within popular culture, must give way to something new—the negation of the logic embedded within modernist conventions becomes the stylistic path of least resistance. Third, technology is still expressed, even fetishized, in its irrational manifestations. Glass is reimagined, no longer merely as the "void" in modernist abstraction, but as the visible and universal boundary between inside and outside; cladding is similarly abstracted as universal surface; structure is bent, angled, cantilevered, hyper-articulated, and so on, using techniques based on distortion or other forms of defamiliarization.

STILL HEROIC

Modern attitudes to construction tend to focus on structure and cladding as "heroic" materials through which the ideas of the designer are made visible. In the postmodern reaction to modernism, such attitudes survive largely intact: critiques of modernist idealism still rely on structure and cladding as expressive formal elements. Yet as building science evolves, the failure to acknowledge an emerging paradigm shift in the actual requirements of building—from the use of relatively unsophisticated enclosure strategies characteristic of modernism to the more subtle application of non-heroic systems based on control layers (to control air, vapor, water, and heat flow) and incorporating issues of sustainability—is increasingly problematic.

MAGIC PILL

At the same time, even as the expression of technology as a manifestation of rationality is subjected to formal critique, technology itself is not actually rejected, but in fact assumes an almost mystical aura. If the engineer of modernism, "inspired by the law of Economy and governed by mathematical calculation, puts us in accord with universal law [and] achieves harmony,"[19] the postmodern engineer rejects the constraints of economy, values ambiguity over harmony, and relies on complex numerical methods programmed within the "black box" of sophisticated analytical software to transcend the limitations of traditional mathematical calculation. "Structure need not be comprehensible and explicit. There is no creed or absolute. . . . It can be subtle and more revealing. It is a richer experience . . . if a puzzle is set or a layer of ambiguity lies over the reading of 'structure.'"[20]

Technology in this context is thought to possess almost limitless power to overcome problems originating in any predetermined form, no matter how arbitrary and illogical. Form, in other words, can be abstracted from virtually all considerations of a technical nature; and technology, much like the digital "improvements" common in photography, music, and film, can compensate for what might have been a hopelessly misconceived or inadequate performance. The singer-songwriter-producer Ben Folds captures this sentiment perfectly in his 2001 song: "I'm rockin' the suburbs / I take the cheques and face the facts / that some producer with computers fixes all my shitty tracks."[21]

The problem with this attitude, at least in architecture, is twofold. First, such technical "solutions," focusing only on internal criteria of success, may lose sight of other criteria external to the immediate problem. For example, a "solution" to a problem of environmental control may require excessive energy use. Second, such an attitude is unrealistic. Unlike structural frameworks or other relatively straightforward technical systems within buildings, the reliability of the building envelope is threatened by thousands of highly complex, and often unpredictable, interactions among building materials and systems subjected to differential movement, chemical reactions, environmental agents, construction and maintenance operations, and so on. Architectural form based upon empirically validated principles of building science—form that minimizes the collisions among these countless variables—has a greater probability of success than does architectural form that either willfully distorts these principles or operates as if such principles can be applied after the fact.

Architects learn to prioritize formal abstraction over utilitarian functionality when they go to school. There is a great deal of anecdotal evidence that such abstraction, independent of serious consideration of technical/functional issues, typifies academic design studio pedagogy: we will look more closely at architectural education in the epilogue.

12
EXPRESSION OF STRUCTURE

The expressive function of contemporary structure has a much smaller role than its utilitarian function, since many, if not most, structural systems are quite literally hidden from view. In traditional residential construction, whether of masonry or light-wood framing, the primary structural elements take the form of walls and floor–ceiling assemblies—typically faced with a thin layer of gypsum board or plaster on inside surfaces, and any number of cladding materials on outside surfaces—and so are often apprehended as the spatial boundaries defining the various rooms of the house, rather than as "the structure." Even when masonry walls are exposed, there is often an ambiguity about their structural status, since the same materials can be, and often are, used as non-structural partitions.

In commercial office buildings, a structural framework of columns, beams, and diagonal bracing elements is also often hidden within the space-defining elements of the building. First, steel structural elements are often coated with some sort of fire-resistant material (reinforced concrete or masonry are already fire-resistant and therefore do not require additional protection). Second, the entire horizontal floor and roof structure, consisting of beams, girders, and corrugated steel decks (in typical steel-framed buildings) or of various site-cast or precast reinforced concrete slab-types, with or without articulated beams or column capitals (in typical masonry or reinforced concrete buildings) is typically hidden above some sort of suspended ceiling system. Third, wind- or seismic-bracing systems are often incorporated within walls defining stair or elevator shafts, so as not to compromise the flexibility of interior spaces or exterior glazed surfaces. Finally, columns, where they do occur, are spaced so far apart, as much as 9–18 meters (30–60 feet) in modern construction, that—even if visible—they no longer appear as part of a coherent system of structure, but merely as additional space-defining elements, or bumps in walls.

That leaves a small minority of buildings in which structure functions expressively. The idea of a contemporary "structural art" was articulated, or practiced, by several notable engineers (or, in some cases, by structurally trained architects such as Frei Otto or Félix Candela), either acting on their own or in collaboration with architects. Perhaps the strangest explanation of the phenomenon of structure *qua* art was given by one of its major apostles, the structural engineer and educator, David P. Billington, who claimed in his 1983 book, *The Tower and the Bridge*, that the proper expression of structure was not only *not* frivolous, but actually was a useful tool in the fight against both fascist and communist impulses:

> In our own age when democratic ideals are continually being challenged by the claims of totalitarian societies, whether fascist or communist, the works of structural art provide evidence that the common life flourishes best when the goals of freedom and discipline are held in balance. The disciplines of structural art are efficiency and economy, and its freedom lies in the potential it offers the individual designer for the expression of a personal style motivated by the conscious aesthetic search for engineering elegance.[1]

The problem with Billington's formulation of structural art as something governed by efficiency, economy, and elegance is that such a view is unabashedly arbitrary, reflecting only the personal bias of the author. Structure may well be considered expressive ("artistic") and simultaneously be inefficient, costly, and inelegant. Peter Rice, one of the great engineering collaborators of the 20th century, when describing the Centre Pompidou and the Sydney Opera House (two of many notable buildings, known for their structural artistry, on which he collaborated as structural consultant), said that "in no way are those buildings representative of fundamental structural approaches. They're using the structure as part of the aesthetic framework in much the same way people did with brick and stone in the 18th and 19th centuries." Rice went on to suggest that his intention was to express something about the "character" of steel or concrete, "even though it may not be a logical structure in the first place."[2] The artist, architect, and engineer Cecil Balmond, as noted in Chapter 9, values "mystery, mysticism, doubt and fluidity,"[3] qualities diametrically opposed to Billington's "efficiency, economy, and elegance."

The question therefore is not, as Billington argues,[4] whether Maillart's reinforced concrete floor system is more logical or more elegant than that of Hennebique (Fig.12.1), but rather *why* elegance is even a relevant concept in a discussion of structural art, and *how* a subjective determination of elegance

12.1 Comparison of François Hennebique's late 19th-century reinforced concrete 1-way slab system with articulated beams and girders (*left*) and Robert Maillart's early 20th-century 2-way slab system with mushroom columns (*right*).

can be made. In the first case, the relevance of structural "elegance" is called into question simply by identifying different, and conflicting, expressive objectives ("mystery" or "doubt") with different expressive functions. In the second case, as E.H. Gombrich suggests, such determinations are constrained by "expectations of possibilities and probabilities" within a given culture. The "history of taste and fashion," he writes, "is the history of preferences, of various acts of choice between given alternatives."[5]

The idea of elegance, in other words, can only be applied to structure through the subjective comparison of available alternatives, rather than by thinking of elegance as an absolute and intrinsic condition of the structure itself. Gombrich, citing the Roman architect Vitruvius, describes the Doric column as relatively more "virile" or "severe" then the Corinthian, not because of anything particularly severe about the Doric column itself, but only in comparison with the flowery Corinthian.[6] In an expressive face-off between the Hennebique system and Maillart's flat slab, it's hardly clear that one or the other will win the prize for being "most elegant." The entire concept of elegance is tied to a subjective connoisseurship of what exactly constitutes a pleasingly graceful style or appearance at a particular time and place, and—as with all questions of taste—multiple competing visions exist, often representing the interests of competing social or economic strata within a given society. For the record, I prefer the Hennebique.

Structural efficiency and elegance are often validated by reference to natural or biological structural forms. D'Arcy Thompson, the Scottish biologist and mathematician, wrote over 100 years ago in *On Growth and Form* that "the form, then, of any portion of matter, whether it be living or dead, and the changes of form which are apparent in its movements and in its growth, may in all cases alike be described as due to the action of force. In short, the form of an object is a 'diagram of forces . . .'"[7] But unlike such naturally evolving forms, building structure is constrained by a persistent characteristic of human behavior. We prefer to inhabit the kind of flat, horizontal surfaces that typify the environments in which we evolved: "The literal basis of the terrestrial environment is the ground, the underlying surface of support that tends to be on the average flat—that is to say, a plane—and also level, or perpendicular to gravity."[8] The abstract desire for structural efficiency, economy, and elegance cannot easily be detached from this onerous precondition. Natural forms certainly co-evolve in ways that influence their structural form—the supporting components of many vertebrates, for example, are composed of a variety of curved compressive elements (bones) held in dynamic equilibrium by elements in tension (tendons, ligaments, and muscles)—but there are no natural analogues to the perfectly horizontal bending structures supported by vertical compressive elements characteristic of human construction. Not only are the horizontal surfaces in buildings constrained by the need for horizontality on the walking side but, to maximize the efficiency of mechanical services and to minimize typical floor-to-floor heights, they are often also constrained by the need for horizontal plenums and coverings (ceilings) on their underside. Furthermore, the manufacturing processes of steel and wood beams favor prismatic cross-sections (*rectangular* for wood, both because of how it is cut and because of its parallel "grain"; *H-shaped* for steel, both because of how it is hot rolled and because such a shape optimizes its strength and stiffness) rather than cross-sections that vary along the length of the span. For this reason, expressive structural form is often relegated to heroic long-span roof structures for which horizontal walking/working surfaces are not required, or to the overarching form of tall buildings, in which the necessary array of horizontal surfaces is subsumed within the larger structural project of resisting wind loads or seismic ground motion.

Structural expression is thus inextricably tied to cultural expectations, which are in turn informed not only by what options are considered possible, but also what options are considered "normal" or "appropriate" in a given situation. As an example, the same form of the Doric column that was described by Gombrich as "severe"—at least when expressed on the scale used by Vitruvius—takes on an entirely different meaning when it is resurrected, almost 2,000 years later, in the Chicago Tribune Tower competition of 1922 (Fig.12.2). Adolf Loos's entry invokes the Doric form, not in relation to other possible Greek orders (e.g., the Corinthian or Ionic), but rather in relation to more modern and, therefore, *non-traditional* forms. Of course, it is not really possible to know with any certainty either what Loos intended, or what the form of the tower expresses to random beholders. On

12.2   The Doric column, per Vitruvius, expresses "severity" (*left*) within the Temple of Zeus at Olympia, Greece; in a different context— Loos's Chicago Tribune competition entry (*right*)—the column's expression is informed by a radically different context.

the one hand, it is true that Loos's choice of the classical motif seems to have been informed by his stated concern that contemporary and "nontraditional forms are only too quickly superseded by new ones," leading to a situation where the "owner soon realizes that his building is no longer fashionable."[9] On the other hand, it is also possible that an element of irony is at play; Loos, according to Anthony Vidler, "is always serious but never deadly so."[10] Critics and other beholders of the project have variously suggested that the tower might be understood "as a joke, a caustic critique, and a sophisticated essay rich in metaphorical allusions," or that it "expresses the Tribune's growth and power, as it did that of the Roman Empire; it playfully alludes to a newspaper's printed columns; it suggests that the Tribune is a pillar of society; it refers to the columnar metaphor describing the skyscraper's tripartite elevation; it takes a critical stand against the American city; it is Dada; it is ironic; it is utterly empty of meaning."[11]

Whereas Loos represented a structural idea (the column) without revealing any of the *actual* structural elements that would have been necessary to hold up his tower, it is certainly possible for structural elements—like traditional stone columns—to be literally visible. Yet exposed structure expresses structure only in the most trivial sense: it simply *is* structure. What provides structure with the potential for having meaning can neither be discovered merely by *seeing* its outward form, nor by examining the physical properties and behavior of its beams, columns, walls or slabs. As Juan Pablo Bonta has argued: "The materials of painting are not paints, those of music are not sounds, those of architecture are not stones, any more than the material of literature is ink. The materials of these arts are not inert matter but the creation of man, charged with the cultural heritage of a community—no more, but certainly no less than language."[12]

One of the more famous modern illustrations of an explicit desire to *express* structure, irrespective of whether the actual structure is exposed or hidden, shows up in several buildings at the Illinois Institute of Technology (I.I.T.) in Chicago designed by Mies van der Rohe and constructed in the 1940s and 1950s. The first to be built—the Minerals and Metals Research Building (1941–1943)—has an exposed steel frame with glass and brick infill, along with various supplemental exposed steel elements designed to engage the non-structural brick and glass components. Certainly, the literal exposure of structural steel columns plays a role in its expression but, as

12.3   The famous steel corner at Alumni Memorial Hall (1945–1946), designed by Mies van der Rohe, is shown as it appears (*left*) and how it is actually constructed as cladding (*right*).

the architectural historian Reyner Banham argues, it was the refinement of Mies's formal "grammar" that was crucial: "The steel is not only made visible, but the manner of its assembly is made manifest, so that the outline grammar of it is filled out with detailed usages."[13]

Yet in his critique, Banham exaggerates the prevalence of "visible steel framing" on the I.I.T. campus. In fact, of the 19 buildings Mies designed at I.I.T., only five have exposed steel structure. Many have reinforced concrete frames and several, including Alumni Memorial Hall, employ steel that is, in fact, fireproofed (i.e., completely covered by concrete), so that what appears as visible steel structure on the facades is merely cladding (Fig.12.3).[14]

The cladding expresses structure by covering the actual structure in a manner that *looks like* structure—much like Mies's earlier use, in the 1929 Barcelona Pavilion, of "10mm thick steel angles . . . bound by rivets to a steel spine to form a compound column [that] was finally clad in chromium-plated steel with a screw-fixed cover plate to hide the join"[15]—and not, as Franz Schulze argues in his biography of Mies, by covering the actual structure in a manner that expresses the merely *symbolic* content of the cladding.[16]

What is *expressed* in the expression of structure is not the actual structure, but a set of culturally determined beliefs about structure. For example, Louis Sullivan, writing about the potential of the newly invented steel frame, described its appeal and inspiration as lying in "the suggestion of slenderness and aspiration, the soaring quality as of a thing rising from the earth as a unitary utterance, Dionysian in beauty."[17] Claude Bragdon, in his foreword to Sullivan's autobiography, credits Sullivan with being "the first squarely to face the expressional problem of the steel-framed skyscraper."[18] Yet a comparison with the actual steel frame shows how Sullivan's *expression* of structure not only differs from the structure itself (Fig.12.4), but reflects his own subjective values in relation to prevailing cultural expectations. What was characteristic of Sullivan's day gave way to new forms of expression, in spite of the fact that the actual structural frame behind the expressive facade looked more or less the same.

The actual behavior of a structural system depends to a large extent on loads applied, types of connections between structural members, material strengths and relative stiffnesses, and so on, factors which are commonly hidden from view and hard to evaluate by external observation.

12.4   In Adler & Sullivan's Guaranty—now Prudential—Building (Buffalo, NY), the true structural bay is revealed only at the ground floor levels.

Expression of structure, on the other hand, deals with notions about structure that may have only a superficial correspondence to the actual structure and its behavior.

And even when the expression of structure derives from the actual structural system, as in SOM's Hancock Building in Chicago (Fig.12.5, *left*), it is still important to distinguish between the structure and its expression, since they retain their independence and their separate purposes. The articulation of trusswork on the building facade may tell an educated observer something about how lateral forces can be optimally resisted in a high-rise building, but its expressive intent is not so literal nor so limited in its appeal. Rather, the expressive content as understood by a beholder is more likely to be metaphorical, referencing trussed forms familiar from other contexts so that, perhaps, an image of strength, utility or industrial technology might be evoked. Presenting this trusswork as a key element of the building's architectural design therefore has little to do with the utility of the real trusses in performing their structural function. Where a different expressive intention is at work, such as in the Citicorp tower in New York (Fig.12.5, *right*), the chevron trusses on the face of the building are simply covered by the building's skin.

12.5 SOM's Hancock Building in Chicago (*left*) and Stubbins's Citicorp Center in New York (*right*) both contain trusswork on their outer surfaces. SOM "expresses" this structural system; Stubbins's trusses are concealed by the building's skin.

Not only is the expression of structure different from structural behavior, but the actual behavior of structural elements and systems is not at all self-evident: all structural action takes place "beneath the surface" so that our view of structure is, literally, superficial. We do not see tension in a suspension bridge cable or compression in a stone column. Structural considerations may constrain or may inspire the invention of architectural form, but in most cases, the primary decisions about form arise from other considerations.

And even when a structural solution may seem uniquely appropriate to a given form—for example, the Eiffel Tower understood as the physical embodiment of the bending moment diagram associated with horizontal loading of a vertical cantilever—it is often the expressive possibilities of the structure, rather than any unique merit it may possess as a structure, that underlies its appeal. The architect Eero Saarinen, far from being forced into the design of his Dulles International Airport Terminal Building because of structural considerations, arrived at his structural system out of formal considerations. His concern, according to Seymour Howard, was that a "strong form that seemed to rise from the plane and hover over it would look best."[19] In fact, according to Howard, the forms have little to

12.6 Saarinen's Dulles International Airport Terminal Building: the forms have little to do with structural efficiency but are designed from the point of view of architectural and structural expression.

do with structural efficiency, but are designed from the point of view of architectural and structural expression (Fig.12.6).

Rem Koolhaas's short preface to Cecil Balmond's 2002 book, *Informal*, celebrates the arbitrary and the mystical. In doing so, it also provides some clues as to how contemporary structural expression may damage architectural utility, in particular, by making the case that Balmond "has destabilized and even toppled a tradition of Cartesian stability—systems that had become ponderous and blatant."[20] Of course, it is not entirely fair to criticize Koolhaas's "Preface" as if it were intended to be taken literally, since it serves less as a logical argument and more as a poetic evocation of the *feeling* he gets in the presence of defamiliarized structure-enabled geometries. And while structural expression can coincide with structural efficiency, as Billington advocated, it is more likely to result in gross inefficiency when it aligns with and supports the *appearance* of instability, as Koolhaas and Balmond advocate. Four types of such structural inefficiency and dysfunction—increased cost, cracking of adjacent material, thermal bridging, and dysfunctional geometry—are discussed below.

EXCESSIVE MATERIAL AND COST

Structural cost, per se, is not necessarily a threat to architectural utility. In some cases, the opposite is true—for example, where relatively more expensive long spans, by reducing the number of internal columns, might facilitate flexibility within a space. Nor is it necessarily problematic when works of architecture are expensive. In fact, being expensive is often useful in establishing a work of architecture's credibility (see Chapter 15). That being said, there are at least two ways in which structural cost may well undermine utility. First, if only a finite amount of money is available for a particular project, then an increased (and gratuitous) cost for structural expression counts as an *opportunity cost*: that is, other useful things may well be sacrificed since the project's budget for those useful things must be reduced to the extent that the cost of structure is increased. Second, a gratuitous increase in the amount of materials and resources used for a building is antithetical to "sustainable" practice. This is because more energy is expended and more global warming gases are produced in the manufacture, transport, and erection of structurally inefficient buildings. In particular, the manufacture of steel and concrete creates enormous quantities of global warming gases (5 percent and 4 percent of global CO_2 emissions respectively[21]). Countering this through the "sustainable" use of fly ash in place of cement or through the use of recycled structural steel simply shifts the problem to other non-sustainable practices: coal-burning electric generation (from which fly ash is obtained) or planned obsolescence leading to junked automobiles (from which wide-flange structural steel sections are obtained).

Although Balmond has claimed that deviant and unconventional structural geometries can actually be *more* efficient—that "interruptions to 'sameness' do not mean heavy penalties" and that "a specific framing with angularities, inclinations or whatever, may be cheaper"[22]—this is rarely the case. For example, consider a simple orthogonal one-story braced frame that is deliberately distorted in five-degree increments in order to represent a contemporary form of structural expression (Fig.12.7). For the spans and loads assumed, the amount (weight) of steel needed when the frame is skewed only 20 degrees from the vertical is almost *doubled*.

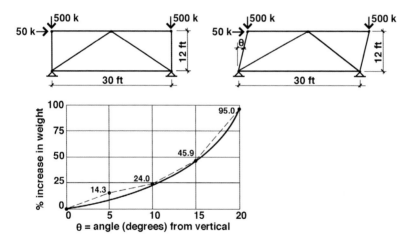

12.7 The weight (cost) of steel almost doubles in this simple braced frame as its inclination from the vertical increases from 0 to 20 degrees. Calculations by the author, assuming pinned connections, ASTM A992 steel wide-flange sections, vertical loads of 500 kips (2224 kN), a horizontal force of 50 kips (222 kN), with the design of compression and tension members based on the *Steel Construction Manual*, 14th edition, AISC (ASD method) except with only yielding of tension members considered (i.e., no consideration of shear lag or bolt holes).

In reality, the cost/weight penalty for structural expression can be even worse than in the hypothetical and schematic example cited above. OMA's Milstein Hall, for example, uses "1,125 tons [1.02 million kg] of steel . . . including five trusses that support the building's massive cantilever" to support a floor area (excluding the basement, framed entirely with reinforced concrete walls and slabs) of about 2,880 m² (31,000 square feet). This works out to more than 342 kg per m² (70 pounds of steel per square foot) of floor area.[23] To put this in perspective, the unit weight of two-story Milstein Hall is *more than double* that of the 100-story Hancock Center (Fig.12.5, *left*), a building intended to be both structurally expressive and—unlike Milstein Hall—structurally efficient, using only "29.7 pounds of steel per square foot of area [145 kg/m²]."[24] Ziad Shehab, an associate with OMA, justifies the structural extravagance of Milstein Hall on the basis of its didactic and phenomenal value ("The way this system of trusses expresses the different forces is something the students will be able to see and experience"[25]), as if structural forces present themselves, in all their complexity, on the surface of exposed steel frameworks. Unsurprisingly, the architects do not mention lost opportunity costs, the reduction of functional flexibility, and the environmental penalties from thermal bridging and excessive material use.

CRACKING OF ADJACENT MATERIAL

When loadbearing structural elements come into contact with cladding or concrete basement slabs (those cast directly on ground), it is necessary to consider how they move in relation to one another. Such movement might be caused by live, wind, or seismic loads; by thermal expansion and contraction; by chemical changes over time; by changes in ambient moisture conditions, and so on. Ordinary structural systems account for such movement by incorporating expansion or control joints, so that movement can occur without cracking of adjacent materials. However, where a particular mode of expression is in conflict with the formal manifestation of such joints, something has to give. As an example, the interaction of structure and cladding in Mies van der Rohe's Minerals and Metals Research Building at I.I.T. was not properly taken into consideration, so that, according to Carsten Krohn, "damages started to appear over time

". . . The continuous band of the masonry plinth was structurally connected to the steel frame behind, causing cracks to appear in the brickwork at the column lines due to the differential movement of the materials."[26]

THERMAL BRIDGES

The use of inordinate quantities of energy (to compensate for heat loss and heat gain), while triggering problems with occupant environmental comfort, was rarely considered in so-called New Brutalist designs, a class of buildings designed on the basis of constructional and structural expression that gained much notoriety in the 1950s and 1960s. Because the ethos underlying the style required that the actual and heroic materials constituting the cladding and structure be visible both from the exterior *and* the interior, the idea of including continuous control layers—such as insulation—into such a schema presented an insoluble conflict. Separately articulated insulation or vapor control layers, by covering the structure and cladding, would interfere with the heroic ("honest") expression of those materials. Reyner Banham, writing about the Hunstanton School in Norfolk, designed by Alison and Peter Smithson in 1949 and completed in 1954, put it this way: "Walls that are brick on the outside are brick (the same brick) on the inside, fairfaced on both sides. Wherever one stands within the school one sees its actual structural materials exposed, without plaster and frequently without paint."[27]

Exposed steel columns and large areas of glass also create thermal bridges in such buildings, with enormous amounts of heat loss and heat gain enabled not only by the movement of heat through highly conductive materials like brick, concrete, and—especially—steel, but also by radiant energy transfers through the glass. Because the "façades which surround the classroom area were structures with glazed panels of the same height as the spaces they protected" in the Hunstanton School, they encouraged "the entrance of natural light and also the heat of direct sun in summer and the cold of winter. This meant unfavourable conditions for the students for a large part of the year."[28]

Thermal bridges occur not only through structural columns or girders that are expressed *within* exterior walls, for example, in the Smithsons' Hunstanton School or in some of Mies's buildings at I.I.T. They also show up in uninsulated concrete expressed as structural walls and frames, or in columns expressed as *pilotis* holding up a building's superstructure. For example, I.M. Pei's Johnson Museum at Cornell University (1973) consists of uninsulated reinforced concrete walls and single-pane glass, a classic instance of thermal arrogance (Fig.12.8). The museum was officially opened in May 1973, just five months before the Organization of Arab Petroleum Exporting Countries instituted an oil embargo that precipitated the first of a series of energy crises leading directly to the implementation of energy codes intended to prohibit precisely that kind of energy-squandering building. Yet energy-squandering buildings, with exposed structure and thermal bridging, continue to be built.

Long after the American Society of Heating, Refrigerating and Air-Conditioning Engineers (ASHRAE) and the Illuminating Engineering Society (IES) jointly issued their first *Energy Standard for Buildings Except*

12.8 I.M. Pei's Johnson Museum of Art at Cornell University in Ithaca, NY is a dramatic and uninsulated reinforced concrete structure in which the entire exterior wall—including glass as well as the structural concrete itself—acts as an enormous thermal bridge.

12.9 Studio Gang's Aqua Tower in Chicago, enclosed only by glass and projecting concrete balconies, acts as an 82-story heat exchanger.

Low-Rise Residential Buildings (Standard 90.1) in 1975 in response to the 1973 energy crisis, buildings such as Studio Gang's Aqua Tower in Chicago (2010) continued to prioritize structural expression at the expense of energy conservation (Fig.12.9). This extreme—but hardly anomalous—example of thermal bridging was described by Joseph Lstiburek in the July 2012 *ASHRAE Journal* as "an orgy of glass and concrete. It is a thermodynamic obscenity while it takes your breath away. An 82-story heat exchanger in the heart of Chicago."[29] A final example of structural expression that results in thermal bridging is OMA's Milstein Hall at Cornell University (2011). In this case, the building is lifted off the ground by 14 enormous and uninsulated steel columns that, of necessity, penetrate the insulated underbelly of the building to connect with the rest of the superstructure, effectively providing an unimpeded pathway for heat loss or heat gain,

12.10   The exterior steel columns in OMA's Milstein Hall at Cornell act as thermal bridges by penetrating through the insulated soffit.

depending on the season (Fig.12.10). Steel being an extraordinarily good conductor of heat, these columns—even with a combined cross-sectional area of just over 1.6 m² (17 square feet)—increase heat loss/gain through the soffit by about 10 percent. These buildings continue the ethos of New Brutalism, even if the "Brutalist" brand is no longer invoked. They demonstrate how the desire for structural expression may undermine utilitarian considerations of environmental control.

DYSFUNCTIONAL GEOMETRIES

While it may seem counterintuitive that a structural design can have a negative impact on the utilitarian function of a building by virtue of its geometry, there are, in fact, several ways in which the desire to *express* something about structure may come into conflict with architectural utility. At the extreme is Peter Eisenman's House VI (1975) in Cornwall, Connecticut, where the desire to express structure was literally made independent of actual structural necessity and behavior. Subsuming structural and other elements within a conceptual framework in which utilitarian considerations are suppressed, it is hardly surprising, as Robert Gutman wrote in 1977, that "easy conversation during meal times is hard to sustain because of the notational columns that for no structural reason descend into the only convenient space for a dining table."[30] In fact, not only do many of the elements that Eisenman expressed as structure "have no role in supporting the building planes," but some structural elements that were added because they were actually necessary demonstrate "the consistency and force of Eisenman's construction [in] that it is immediately apparent they don't belong in the building."[31]

A similarly gratuitous expression of structure occurs in OMA's Milstein Hall, where an inclined reinforced concrete column, having no structural

12.11 Enormous rigid-frame "trusses," visible behind the curtain wall, enable OMA's Milstein Hall at Cornell University (2011) to cantilever over University Avenue.

function, created ADA-compliance issues that were ultimately addressed only by the addition of cane-detection bars (discussed in Chapter 4). OMA, working with structural consultant Robert Silman Associates, also compromised the building's utility by cantilevering the second floor 15 meters (50 feet) over an adjacent street (Fig.12.11). Even with the additional weight of steel needed to implement this audacious cantilever, discussed above, the flexibility of the second floor is forever compromised because occupancies with heavy live loads such as library stack areas—originally envisioned as a possible programmatic component of this large floor plate—can no longer be placed in the cantilevered zone since their weight would cause excessive structural deflections.

Perhaps the most obvious way in which structural geometry can compromise utility occurs in auditoriums and stadiums—as described in Chapter 2—where columns designed to support mezzanines or roofs block views of the stage or the field of play. Yet one tends to forgive the architects and engineers of such dysfunctional geometries, at least in older structures, since they were consistent with prevailing technical limitations, and therefore also with cultural expectations, corresponding to lower material strengths (at least for steel and reinforced concrete) and less sophisticated methods of structural analysis. Rather, it is the gratuitous and deliberate *expression* of structural dysfunction that is here criticized.

13
EXPRESSION OF SUSTAINABILITY

It seems trivial to examine the expression of normative building types—"gas station," "office building," and so on—in terms of their utilitarian function. And it seems inappropriate, if not entirely futile—since I am neither connoisseur nor critic—to speculate about the subjective expression of idiosyncratic buildings (Architecture with a capital "A") in relation to their underlying utilitarian functionality. There is, however, one class of utilitarian building—a class that includes everything from gas stations to office buildings—in which architecture often devolves into generalized forms of expression, irrespective of the building's particular occupancy or type: the so-called green, or sustainable, building.

Buildings that seek to *express* their sustainability often utilize similar formal and material tropes in two broad categories: natural and industrial. Nature is a surprisingly persistent theme in sustainable building design, presumably because it expresses the ideal of a sustainable planet, one *in* which—and *with* which—humans could live in harmony. Such an interest in nature shows up in the use of (1) curved forms, since straight lines might be construed as an expression of human arrogance; (2) relatively unprocessed materials such as wood, bamboo, mud brick, and fieldstone; (3) fabric membranes, which evoke a nomadic hunter-gatherer lifestyle, i.e., one in which humans were closer to nature; (4) an abundance of daylight, i.e., passive solar energy; and (5) plant material—even if only a monoculture consisting of sedums set into a thin layer of engineered soil medium—covering walls or roofs.

On the other hand, industrial and technologically sophisticated forms and materials also show up as expressive elements in sustainable architecture, for example, in the use of (1) wind turbines and photovoltaic solar panels to capture energy from wind and sun; (2) glass—lots of expensive, high-tech, spectrally selective, double- or triple-glazed insulating glass—primarily to enable daylighting, whether or not this actually represents an energy-efficient (sustainable) deployment of resources (see Chapter 5); and (3) other high- and low-tech devices, often employed to enable the expression of daylight, including such things as light shelves (to bounce incoming light further into the building interior) and automatic or fixed shading devices (to mitigate the problem of glare).

One might think that simply *being* sustainable would be enough, but this is clearly not the case. The utilitarian functions of sustainability—to create healthy indoor environments; to reduce the use of fossil fuels and, therefore, the production of greenhouse gases; to limit the use of potable water; and to harvest renewable raw material without damaging natural ecosystems (or to recycle nonrenewable material)—are not necessarily consistent with corporate profitability and international economic competition and so, unless required by governmental intervention in the form of energy codes, building codes, and zoning ordinances, they are not likely to be taken seriously. In this vacuum, however, the *expression* of sustainability has emerged as a value-adding economic strategy for both state and corporate entities, primarily as that intangible asset known in accounting practice as "goodwill."[1] Disingenuously expressing the idea of sustainability, rather than actually creating the conditions for sustainability, is often labeled "greenwashing," the impetus for which is parodied brilliantly by cartoonist Rob Esmay, who draws two executives staring out their office window at billowing industrial smokestacks, one remarking wistfully to the other, "Can't we just dye the smoke green"?[2]

THE HANNOVER PRINCIPLES

The architect William McDonough and other members of his office wrote (he prefers to use the word "assembled") *The Hannover Principles* as a design guide for the 2000 World's Fair in Hannover, Germany, to "encourage the design professions to take sustainability into consideration."[3] While there is some interest in the utilitarian function of sustainability, the book is primarily concerned with offering advice about the *expression* of sustainability. To that end, the book consists of nine principles ("maxims") intended to inspire participants in the Fair, followed by guidelines and other supplementary material (including a more "sustained" discussion of sustainability). The principles are all idealistic; they deal not with the reality of building constrained by profitability and competition, but rather with a fantasy landscape "based on the enduring elements of Earth, Air, Fire, Water, and Spirit."[4] Similar pre-scientific categories appear in Hindu,

Japanese, and Greek ancient philosophies; the use of these terms to frame the discussion of sustainability foreshadows a denial of, resistance to, and denigration of science-based knowledge.

The principles, summarized below, betray a moralistic, anti-rational, and pro-business standpoint. This is hardly accidental: forms of expression do not evolve in a vacuum but are validated within particular cultures to the extent that they accomplish an ideological mission—a mission that serves the interest of whomever is paying the bills. Whether or not the authors articulate, or even understand, this function is irrelevant. Invoking morality and mysticism on the one hand, and denigrating science, technology, and social planning on the other hand, provide ideological cover for the continued exploitation of both human and environmental resources.

Principle No. 1: Insist on rights of humanity and nature to coexist. This principle frames the coexistence of humans and the natural world in terms of "rights." But what exactly are rights, where do they come from, and what is their purpose? In his book on the evolution of rights and liberal theory, Ian Shapiro convincingly shows

> that the principal reasons for the tenacity of the liberal conception of individual rights, problems and all, are ideological: its Cartesian view of the subject of rights, its negative libertarian view of the substance of rights, its view of individual consent as the legitimate basis for rights, and its essentially pluralist and utilitarian conception of the purposes of rights have, in their various formulations, combined to express a view of politics that is required by and legitimates capitalist market practices.[5]

Market practices, of course, involve the exchange of property, a practice which turns out to benefit some while impoverishing others. Clearly, a power is needed to enforce the voluntary exchange of property that takes place in such market economies and that constitutes its fundamental principle.

> By granting rights, the state is using its power to ensure that every relationship between citizens satisfies the principles of its rule, nothing more. . . . The 'nature' that demands constitutional rights for humans is

the world of competition, in which property does not leave much room for mutual respect. The *positive* determination of what is *human*, which the state bestows on everyone, has a purely *negative* content.[6]

McDonough's discussion of rights not only abstracts from any consideration of purpose and power, but also idealizes the result of this coexistence as something potentially "healthy, supportive, diverse and sustainable."[7] Health, support, and diversity do, in fact, enter into the calculations that underlie governmental decisions to support sustainable practices, but only to the extent that they "sustain" the profitable exploitation of humans and natural things. Such calculations—for example, pitting the competitive success of nation-states against the potentially catastrophic consequences of global warming—are both ubiquitous and insidious; politicians and media routinely hold the latter hostage to the former as if such priorities were self-evident. As I write, tariffs are being imposed on imported solar panels by a Republican president, based on calculations about the cost of (imported) renewable energy versus the benefit for American workers and corporations: "On Monday, the Trump administration announced that it would impose steep tariffs on imported solar panels, which could raise the cost of solar power in the years ahead, slowing adoption of the technology and costing jobs. Mr. Trump has long championed trade barriers as a way to protect United States manufacturers from foreign competitors."[8]

This is clearly not just an artifact of a particular political party gaining power. During the previous Obama administration, for example, the logic of promoting domestic jobs and economic growth, while dealing with perceived threats to national security, also informed decisions about sustainable practices. For example, Obama argued that the U.S. could "become the world's leading exporter of clean energy. We can hand over the jobs of the future to our competitors, or we can confront what they've already recognized as the great opportunity of our time: The nation that leads the world in creating new sources of clean energy will be the nation that leads the 21st-century global economy."[9] The modest initiatives proposed and implemented during that administration were always justified on that basis and were never designed to actually "avoid a catastrophic rise in sea levels."[10]

Principle No. 2: Recognize interdependence. This is essentially the same as the first principle dealing with coexistence.

Principle No. 3: Respect relationships between spirit and matter. Corporate entities and their designers are asked to take into account "community, dwelling, industry and trade in terms of connections between spiritual and material consciousness."[11] This advice is readily accepted by those entities seeking to mask their actual contributions to environmental and human damage—contributions that are unavoidable within a competitive framework defined by the life-and-death struggle for corporate survival—with a mystical appeal to some "higher" principle.

Principle No. 4: Accept responsibility for the consequences of design. This serves as a moral admonition to those competing within capitalist economies within which human and environmental damage are well documented. The system itself, we are told, should never be held accountable: rather, it's *your* fault (so *you* need to accept responsibility).

Principle No. 5: Create safe objects of long-term value. This is a puzzling principle to include in a set of sustainability guidelines. The clear implication is that safe objects of long-term value are *not* the default product of conventional architectural design based on codes, regulations, and practices that have evolved within democratic governments supporting capitalist economies. Furthermore, this principle suggests that it is the responsibility of architects and the property owners who hire them to voluntarily create such things based on a heightened sense of moral righteousness, rather than to work towards the abolition of the conditions which make such objects the exception rather than the rule. The idea that voluntary action of individuals can overcome countervailing tendencies rooted in the competitive need to reduce costs of production (tendencies that historically have worked *against* the creation of safe objects of long-term value) is itself rooted in the type of market-driven, libertarian ideology that pervades McDonough's book.

Principle No. 6: Eliminate the concept of waste. That is, emulate "natural systems, in which there is no waste."[12] There are two problems with this advice. First, waste is inherent in all biological and production processes. If such waste is then transformed into something useful within the human sphere, or subjected within nature to processes of transformation, one still hasn't abolished waste in the first instance. Second, rather than emulating the blind processes characterizing natural systems, modern human societies have found it necessary to develop purposeful strategies for dealing with waste. In nature, bears shit in the woods; within dense human settlements, expensive and technologically sophisticated waste-water treatment plants must be built. Even so, eliminating waste is different from eliminating the *concept* of waste. The former is a technical and economic problem in which the costs of waste reduction or "recycling" are weighed against the benefits; the latter is pure ideology. In fairness to McDonough, he seems to have retreated somewhat from the concept of no waste, at least as a slogan; in answer to a question about his approach to a "zero-waste" universe, he replied, "I wouldn't use that phrase. If I said zero waste, then it makes it sound like I don't like waste. I love waste!"[13]

Principle No. 7: Rely on natural energy flows. "Human designs should, like the natural world, derive their creative forces from perpetual solar income."[14] This is misleading on a number of counts. First, many sources of energy used in "human designs"—those based on carbon or hydrocarbon fuels, whether wood, coal, oil, or natural gas—are already derived from "perpetual solar income"; second, even if we understand "perpetual solar income" as the direct use of the sun's energy (or the use of renewable, plant-based, fuels), this still excludes from consideration other renewable energy sources such as geothermal and tidal; third, non-human life forms constituting the "natural world" rely on solar-derived energy just as humans do, and are also constantly running into "problems" of fuel (food) supply shortages. Idealizing the natural world as a place of ecological stasis and bliss sheds no light on the human condition.

Principle No. 8: Understand the limitations of design. With this principle, designers are asked to "practice humility in the face of nature."[15] After all, architects cannot solve "all problems" and nothing lasts forever anyway. This is just a repackaging of ancient mythology and postmodern assertions implying human arrogance, the danger of knowledge, and the evils of technology. Its underlying content is that our inevitable failures (since we cannot solve all problems) shouldn't bother us (practice humility) as we emulate nature (our "model and mentor") and eschew science, planning, and collective action.

Principle No. 9: Seek constant improvement by the sharing of knowledge. This final principle is an example of the underlying idealism of the text, in that competition between private businesses ensures that knowledge is a resource reserved, to the extent possible, for private gain. Patents and copyrights turn knowledge into intellectual property. Trade secrets are protected jealously. In other words, knowledge is limited because those who have it tend to view it in a proprietary manner and are reluctant to share it. Competing manufacturers vying for market share may not be inclined to publish information that objectively compares their products with others. Even the possibility of gaining knowledge from structural design failure is often constrained because "the commercial nature of engineering works against the wide dissemination of accounts of human error" including, for example, "the practice of sealing the testimony of legal proceedings dealing with liability over design failures."[16]

The five mystical elements of the guidelines, cited earlier, are used as ad hoc placeholders to organize various strategies and platitudes concerning sustainability. For example, Earth is not only described as "context and material" for buildings but also as the material basis for the development of an appropriate "aesthetic" attitude. This is to be accomplished by wrapping buildings in forms of expression that allow them to serve as "a didactic tool to demonstrate that sustainable thinking can be put into practice in the real world." Building materials should be "considered for their broadest range of effects, from emotive to practical," while local traditions and production should be mined to "emphasize the regional, cultural, and historical uniqueness of the place."[17]

McDonough is hardly the only architect/writer who values the didactic or expressive qualities of sustainable building. Richard Ingersoll, for example, makes essentially the same point:

> The question of what a building looks like, what other buildings or natural things it reminds you of, and what it represents is still of primary importance. This is why the rhetorical function of architecture is so

important. A good building must convince one that it is good—it must have appeal as a cultural product as well as a phenomenal, sheltering device.[18]

Yet while Ingersoll still presumes that a utilitarian functionality must underlie a building's expressive appeal, McDonough's Earth guidelines say very little about actually *being* sustainable. Instead, *utilitas* has been replaced with *venustas*; the prosaic utilitarian function of creating and preserving the necessary conditions for human survival—presupposing a scientific understanding of both human and environmental resources— has been seamlessly converted into the project of *selling the idea* of sustainability.

One "sells" an idea by appealing to emotions, rather than logical reasoning. It is therefore not accidental that an anti-rational bias permeates this text, emphasizing the fallibility and limitations of human knowledge and social planning: "No one knows the right answers to the challenge of sustainability as of yet."[19] "The best examples of it [sustainable development] come from simpler societies . . . But no simple return to vernacular architecture can help us now."[20] "Quality of life needs to be implied in the design itself, not legislated by a list of rules."[21] "The built fabric of our world . . . encourages us to imagine that we comprehend systems more complex than we can ever know."[22] "We gauge the success of a design by the experience of it through time. It cannot be judged against a pre-existing checklist of criteria."[23] (In other words, our "experience" of the design is considered an acceptable means of judging, as long as we have no objective criteria in mind!) "The idea of efficiency, of minimizing this or maximizing that, reinforces the limitations of mechanistic thinking, which imagines everything we do or experience to be part of a quantifiable system."[24] Instead, the text extolls "the unplanned, the fortuitous, the places evolved without any imposed and directing idea."[25] "Never has a world exposition chosen to celebrate the fact that humanity does not know very much about the world."[26] "The evidence is clear from the record of our [twentieth] century: claims to plan all aspects of the environment have failed . . ."[27] (In other words, "planning" itself is the culprit, rather than the capitalist exploitation of natural and human resources.) McDonough then cites Christopher Alexander's *Timeless Way of Building* which, he argues, "succeeds because he speaks, Zen-like, circling around the subject rather than holding it up for all to examine."[28] What is needed, in other words, is not a scientific understanding and organization of human society in relation to its environmental context, but rather a kind of poetry that might find "the truth of an integrative kind of beauty which is so impossible to describe."[29]

This anti-rational sentiment is hardly unique to McDonough's *Hannover Principles*; Anthony Vidler identifies an

> antimodern discourse that, since the early 1930s, had been gaining ground with critics skeptical of 'progress' and its supposed benefits. Philosophers on both the right and left of the political spectrum contributed to this sensibility, from Theodor Adorno to Martin Heidegger, Max Horkheimer to Hans Sedlmayr, which amounted to no less than a concerted attack on the founding premises of modernism . . .[30]

So much for Earth. Air and Fire are treated rather literally, in that the consideration of "atmospheric effects" of design is *not* meant to evoke ethereal modes of expression but rather the building's impact on global warming and ozone depletion. Also mentioned in the context of "air" are air pollution, indoor air quality, noise (presumably since it may travel through air), ventilation, wind, and so on. Fire is pretty much taken to stand for "energy." Once that equation is established, sustainable designers are encouraged to prioritize "on-site renewable energy sources" which avoid "fossil fuels or remote electrical generation"—in other words, to *avoid* using fire as a source of energy.[31]

Water is also treated mostly as what it is, with practical suggestions on how to use it efficiently ("sustainably"), although designers are also urged to find ways to "celebrate the profound value of this resource on both material and spiritual levels . . ."[32]

Spirit is invoked to once again excuse the chaos and damage corresponding to profit-driven development: "Building on the principle of humility, the design philosophy here should realize its *inherent limitations in trying to plan and direct* both human and natural processes." Planning and direction are ruled out but, perhaps in compensation, participants are advised that their design "*must present an aesthetic statement* which sets up human society as a conduit toward the further understanding of nature, not as an affront or an enemy to it."[33]

Consistent with the anti-rational bias of the text is the manner in which sustainability is reconciled with capitalism:

> Sustainability is a loaded and slippery term. It names those activities which can be continued far into the future, defining a way of life that will last. The trouble is that it is nothing new—business and industry have always hoped that whatever course they choose will be the sustainable course, one that will not push them out of business. In a sense, there is no practical need to scold business too much. If environmental considerations are something that can really be addressed, they have to encourage business activity, rather than forbid it.[34]

In other words: don't try to explain sustainability. Actual knowledge is impossible. Don't blame business for environmental and human damage; possibly nothing can be done about it anyway. And whatever is attempted must be consistent with the needs of those businesses which, desiring nothing but unending profitability, are sustainability's natural partners.

That the goal of sustainable development is to sustain exploitation is at once denied and proudly demonstrated. Maintaining a sustainable level of poverty in the Brazilian city of Curitiba is held up as an "inspiring example" of a "truly sustainable community." Garbage there is exchanged "for food and bus vouchers in the poorer parts of town" to encourage recycling; such measures result in a city that is "a favored site for new industries of local and foreign origin."[35] Glorification of "successful" unfettered development is later contradicted by a moral critique of both production and consumption that not only abstracts from the actual preconditions for sustained capitalist production, that is, the accumulation (growth) of privately held wealth, but simultaneously misrepresents damage to humans and environments as a consequence of the *scale* of exploitation, rather than the exploitation itself: "Sustainable development in the end recommends the leveling-off of increases in population and resource consumption. It will finally require a redefinition of values and a commitment from consumers to want and buy less, a pledge from industry to make less, and from builders to build less."[36]

Critiquing the Hannover Expo in 2000, Ralf Strobach, secretary of Hannover's Citizens' Initiative for Environment Protection, stated that: "For a long time, companies were unsure if they would be putting money in an eco-show or a showcase for their latest inventions."[37] *The Hannover Principles*, with its predictable blend of morality and capitalist ideology—invoked to explain and advocate for a sustainable world—thus perfectly reflects this confusion. The contradiction of the "green building" project, seeking to reconcile its idealistic goals with an economic system in which global competition for supremacy (or for survival) turns human and environmental exploitation into a virtual "law of nature," is becoming increasingly difficult to sustain.

14

THE COMMUNAL BEING AND THE PRIVATE INDIVIDUAL

Humans in developed capitalist societies, as a young Karl Marx argued in 1844, live two lives:

> Where the political state has attained its full degree of development man leads a double life, a life in heaven and a life on earth, not only in his mind, in his consciousness, but in *reality*. He lives in the *political community*, where he regards himself as a *communal being*, and in civil society, where he is active as a *private individual*, regards other men as means, degrades himself to a means and becomes a plaything of alien powers.[1]

This split personality manifests itself in the realm of art and architecture, where one finds both types of expression—the idealism of the communal being as well as the self-interested behavior of the private individual—but not necessarily so neatly bracketed within the two realms of man's "double life." Rather than finding the expression of freedom, democracy, equality, and community exclusively in the public (communal) domain and the expression of wealth, power, and status exclusively in private or corporate architecture, *all* forms of expression may at times appear in *all* buildings. Each individual, corporate, or public entity manifests this split identity, so the types of expression consistent with both sides (i.e., both the private/ self-interested and political/communal) may well show up in commercial buildings and private residences; while public or communal architecture also exists in a competitive environment—cities and states engage in economic competition against other cities and states; nations engage in global competition against other nation-states—so that symbolic evidence of wealth and power often becomes fused with the ideals of democracy, freedom, and community in public architecture.

While architecture's materials and geometries do not contain *within themselves* symbolic or expressive content, there is, nevertheless, some objective basis for identifying freedom, democracy, equality, community, wealth, and power as common expressive tropes. For example, when the Romans deployed "massive monolithic columns," not only were they "a symbol for the domination of Rome, [but] an equal degree of *power was displayed in their transport and erection*."[2] In other words, the necessary expertise, wealth, and power that made these structures possible was understood at the time—immediately and objectively, by rich and poor alike—not by decoding messages hidden in the forms, or by accessing repressed or unconscious psychological motivations, but simply by observing and drawing logical conclusions from the size and weight of the stones, and the effort (requiring wealth and literal power) necessary to quarry them, transport them, and erect them.

FREEDOM

In the Metropolitan Museum of Art's "Epic Abstraction: Pollock to Herrera" show, which opened in 2018 in New York City, the following curatorial text appeared on the wall: "Abstract Expressionism was promoted as exemplary of American democracy and freedom during the early years of the Cold War, and Pollock's art began exerting an international influence in this context. He reinvented the medium of painting as experiential, a kind of performance. Well over fifty years after their creation, these works retain their audacious dynamism and sense of daring."[3] From these three sentences may be gleaned many of the principal means and purposes relating to the expression of democracy and freedom. Most importantly, there is Pollock's "audacious dynamism and sense of daring" which expresses the ideal of freedom precisely by breaking conventions. To repeat and reprise what has gone before is, of course, just as valid an exercise in freedom as to break boundaries and defy conventions; freedom is, after all, the ability to do whatever you want to do (albeit subject to your control over the property that you are *doing* something to, while not transgressing the boundaries of someone else's property). But doing nothing new or daring, while an *example* of freedom, is not typically a viable *expression* of freedom. In other words, the *ideal* of freedom is to break free of existing constraints, and not merely to use one's property to further one's own interests, against all others. It is that ideal that is expressed in paintings such as Pollock's.

According to the curatorial gloss, this expression of freedom was "promoted . . . during the early years of the Cold War." This shows that ideals of freedom can be deployed as propaganda, not only to reinforce and express competitive values within the home country, but also against rival economic systems. And the use of art (or architecture) as propaganda has no necessary or intrinsic relationship to the actual formal characteristics of the work itself. Deborah Howell-Ardila, citing another instance of Cold War competition, argues that "built forms convey no inherent political meaning; the same modernist style of the FRG's [West Germany's] first transparent (and thus 'democratic') Bundestag in Bonn, for example, had been used to fine effect by Benito Mussolini for the fascist party headquarters in Como, Italy."[4] Not only that, "two heroes of the modern movement, Walter Gropius and Mies van der Rohe (both of whom played prominent roles in shaping the new 'democratic' architecture of the FRG) had entered Nazi-sponsored design competitions . . . thus acknowledging the flexibility of architecture's political significance."[5]

In extrapolating from painting to architecture, there is only one minor disclaimer. Architecture, unlike painting, is not only a means of expression, but is also a vehicle to support various utilitarian activities. This, by its very nature, constrains the unfettered expression of freedom, but also, paradoxically, makes that expression—where it occurs—all the more potent. As an example, consider the rebuilding of the World Trade Center towers in New York City. Daniel Libeskind's unbuilt proposal, "a sharp-angled skyscraper, topped with a twisting spire,"[6] deploys two modes of expression, each of which gained quite a bit of public support. One type of symbolism is gratuitous and inane, that is, setting the tower's height at exactly 1,776 feet. This height references the date of America's Declaration of Independence, at least when measured in imperial units; the same height expressed as 541 meters would be perceived as unremarkable, unless one was commemorating, for example, the year when "Bubonic plague appears suddenly in the Egyptian port of Pelusium."[7] The other form of expression is more analogous to Pollock's "audacious dynamism and sense of daring": the unexpected distortion of the tower's form from what is considered economically, structurally, and functionally appropriate.

Yet although Libeskind won the competition for the new World Trade Center master plan, his expressive "Freedom Tower" design, intended by the competition's organizers only to illustrate the potential of the master plan, was never seriously considered. "There was no guarantee that the architecture from the master-plan competition would be built; it was intended to get people excited about a master plan. . . . In fact, by the time Libeskind had won, [developer Larry] Silverstein had already hired David Childs, an architect at Skidmore, Owings, and Merrill." Whereas Libeskind's proposal was an inefficient and expensive expression of freedom, Childs's design was precisely the opposite, prioritizing structural and functional efficiency. Even the name, "Freedom Tower," was replaced with something explicitly conservative and nostalgic: "1 World Trade Center." Michael Kimmelman, architecture critic for the *New York Times*, contrasted the expression of freedom that could have been—"to show New York's indomitable spirit: the defiant city transfigured from the ashes"—with the attitude actually taken, one that "implies (wrongly) a metropolis bereft of fresh ideas." For Kimmelman, having "fresh ideas" can be understood at the scale of architecture—through a building's unconventional ("fresh") design—but also at the scale of the master plan, for example, by incorporating "housing, culture and retail, capitalizing on urban trends and the growing desire for a truer neighborhood, at a human scale."[8] However, only the former can be understood in terms of the *expression of freedom*; the latter is simply the critic speculating about the utility of deploying mixed occupancies on the site.

Instead of acknowledging the essence of defamiliarization as the expression of freedom, historians and critics often prefer to wallow in the subjectivity of psychological or pseudo-scientific speculation, whether invoking Freud's speculative theories of a death drive or Sigfried Giedion's "cosmic" vision linking art and Einsteinian relativity. The point is not to validate what architects or beholders *think* about their motivations or intentions in creating or interpreting defamiliarized buildings; on the one hand, one cannot peer into someone's brain to uncover a "true" motive; on the other hand, whether a motive is articulated at the moment of creation or extracted on the psychoanalyst's couch only reveals to what extent that motive has been informed by personal experience or appropriate cultural frameworks. Immersed within an architectural culture in which defamiliarized formal strategies have become prevalent, the desire—the *necessity*—of architects and beholders to compete within that culture will, in and of itself, motivate them to internalize the critical frameworks that have emerged within that culture. These critical frameworks are adopted—like the phenomena they purport to explain—not because they are *true*, but because, within their own competitive critical sphere, they have proven themselves effective in promoting a particular stylistic tendency.

The point, then, is to find an objective explanation of defamiliarized architectural production within modern capitalist democracies that does not rely on the self-serving subjectivity of critical artistic frameworks. And this brings us to the observation that *all* instances of the avant-garde can be explained as expressions of capitalist freedom. Those architects and their clients who choose to deviate from cultural norms by defamiliarizing their architectural production do so, first, in a competitive environment where being noticed (having *notoriety*) is deemed useful and, second, where freedom—the permission (compulsion) to do what one wants with one's property—is enshrined as a basic tenet of capitalism. Thus, the idealization of freedom as a heroic refusal to accept bourgeois conventions, rather than representing some threatening or revolutionary impulse, has an entirely reactionary content. This is not because the freedom being invoked is an illusion, but, to the contrary, precisely because it is real and oppressive. As explained by Karl Held and Audrey Hill, "freedom and equality are hardly an idyllic matter."[9]

DEMOCRACY

If the expression of freedom in art and architecture is clearly linked to the *reality* of freedom in capitalist democracies, examples of the expression of democracy in art and architecture are harder to find and more difficult to explain. Of course, one can cite the trivial case where buildings that house democratic institutions come to symbolize the idea of democracy: "For at least 2,500 years," according to Deyan Sudjic, "people have assembled to participate in and observe democracy in action. The environments in which democratic debate takes place can be seen as a *physical expression* of mankind's relationship with the ideals of democracy."[10] Yet, even in those cases, it is not clear that "democracy" itself is being expressed. Instead, it may be that the formal qualities of legislative (parliament) buildings, for example, are more likely to express intimidation, authority, and legitimacy than the ideals of democracy. Sudjic admits as much when he argues that the "classical language of architecture has been used more than any other to create monumental parliamentary buildings that both inspire and can also *intimidate* in their representation of the democratic ideal"; or that "the architectural language ... relied upon an established political tradition to reflect its *authority*. None more so than the fledgling United States of America which looked to Greece and Rome to *legitimise* its own republic."[11]

In the same way, the mere provision of a gathering place, whether indoors (the "town hall") or outdoors (the "public space"), is still often conflated with the ideal of democracy: "In 2011, Occupy Wall Street and Cairo's Tahrir Square protests sparked the publication of a spate of architectural texts on the use of public space, the rise of a democratic network culture, and the rethinking of public policy."[12] Yet such spaces express democracy, not because there is anything particularly "democratic" about their form or structure (except for the trivial fact that they *can* physically accommodate large groups of people) but because they have become associated with specific protest movements that have, in turn, been linked with the ideal of democracy.

The idea of a democratic architecture has also been applied to buildings that are pleasing to, or used by, the masses, whether libraries, shopping malls, or railway stations. Joan Ockman, for example, asks if Rem Koolhaas's "radical gesture" of "overturn[ing] all the established hierarchies" at the Seattle Public Library was "a democratizing one, an effort to make an august public institution more crowd-pleasing and friendly?"[13] Aaron Betsky argues that "our railroad stations are our contemporary architecture of democracy [because] they are open and accessible, they are shared spaces, they bring us together, and they celebrate all that gathering and connecting with grand and often beautiful structures."[14] Koolhaas himself writes with unbridled condescension about the unending interior maze within airports and shopping malls that serves as "an architecture of the masses" and "one of the last tangible ways in which we experience freedom."[15] Yet equating democracy or freedom with mere gathering, access, or movement is unconvincing, and Ockman's claim that "democratic architecture in late-capitalist society ... has shifted over the last half century from a culture of monuments to one of spectacles"[16] is both irrelevant and misleading. Examples of public gatherings, access, and movement—framed by architecture as spectacle—are hardly unique to modern democratic states (think of medieval cathedrals, markets, and fairs; or Roman games with their animal entertainments and executions; or festivals and celebrations in fascist Italy).

In fact, the word, "democracy" is most often simply added whenever freedom is discussed, since they are bound together in practice: Louis Sullivan, for example, makes this clear in an article directed at "The Young Man in Architecture" in 1900, defining democracy in terms of both freedom and restraint: "It is of the essence of Democracy that the individual man is free in his body and free in his soul. It is a corollary therefrom, that he must govern or restrain himself, both as to bodily acts and mental acts; that, in short, he must set up a responsible government within his own individual person."[17]

The linkage of democracy with freedom shows up, as we have already seen, in the Metropolitan Museum's claim that "Abstract Expressionism was promoted as exemplary of American democracy and freedom." On the one hand, freedom—to do what one wants with one's property, especially when defying cultural conventions—is clearly expressed in Abstract Expressionist paintings. But on the other hand, there are no obvious elements in such paintings that correspond to the idea of democracy—literally "rule by people" as translated from the Greek. Neither representative government, elections by majority vote, the checks and balances of legislative, executive, and judicial branches, nor any of the other conventional trappings of democracy appear, however metaphorically, in these paintings. The sociologist Herbert Gans makes the same argument in his response to Ockman's essay on democratic architecture: "Architects design buildings, but their buildings do not engage in politics, vote, or give money to campaigning politicians. They simply house a variety of human activities, including political ones, but these could be democratic, fascist, or communist, even if they were designed by an architect active in democratic politics."[18] If freedom is the concept made visible by defying convention, democracy, invisible as a concept in its own right, comes along for the ride.

DEMOCRACY AND TRANSPARENCY

Ever since U.S. Supreme Court Justice Louis Brandeis argued in 1913 that "publicity is justly commended as a remedy for social and industrial diseases, sunshine is said to be the best disinfectant, electric light the best policeman," the metaphor of transparency has become a popular ideological trope for democracy, although certain limitations and even negative consequences of transparency have also been noted. For example, "if the power of transparency is based on the 'power of shame,'" according to political scientist Jonathan Fox, "then its influence over the really shameless could be quite limited."[19] Additionally, and precisely *because* transparency has become a factor in their operations, "democratic governments have incentives to obfuscate evidence."[20] This "dark side" of transparency gets even darker, since "one person's transparency is another's surveillance [and] one person's accountability is another's persecution."[21]

As an expressive architectural element symbolizing democracy, the metaphor of transparency has not been particularly common. Where it does show up, most famously in the reconstruction of the Reichstag in Berlin by Foster + Partners in 1999, the architect's disingenuous claim that "within its heavy shell it is light and transparent, its activities on view"[22] is contradicted by other observers. The architect and scholar Hisham Elkadi argues, for example, that "while glass seemingly provides a wider transparency and a social transformation, it actually denies any real interaction. . . . In fact, the glass dome of the Reichstag has replaced one form of presentation of power with another illusive and more subtle one. The transparency of glass is used in this case to conceal the contemporary powers of the Reichstag; the dome is a reference to tradition in order to conceal tradition."[23]

Peter Conradi framed a similar argument against the Bundestag in Bonn designed by Günther Behnisch in 1992:

> The assertion that glass is transparent and therefore democratic is just as silly as the assertion that stone is not transparent and therefore authoritarian. It would be banal to assume that the transparence of Behnisch's new Bundestag . . . creates more democracy . . . Even in this see-through hall, the tax law of 1995 remains an incomprehensible, impenetrable piece of politics. The tactical evasions of a Wolfgang Schauble do not become more transparent in a glass assembly room.[24]

EQUALITY

Democracy is sometimes used as a stand-in for the ideal of equality—of a non-hierarchical society where everyone gets the same things. The architectural manifestation of this democratic ideal of equality consists of a non-hierarchical array of units in which repetitive functions, all with the same underlying geometry, can be housed. This is, however, not even remotely close to representing what equality means within democratic states. It confuses what bourgeois economists derisively call "equality of outcome"—the idea that governments ought to redistribute wealth to eliminate or reduce distinctions between rich and poor—with what they typically advocate under the rubric of "equality of opportunity." This latter version of equality necessarily creates losers and winners, being nothing other than the requirement to compete, and is consistent with freedom, liberty, and the equal application of law. Yet even the ideal of equality is not easy to express in works of architecture, since hierarchy—ordered difference—is inherent in much of what is built, irrespective of the architect's intention: *up* is different from *down*; *high* is different from *low*; *edges* are different from *middles*; *south* is different from *north*; and so on. The corner office, a paragon of unequal and hierarchical space, is inherent in rectangular office plans and, to that extent, precludes formal equality in such buildings. Perhaps the clearest expression of the ideal of equality shows up in apartment houses, hotels, jails, strip malls, and suburban housing developments—that is, in architectural and urban forms where repetition of a standard module is consistent with the utilitarian functions operating within the overall composition.

Yet this vision of a non-hierarchical democratic order based on the ideal of equality is at odds with the most famous articulation of a democratic architecture. For Frank Lloyd Wright, democracy did not mean equality of outcome, but rather signified an individual's freedom to choose, within an idealistic and idiosyncratic version of capitalism based on "ground free in the sense that Henry George predicated free ground" and "money not taxed by interest but money only as a free medium of exchange."[25] As to how those "democratic" ideals would be expressed, Wright could only point to his own buildings, for example, his Usonian projects, as "expressing the inner spirit of our democracy, which by and large is not yet so very democratic after all."[26] Yet it is clear that Wright was not interested in obliterating class distinctions or creating a one-size-fits-all template to express the ideal of democratic equality. "In the buildings for Broadacres," he argued in 1935, "no distinction exists between much and little, more and less. Quality is in all, for all, alike. The thought entering into the first or last estate is of the best. What differs is only individuality and extent. There is nothing poor or mean in Broadacres."[27] What Wright means—by suggesting that "no distinctions exist between much and little, more and less"—is *not* that one should eliminate distinctions between "much and little, more and less," but rather that one should imbue all the architecture in Broadacre City, no matter its size, with the same *quality* of design. *Quantitative* differences— class differences—are not abolished or suppressed; equality of outcome is never the goal.

Christian Norberg-Schulz, like Wright, agrees that "democratic" architecture should *not* be concerned with the expression of equality. Unlike Wright, who had no problem with the expression of social inequality, Norberg-Schulz is concerned that class differences within capitalist society constitute a social embarrassment that should be suppressed, although differences in occupation—function—remain worthy of expression, except in the domestic sphere:

> In a democratic society it may not be right to express differences in status, but it is surely still important to represent different roles and institutions. Our individual roles should probably not show themselves too much in the dwellings, as this would contradict the democratic equality of private persons. But our places of work should be differentiated to show that the individual roles participate in varying phenomenal contexts. The surgery of a physician should not only be practical, it must also appear clean and sanitary. In this way it calms down the patient. The office of a lawyer, on the contrary, should soothe the worried client by appearing friendly and confidence inspiring, at the same time as it expresses that the lawyer is an able man.[28]

What Norberg-Schulz advocates is an architecture of explicit manipulation, referencing techniques more commonly associated with advertising and persuasion: it is not enough for architecture to merely function. Architectural expression must also alter the mental and emotional state of building occupants so that they are better able to assume the roles assigned to them by the architect, presumably acting on behalf of the building's owner or tenant. While it is possible that the surgery actually *is* clean and sanitary in addition to *appearing to be* clean and sanitary, and while it is possible that the lawyer *is* actually competent in addition to *appearing to be* competent, it is easy to see how this attention to the techniques of appearance and persuasion, made independent from real performance and behavior (utilitarian function), can lead to all sorts of deceitful, if not dangerous, practices.

COMMUNITY

Stone, as exemplified in the prior discussion of Roman monoliths, often celebrates and expresses wealth and power. Yet stone can also be deployed as an idealization and expression of community. This occurred in postwar Berlin, in reaction to the alleged "inhumanity" or "superficiality" of modernist architecture and urbanism, to which stone's apparent solidity—and a renewed interest in traditional (although criticized as "nostalgic") community and pedestrian-friendly urban design—was offered as an antidote. Yet, like the facile equation of transparency and democracy, even such seemingly benign references to traditional stone-faced architecture can be fraught with controversy. Hans Kollhoff, for example, complained that—at least in the context of postwar Berlin—"every architect who takes a stone in the hand is accused of being a fascist."[29]

The expression of community is thus invariably double-sided, with the ideological battles fought in postwar Germany over the alleged political content of merely formal arrangements hardly an isolated exception. On the one hand, the expression of community, like that of democracy, can occur simply when utilitarian forms designed to accommodate groups of people (communities) become associated with that activity. This happens, for example, in sports stadiums, where a community of fans gathers to cheer on their local team, or even in the parking lots outside the stadiums, where community members gather for "tailgate" parties. Yet even, or especially, in such cases, the dark side of community is easy to spot: the community of fans is often explicitly antagonistic to fans of the opposing team, with taunting or physical altercations commonly encountered.[30]

Architects may adopt explicit formal geometries that have come to "mean" or express the ideal of community—things like front porches or stoops that occupy and define a semi-public space between the explicitly public right-of-way (street) and the private domain of the house or tenement building—based on the memory of cultural practices from prior times. But, as noted in Chapter 7, times have changed, and the historic sense of community embodied in urban patterns associated with specific building elements like porches and stoops is increasingly anachronistic. Where actual community does persist, it is always on an *exclusionary* basis—this is made unambiguously clear when politicians or community leaders talk of the "black" community, the "LGBTQ" community, the "alt-right" community, and so on. Even where the ideal of community is invoked on an apparently inclusive basis, for example, when the concept of a "people" is invoked, this national community—"the totality of a country's inhabitants whom a *state power* defines as *its members* . . . regardless of the natural and social differences and antagonisms between them"[31]—is, nevertheless, explicitly, and ruthlessly, exclusionary with respect to the other "peoples" of the world, with whom they are forced to compete.

Thus, the architectural expression of community is mostly self-evident and trivial in buildings like community centers, stadiums, or other community gathering places where the sign on the door and the purely utilitarian organization of form and space—rather than any explicit symbolic system of meaning—create a de facto expression of community, having become associated with the *reality* of community gathering that takes place therein. On the other hand, where explicit symbols of community are deployed, such as porches and stoops intended to invoke a memory of what once might have functioned as a communal street, they tend to become merely anachronistic *expressions* of community, betraying the absence of actual community.

WEALTH AND POWER

Not only wealth and power, but the *lack of* wealth and power, can be expressed in works of architecture. For example, material qualities that appear to be cheap or ubiquitous lend themselves to architectural expression in two ways: first, when a material's cheapness or ubiquity is consistent with the building's function; and second, when a material's cheapness or ubiquity is self-consciously deployed as a form of irony. An example of the former is traditional public (social) housing, where being cheap and common is implicitly part of the design brief. The idea is to attach a stigma to the building itself because "anything well-designed will be too appealing to eligible tenants, thus discouraging them from ever leaving. So affordable housing should not only be cheap, it should look cheap."[32] An example of the latter is Frank Gehry's early use of corrugated metal, sheet metal, or chain-link fencing as part of building enclosure systems, or his later use of cheap plywood as a finished interior surface within expensive and culturally sophisticated buildings.

Materials that appear to be expensive and unusual (rare), or that require the deployment of great effort to transform them from their natural state, also lend themselves to architectural expression, primarily as manifestations of wealth and power (and, as argued by John Ruskin, as representations of devotion or sacrifice). But none of this is absolute; a material such as glass, to take but one example, can express wealth and power yet can also be used in modest and prosaic ways.

Because glass is cheap and ubiquitous in modern culture, it may not be self-evident how it can still be deployed as a sign of wealth and status. In fact, there are two primary means: first, by using large and non-standard (i.e., expensive) sizes, often with sophisticated metallic coatings or tints, laminations, fritting, or various types of heat strengthening; and second, by "capturing" particular types of views that only money can buy—whether urban (with the city viewed from a dizzying height, abstracted from the noise and smells of the quotidian work force below and transformed into a silent and sublime expression of human power) or natural (with large expanses of meadow, woods, ocean, lake, or stream providing the same sense of the sublime).

There are many manifestations of these expressive strategies, and numerous variations determined, in part, by whether the transparent surface is viewed from the inside looking out as opposed to looking in from the outside; and there are also variations in both of these points of view (i.e., inside looking out versus outside looking in) depending on relative levels of illumination on the inside versus the outside, levels that are typically inverted during the daytime and nighttime hours. Glass may well cease being transparent, and appear reflective or opaque, from the vantage point of an observer looking from an environment with higher levels of illumination than the environment on the far side of the glazed surface. Thus, a glazed building enclosure may appear impenetrably black when viewed from the outside on a sunny day; the same enclosure may appear entirely transparent when viewed from the same vantage point at night if the interior spaces are illuminated. Similarly, glazed surfaces may block views of low-lit exteriors when viewed from well-lit interior spaces, while permitting views of sunny outside spaces during the daytime.

In Figure 14.1, four expressive strategies for the use of glass are illustrated. The first involves an expression of transparency that establishes visual continuities between exterior and interior spaces. Most commonly, walls and floors—and sometimes ceilings (soffits)—are extended from an inside space to an outside space, with the glazed boundary (enclosure) that separates inside from outside visually minimized. In this way, the idea that the outside is *outside* the inside and that the inside is *inside* the outside, is defamiliarized, or called into question, by the use of large and expensive surfaces of glass. Aside from the expression of *expense*, common to all strategies by virtue of the size and sophisticated composition of the glass itself, the expression of *property* is made explicit, at least to the extent that the walls used to express spatial continuity between inside and outside also create a bounded domain from which all others are physically excluded. Mies van der Rohe's various Court House projects from the 1930s and 1940s, in which interior spaces flow seamlessly into bounded gardens (Fig.14.1a), are perhaps the best examples of this first case, although the essential ideas show up in many other built works.

The second case is similar to the first, in that the enclosure plane is meant to disappear. However, rather than using this transparency to create a sense of interior and exterior *spatial continuity*, transparency is here used to link the interior to a spatially separated, but particularly *sublime*, exterior, whether consisting of city, park, farmland, forest, lake, stream, or ocean. The first case may well be triggered by a desire for privacy and enclosure, since exterior space can be contained with walls that begin inside and extend outside, seemingly without interruption. The second case also achieves privacy, but not by enclosure. Instead, privacy is achieved by literally taking ownership of sufficiently vast amounts of property from which curious onlookers are excluded, or by gaining *metaphorical* ownership of the view itself—perhaps by an adjacency to vast distances that cannot be easily inhabited (lakes, oceans, and so on) or by building high enough above adjacent structures to preclude surveillance from below. Of course, it is possible to "own the view" using only conventional windows, but the most dramatic expression can be found with large expanses of glass as occurs, for example, in Pierre Koenig's Stahl house in the Hollywood Hills, looking over the city of Los Angeles (Fig.14.1b).

The third case aims not so much to link exterior and interior space, but rather to frame the solid (opaque) elements of the enclosure system as figural, or sculptural, objects. As in the first two cases, the necessary continuity of enclosure is established by glazing elements that—even while joining together the solid elements—are meant to visually disappear. The difference is that in the first two cases, the enclosure "plane" is meant to disappear completely so that the exterior is brought into focus (or the interior, when viewed from the outside), whereas in the third case, the *solid* portion of the enclosure system itself is meant to be viewed as a figural

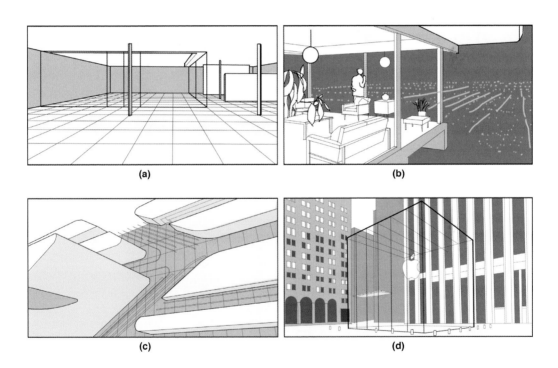

14.1   Four manifestations of transparency: (a) expressing visual continuities between outside and inside in Mies van der Rohe's Row House with Interior Court project from about 1938; (b) linking the interior to a spatially separated, but particularly sublime, exterior in Pierre Koenig's Case Study House #22—the Stahl House—in Los Angeles from 1959; (c) framing the solid (opaque) elements of the enclosure system as figural, or sculptural, objects in Zaha Hadid's Pierresvives in Montpellier, France from 2012; and (d) defamiliarizing structure and enclosure in the form of an all-glass box in Bohlin Cywinski Jackson's Apple Store, Fifth Avenue in New York City from 2006.

object, and any exterior spaces, while visible from the interior (or interior spaces, even if visible from the exterior), are not directly relevant to the figure-ground or solid-void experience of the enclosure system. Zaha Hadid utilizes this framing device in the Pierresvives building in Montpellier, France (Fig.14.1c), a combined archive, library, and sports department within an articulated enclosure.

The fourth case requires an enormous investment in material and in engineering to overcome the inherent brittleness of glass—a property that under ordinary circumstances precludes its use as building structure. Here, the building enclosure is not so much made invisible (since it is precisely the heroic gymnastics of the glass that is intended to be foregrounded) as it is made *incredible*. The already canonical example of this type of expression is the Apple Store on Fifth Avenue in New York City (Fig.14.1d), designed by Bohlin Cywinski Jackson in 2006, and then redesigned and rebuilt with even fewer structural glass elements in 2011.

It is possible to use two or more of these strategies in various combinations, or to invent other formal devices utilizing glass that transcend the default expectation of being a mere window in a wall. And it is certainly true that all of these and other applications of glass may well express countless other things—not only ideas about wealth, power, democracy, and freedom—to those who design them and to those who behold them. Large expanses of glass in all these cases are not only expensive to build, but also impose an energy penalty and contribute to global warming—negative consequences similar to those discussed in relation to thermal bridging in Chapter 12.

15
FASHIONABLE BUILDING

Free competition is the real development of capital. By its means, what corresponds to the nature of capital is posited as external necessity for the individual capital; what corresponds to the concept of capital, is posited as external necessity for the mode of production founded on capital. The reciprocal compulsion which the capitals within it practice upon one another, on labour etc. (the competition among workers is only another form of the competition among capitals), is the free, at the same time the real development of wealth as capital.

(Karl Marx[1])

Architectural theory can never stray very far from the Vitruvian functional triad of *firmitas*, *utilitas*, and *venustas*—firmness, commodity, and delight in Henry Wotton's 17th-century translation—especially if *venustas* is taken in its broadest sense to include all manner of expression, ethics, and beauty. Yet there is an aspect of *venustas* that is really more of a *meta*-function, in that it transcends the mere acknowledgment and analysis of expression, ethics, and beauty, however those terms may be understood, and instead seeks to explain the *overarching purpose* of architecture within society. Even if we accept the fact that both architects and building users find buildings expressive, beautiful, delightful, symbolic, or pleasurable in various degrees—and consider such qualities to be the function of *venustas* (i.e., to be expressive, delightful, symbolic, and so on)—there is still an important question left unanswered: what is the *function* of the function of *venustas*? In other words, what explains the phenomenon of architecture, where the word *architecture* is used as a shorthand for those buildings that embody the function of *venustas*?

The short answer to this question—adding to Vitruvius's Latin place holders—is *pecunia*, a term which refers to money or, within civil law, to "every thing which constituted the *private property* of an individual, or which was a part of his fortune; a slave, a field, a house, and the like, were so considered."[2] In modern capitalist democracies, architecture is property; and private property, in turn, is the essential form of wealth in contemporary society.

Thus, to explain the function of architecture within society—its *purpose*—one needs a theory that explains the phenomenon of architecture as property, addressing the question of why there is architecture in the first place. Such a theory of architecture differs not only from the kind of critical theory that tells us what's good and what's bad, but also from the kind of surveys that outline what various architects want to do (i.e., what their intentions are) and how people react to the forms they create.[3] In other words, a meta-theory of architecture needs to abstract from the many competing formal, spatial, behavioral, or psychological aspects of particular architectural styles or tendencies, and instead explain the phenomenon of architecture itself. In doing so, the subjectivity of critical analysis does not necessarily lose its relevance but is subsumed within the overarching and objective meta-theory.

We start with the world of individual ownership, where each person uses his wealth *against* all others, and in turn is excluded from the private wealth of everyone else; this world is, of necessity, a world of competition. Architects compete against architects; students compete for grades; workers compete for jobs; etc. Competition is inherent in the relations of production called capitalism; it permeates every aspect of our lives. Moreover, competition appears as an external necessity—one cannot decide to play with a different set of rules. Even the American Institute of Architects (AIA) urges its members to compete *against each other* by sponsoring "How To Win" seminars.[4] The various manifestations of *venustas*, for which I will substitute the word "fashion" in what follows—fashion being used in the sense of "a prevailing custom, usage, or style"[5]—are strategic elements deployed in this competition.

It is not necessary to itemize the ever-changing array of styles and aesthetic/formal tendencies to acknowledge the importance of fashion within architectural pedagogy and practice. Nor is it necessary to correlate the degree of corporate or individual aesthetic sophistication with particular stylistic preferences, where terms such as "sophistication" and "connoisseurship" are, unsurprisingly, claimed by the elites for themselves. The purpose of fashion is competition, within all levels of class, wealth, and power. People use fashion to compete.

The utility of fashion for competition has two aspects. First, architectural fashion provides visual clues that indicate one's "membership" within a group, class, or subculture. Second, within a particular group (or class, or subculture), fashion acts as a means of competition. Since the first aspect is a prerequisite to the second—it is necessary to be *in* a group, acknowledged as being *in* fashion, before one can compete within that group—the utility of fashion for competition is absolute and unequivocal. That the same phenomenon shows up in various non-human species, for example, in the sexual ornaments and displays of certain birds, can be taken as evidence in support of the argument, but also as evidence of its dysfunctionality: according to Richard Prum, there is no necessary evolutionary benefit in the use of fashion within avian culture, other than enabling sexual selection (i.e., competition) on the basis of arbitrary aesthetic criteria. And these criteria may well be maladaptive, "resulting in a worse fit between the organism and its environment."[6] This insight was brilliantly captured by Theodor Geisel (aka Dr. Seuss) in his 1958 story about "a girl-bird named Gertrude McFuzz"[7] who, competing with another female bird, decides to grow dysfunctional quantities of tail feathers that ultimately prevent her from flying. E.H. Gombrich argues that such unintended and disastrous outcomes of competition, characterized by a "threat summed up in the word 'escalation,'" are often found in human societies.[8]

Just as various aesthetic ("fashionable") practices have evolved within avian societies that enable members to self-identify and compete within their species, individual humans who are competing (i.e., seeking, first, to identify themselves within a particular subculture and, second, to compete within that subculture) inevitably discover that they need to wear appropriate (fashionable) clothes, style their hair in an appropriate (fashionable) way, and so on. Fashionable buildings are commissioned and designed for the same reason. To the extent that buildings are needed for their utility only, that is, where their quality as fashion isn't useful, we find utilitarian (i.e., *non*-architectural) building. That one period's utilitarian "style" becomes another's high art does not alter this conclusion; it only shows that it is not the content of the fashion that counts, but only the fact that it *is* fashion. The reason that fashion must change is the same as its purpose: competition. A static and universal style of art would be useless for competition since everyone would soon be able to understand and make use of it. Therefore, once fashion becomes commonplace, it has already been replaced by a new avant-garde. The vicissitudes of fashion, and the inevitable death and replacement of avant-garde styles, are often noted, even if the underlying motivation—serving as an aid to competition—is not acknowledged: "The final phase of a fashion is its death, when it becomes *poncif*, literally a 'pounced drawing' and figuratively a 'commonplace piece of work.' At this point it may either be overthrown by another fashion challenge or consumed as part of a generic style."[9]

In spite of some parallels with non-human species, the phenomenon of a permanently evolving avant-garde cannot be explained by analogy to the mutations and adaptations through which living creatures co-evolve within their environments. Such an argument is proposed by architect-theorist Patrik Schumacher, who writes that "the sole responsibility of the avant-garde architect is to mutate and give innovation a chance ... The client's immediate interests are served only inasmuch as they coincide with the new, generalizable interests of contemporary civilization that the avant-garde exploration tries to address. In the absence of this coincidence, the client might find some compensation by exploiting the innovative thrust of the project for the promotion of his reputation."[10] Schumacher argues that the avant-garde project is undertaken primarily for the improvement of society ("contemporary civilization") and only secondarily to benefit the client who commissions and pays for it ("the client might find some compensation. . ."). But the client's interest in such a project—whether the client is corporate, governmental, or just a status-seeking individual consumer—*is* the reason that such projects are commissioned, paid for, and built. The client's interest, and therefore the *function* of this type of architecture, is to enable competition, not to serve some unspecified "generalizable interests of contemporary civilization."

The fact that advocates of particular architectural styles may not understand the purpose of fashion in their architecture results in a never-ending debate on the *merits* of their favored styles. Whether the debate is in terms of "ethics," "economy," "contextuality," "complexity," and so on, the criticism of last year's model for not solving some particular human problem is always possible, since its purpose never had anything to do with solving that type of problem in the first place. Val Warke argues that:

> As seducer, a fashion may urge the adherents of the established fashion to reevaluate their allegiances by suggesting a plausible, though previously forbidden, variation on the apparently stable style's primary tenets. The fashion as antagonist will confront a popularly

held fashion or style by underscoring the fallacies of the target's basic advertised presumptions and propositions (that is, of its soft-bellied verisimilitude). Since verisimilitude is not verity, it is always sensitive to opposition from similar constructs, particularly when those constructs insist upon their own opposing truth.[11]

Utilitarian buildings are economical; there are no added frills, wasted space, etc. Fashion, on the other hand, costs money. The conspicuous expression of the money it costs is, in fact, a necessary aspect of fashion, as Thorstein Veblen noted in 1899: "The superior gratification derived from the use and contemplation of costly and supposedly beautiful products is, commonly, in great measure a gratification of our sense of costliness masquerading under the name of beauty."[12] One can compete with fashion *because* it is expensive (if it were cheap, anyone could buy it). Perhaps a more accurate formulation would replace the word "expensive" with the word "rare," thereby allowing room for certain creative designers to be fashionably cheap. Gombrich, for example, argues that

> fashion can be described in terms of a rarity game. At one time it may be the display of rare lace that arouses attention and competition, at another a daring décolleté, the height of the coiffure or the width of the crinoline. At various times competition has driven fashion to notoriously foolish 'excesses'—though what we call an excess here is harder to tell.[13]

On the other hand, since the whole premise underlying capitalism is to accumulate private wealth, there is simultaneously an opposite movement away from fashion, toward utility.

At times, one side of the contradiction comes to the fore; at other times, the opposite side. More often, both sides of the contradiction struggle to coexist, often by invoking the architect's design skills, and not just the cost of construction, as evidence of the architecture's fashionable pedigree. Frank Gehry's conspicuous and ironic use of cheap plywood as an interior finish within expensive corporate or institutional buildings, or his earlier use of sheet metal—with details inspired by mechanical ductwork—for exterior cladding, are canonical examples, but are hardly unique. Michael Graves, at one point in his career, also sold fashion on the basis of his "design" skill (i.e., his ability to manipulate color and form), abstracting from the conflict between fashion and utility, a conflict which he dismissed as merely a *moral* dilemma: "I don't know whether lay people know it's gypboard. For many modern architects," he said, discussing quasi-classical column capital motifs in his postmodern Portland Building, "it's a moral question: If it's gypboard, they feel it should be read as gypboard. That doesn't interest me. It's a surface that gains some identification beyond the junk it's made of, by virtue of its color, its texture, its placement."[14]

As tools of competition, both fashion and utility are desired in a positive sense, to the extent that they make a building more valuable to its owner. Yet they also seem to be forced on the owner of the building, since their omission places the owner at a disadvantage with respect to other building owners.

Changes in style are called fashion. Changes in utility are called progress. Stylistic change incorporates and therefore reflects progress (in which technological change plays a major role), but technology is not the *reason* for style. Form follows function *and* form follows fashion. The particular blend of "art" and "utility" varies from building to building and from one period to another, depending on the usefulness of fashion in the particular case. Since fashion costs money, it is applied only to the extent that it is useful. Houston developer Gerald Hines puts it this way: "We try to be on the cutting edge, but we don't want to be unusual for the sake of being unusual."[15]

It is sometimes claimed that the art, or *fashion*, of architecture itself counts as an objectively logical aspect of the building, just as things like structure, insulation, and egress stairs do. People *need* fashion, and developers *profit from* fashion, so it must have some objective standing. This argument is true as far as it goes—one can objectively discuss the purposes and logic of fashion, in spite of its subjective nature. But what one is discussing in this case is not fashion *qua* art, that is, examining a particular object to the extent that its subjective meaning or interpretation is of interest; rather what is at issue is the part that this "art" plays within a larger context, as a means of competition, that is, as a useful expression of wealth, power, or taste. In other words, fashion examined objectively is not criticized on the basis of its subjective merit ("Gehry has crafted one of the most beautiful towers downtown"[16]) but on the basis of its objective purpose ("In fact, apartments [at the Gehry-designed building] are going at a 15% to 20% premium over the average luxury building rental"[17]).

The usefulness of "starchitecture" in adding to a commercial building's value has a relatively short history; architectural critic Paul Goldberger, for example, first discussed the tendency in a 1976 *New York Times* article on Philip Johnson and the developer Gerald D. Hines: "Still, there is no question that the building [designed by Johnson] needs slightly higher rents than its neighbors to make money. Hines gets them (25 to 50 cents per square foot per year more than his competition) by selling the building's architectural quality as an asset; in other words, he makes a profit on prestige."[18] In the same article, Goldberger notes that cultural institutions and governmental entities have, for a much longer period of time, also found architecture useful—he doesn't explain why such institutions have been patrons of architecture, but the motivation is not hard to determine. Architecture reinforces wealth, power, and status in numerous ways that are useful to all sorts of institutions, governmental entities, and individuals. Cathedrals and courthouses awe and intimidate those they are meant to impress; museums announce a world of refined taste and, more recently, are explicitly subjected to a kind of cost–benefit analysis based on the calculation of what it takes these days to get on the international touristic map, the so-called Bilbao effect.

Discussing the art of architecture as an objective attribute of buildings, rather than as a subjective judgment made by critics and connoisseurs, is complicated by the fact that those who subjectively evaluate architecture— even the architects themselves—may have no useful insight into the purpose or reason for their creations. What one typically finds in architectural criticism are combinations, or rather conflations, of facts (not always correct) and judgments. The judgments are subjective and cannot be verified (refuted, or falsified, to use Karl Popper's criteria for evaluation of scientific theory). The facts are of various types—biographical details of clients and designers, formal historical antecedents, physical or material descriptions, and so on. The critic often juxtaposes facts and judgments without differentiating between them, as if they all have the same evidentiary value, or as if facts somehow explain their judgments. Paul Goldberger illustrates this tactic perfectly in his review of "New York by Gehry," Frank Gehry's New York City apartment tower at 8 Spruce Street (Fig.15.1): "But its effect is dramatic, thanks to a curtain wall made up of ten thousand three hundred stainless steel panels, weighing half a ton each, into which are cut twenty-four hundred windows."[19] The facts are these: there are 10,300 panels weighing 1,000 pounds, each made from stainless steel with 2,400 windows. The judgment is this: the effect is "dramatic."

15.1   Frank Gehry's "New York by Gehry" at 8 Spruce Street, New York City.

Of course, the judgment cannot be logically deduced or inferred from those facts, or from any set of facts; the opposite judgment could just as easily be made. For example, here is James Gardner's take on the same stainless steel panels on the surface of the same building: "The metallic cladding of 8 Spruce Street, which seems to be slipping off the surface like grease that puckers, puddles and undulates in its descent, comes off as little more than a big gimmick . . . the undulations along the surface look like halfhearted wavelets."[20] So, is the stainless steel cladding "dramatic" or "halfhearted"? The short answer is this: it all depends on how you *feel* when you look at it, or how you *feel* when you think about it, or how you *feel* when you write about it. And feelings are not always reliable indicators of objective conditions.

Virtually all criticism is merely a transcription of the critic's feelings, albeit hidden deep within critical frameworks (sometimes called "theory") and ornamented with special vocabulary designed to obscure the subjectivity of these critical judgments. Hegel describes such feelings as "the lowest form in which any mental content can exist . . . a mode which [man] has in common with the animal." He goes on to describe precisely the type of subjectivity that renders feelings useless as a logical mode of discourse:

> If one says: 'I feel such and such and so and so,' then one has secluded himself in himself. Everybody else has the same right to say: 'I don't feel it that way.' And hence one has retreated from the common soil of understanding. In wholly particular affairs feeling is entirely in its right. But to maintain that all men had this or that in their feeling is a contradiction in terms; it contradicts the concept of feeling, the point of view of the individual subjectivity of each which one has taken with this statement. As soon as mental content is placed into feeling, everybody is reduced to his subjective point of view.[21]

Criticism, however, is hardly rendered useless because of its subjectivity. In fact, subjectivity is precisely the point of criticism. Critics are valued because they tell the rest of us, or more accurately tell some self-selected subset of "us," how to *feel* about something: you, the interested reader, should like (or dislike) this wine, this pair of shoes, this movie, this work of architecture. Why should I like (or dislike) it? Because I, the critic, like (or dislike) it, and because you (the reader) want (need) to feel the way I feel.

And why do I need to feel the way you feel? Because liking the right things, or feeling the right way about things, is a means of competition—a way of advancing, or even just remaining, within a particular social or economic group. You want to compete, and "understanding" architecture may be useful in that competition (whether that competition is in the social, economic, or any other sphere of your activities). Therefore, you need to be initiated into the subjectivity of this particular field, and you need to be periodically updated with credible opinions about specific and current examples within that field.

If you should somehow, through naivety or bad luck, find yourself attracted to a critical framework that is misaligned with your social or economic aspirations, rest assured that your peers or superiors will quickly notice and provide a correction. If you nevertheless choose to propound your uninformed or poorly informed opinions, you will quickly discover that such a principled stance is never respected within the group and is entirely counterproductive as a useful means of competition: as argued by Gombrich, social taboos regulate and enforce the utility of fashion:

> Debates about artistic merit, though I do not consider them empty, tend to be laborious and inconclusive. What wonder, therefore, that there are few areas where 'social testing' plays a greater part than in aesthetic judgments? The adolescent soon learns that the group can be a dreadful spoilsport if he confesses to liking something that has fallen under a taboo . . . The more seriously art is taken by any group, the more adept will it be in such brainwashing; for to enjoy the wrong thing in such a circle is like worshipping false gods; you fail in the test of admission to the group if your taste is found wanting.[22]

Buildings get built for purposes of *speculation* (built to be sold); or, when built for a specific client, either as means of *production* (factories, office buildings, etc.), as articles of *consumption* (including both buildings for subsistence and, primarily for elites, luxurious buildings), or as ancillary facilities to support that production, consumption, and speculation (governmental buildings, schools, etc.). Yet these categories, even for ordinary production and consumption, are intertwined, with production implying consumption and vice versa.[23] For architecture, the situation is even more complex, since gratuitous consumptive elements—those fashionable formal gestures that decorate otherwise utilitarian sheds or contort such normative structures into ducks[24]—may well be included in buildings intended either as means of production or as necessary articles of consumption. This is because nothing prevents the *public* faces of buildings, even when their underlying construction serves as means of production or as "necessary means of subsistence," from being designed and consumed as "articles of luxury," that is, as ideological billboards supporting those corporate, institutional, or governmental entities for which the buildings are commissioned.[25]

Were it merely a question of utility, architects would be quite superfluous in building these structures; in fact, "utilitarian" buildings of all types can be designed and constructed by the various technical consultants and building trades without the services of an architect being required at all. The distinction between "building" (mere utility) and "architecture" (as art, or as embodying fashion) already admits this possibility. John Ruskin expressed this distinction quite clearly in 1849, arguing that we must "distinguish carefully between Architecture and Building. To build ... is by common understanding to put together," whereas architecture must also "impress on its form certain characters venerable or beautiful, but otherwise unnecessary."[26] Lewis Mumford rejected Ruskin's argument that ordinary buildings needed to be ornamented with painting or sculpture, but nevertheless accepted Ruskin's basic premise, writing in 1951 that "Ruskin's notion, that architecture is more than mere building, was in fact sound." Mumford, however, wanted the *architect*, rather than the painter or sculptor, to treat "the whole building as an image and a plastic form, in order to express, by his modification of pure functional needs, the meanings and values that are integrally related to the structure: underlining the relevant human purposes and values, designing an office building so that it will make the workers in it feel more efficient and business-like, a university so that the students will be prompted to habits of study and intellectual intercourse, a church so that its communicants will feel more indrawn and exalted."[27]

SPECULATION

Where buildings are built in order to be sold (or rented) at a profit, the role of the architect will vary according to the developers' need for "design" (i.e., fashion) in maximizing their profit. Where the buyers of their products need utility only, or where the particular ratio of supply and demand assures them of selling their product in any form, developers will cut down or eliminate altogether the costs of "design."

On the other hand, where the buyers of their products need fashion to compete, where *their* competition forces them to produce "designer buildings," or where they see opportunities to increase the value of their brands by fashionably embellishing otherwise utilitarian buildings, the costs of such design become necessary costs in the developers' calculations. Where the costs of design are justified by the return on the investment, "fashion" becomes a *positive* means for the developer. This is as much true for Miuccia Prada (hiring Rem Koolhaas and others) in the 21st century as it was for Gerald Hines (hiring Philip Johnson and others) in the 20th century. Hines, for example, credited the fashionable architecture he developed in the 1970s and 1980s with higher rents and a 3 percent to 5 percent increase in profits.[28]

PRODUCTION

Showplace factories and sleek corporate headquarters are forms of public relations; they are never built without the assistance of an architect. However, where the profit to be derived from a particular production process is independent of the architectural quality its building possesses, then "non-architectural" building is sufficient.

Both in production and speculation, architecture may simultaneously appear as a positive means to make a profit and as an external necessity forced on its buyer; or it may simply appear as a waste of money. The competition among the owners of buildings assures that architecture is never, however, built purely at the whim of architects.

CONSUMPTION

In order to live, people need shelter, food, and so on. In our society, these conditions of existence are not produced *because* people need them—they are produced and exchanged as private property, and then only to the extent that they realize a profit for their owners. Thus, it is a commonplace to discover that people go hungry when there is food in supermarkets, or that people need housing even when construction workers (and architects!) cannot find work. The fact that capitalists do "produce" useful things for people is not *because* they are useful, but because being useful is a necessary condition for being profitable. This should be self-evident, even if rarely acknowledged. Thus, when Alfred P. Sloan, General Motors's former president, chairman and CEO, wrote in the 1960s that GM's primary mission was "not just to make motor cars" but rather "was to make money,"[29] this self-evident admission was energetically rebutted by corporate apologists, economists, and politicians, who preferred to cite instances of "socially responsible" capital, for example, the feel-good story of Ben & Jerry's ice cream. Yet even in that case, according to Brad Edmondson, "by the late 1990s, consolidation in the ice cream industry made it difficult for Ben & Jerry's to continue as an independent company, even though most board members did not want to sell. Ben became estranged, board meetings resembled legal depositions, and it often seemed that investment bankers were calling the shots."[30]

Speculatively built housing needs to be a useful object of consumption in order to be sold; but because its purpose is not its use, but its profit, we classify it under "speculation." When speculators build *their* homes, however, they spend money, not for profit, but for use: in this case we have building for consumption—hardly the bare consumption for subsistence that underlies all human existence, but rather the consumption of luxury items that applies primarily to elite classes. Yet it is here, where usefulness might seem to be the only criterion, that architecture truly blossoms. The architect-designed private home is the arena in which the "battle of the styles" is fought. Here, the reputations of young architects are made; here, their bold experiments with fashion are carried out; here, the avant-garde establishes its credentials.

That the owners of wealth rarely choose to live in modest and utilitarian accommodations should not come as a surprise, in spite of the fact that spending money on gratuitous and luxurious items is in direct contradiction to their passion for capital accumulation. They need luxury and fashion in their homes just as they need it in their clothes, cars, and so on.[31] Like all forms of competition, it appears as both inner drive and external necessity.

GOVERNMENT BUILDINGS

A capitalist nation-state competes within the international global economy for wealth and power, yet within its own sovereign territory remains necessarily outside the sphere of competition, at least in principle, acting rather as the power that forces competition on its own citizens: "In pursuing their individual advantage the members of a capitalistic society inevitably harm each other, so that they require a power removed from economic life to guarantee respect for person and property. They supplement their negative, competitive relation to each other by jointly submitting to a power that curtails their private interests."[32] In either case, fashionable *public architecture* is the outcome, commissioned to demonstrate (and thus preserve and extend) state power. On the other hand, where the government is only providing the infrastructure of transportation and communication—prerequisites for the growth and existence of private property (which nevertheless appear to the owners of private property as expenses taken from *them*)—it is often satisfied with mere utility. Fashion is here seen as unnecessary embellishment. Of course, there are instances where the spheres of utilitarian infrastructure and fashionable public architecture (e.g., in trains stations and airports) collide. In such infrastructural projects, the boundary between utilitarian elements (railway tracks, platforms, tarmac, bathrooms, etc.) and fashionable elements (primarily the gratuitously grand terminal spaces with which cities and countries advertise their wealth and power in order to compete for business and tourism) is always clearly defined, consistent with the varying needs for utility and fashion.

Just as the apologists for corporate capitalism often deny the profit-seeking basis of their enterprise—by citing alleged benevolent motivations of corporate icons like Ben & Jerry's or, more generally, by maintaining the fiction of a "triple bottom line" in which social and environmental well-being are supposedly balanced against profitability—the apologists of architecture often deny the central role of fashion in their enterprise. Theory, for them, becomes not an explanation of the *phenomenon* of architecture but rather a self-serving and ideological *criticism* of architecture, one that presumes to illuminate "not only an architect's intentions and the mechanisms used to convert those intentions into building forms, but also how people experience those forms given their own knowledge, attitudes, and motivations."[33] In other words, such theory concerns itself only with what architects want to do (their intentions) and how those intentions are implemented. So, if an architect intends to make buildings that are *pyramidal and red*, and if that architect has a design method to accomplish such an intention, this alone—according to the prevailing view—constitutes a theory of architecture.

It should be clear that such "theories" explain nothing about the phenomenon of architecture; they entirely avoid the question of why there *is* architecture in the first place, rather than mere building. Architecture, to be "consumed," must first be "produced," and not merely "intended." The gulf between the production and consumption of architecture, on the one hand, and the mere intention to create architecture, on the other hand, is enormous, and cannot be bridged without large expenditures of capital. Only where fashion is deemed useful for competition, no matter within which class or subculture this competition takes place, is such an expenditure of capital increased to pay for fashionable building—for architecture. Of course, fashion, driven by competition, is not *inevitably* the criterion by which architecture is commissioned, designed, selected, and built. There have certainly been societies in which competition, based on changing fashion, was not a driving force within the culture of building. In Egypt, for example, "the earliest royal monuments, such as the Narmer Palette carved around 3100 B.C.E., display identical royal costumes and poses as those seen on later rulers, even Ptolemaic kings on their temples 3000 years later."[34]

The idea that fashion and competition are driving forces within culture has been advanced by many theorists, but such ideas tend to be resisted within architectural theory. This may be because architectural theorists, following Adorno, tend to idealize the art of architecture, viewing fashion as something beholden to monopoly capital that "threatens the autonomy of the artwork."[35] Such theorists become infatuated (distracted) by all the *particular* "artistic" qualities of the fashionable building—its mode of expression, its relation to prior artistic movements or prior forms, its intentionality, and so on—denying the overarching meta-function of architecture: to enable competition by deploying fashion.

The meta-theory of architecture, based on this meta-function, is deceptively simple: *architecture is fashionable building*. Fashion is a tool, among others, to enable competition. Competition is inherent in the capitalist mode of production: "It is ubiquitous as the principle of the way people deal with each other and as an imperative, anonymous law shaping the behavior of modern individuals."[36] Competition is felt by its subjects in both a positive sense (as an opportunity to make money, to profit, to "win") and in a negative sense (as a compulsion to avoid failure, to survive even as others seek to surpass you). The competition to create fashionable buildings revolves around *pecunia*, flawed arguments based on a psychology rooted in "human nature" notwithstanding. Marx famously stated that "it is not the consciousness of men that determines their existence, but their social existence that determines their consciousness."[37] Karl Popper, otherwise critical of many Marxian formulations, defends this particular argument, writing that: "The universal occurrence of certain behaviour is not a decisive argument in favour of its instinctive character, or of its being rooted in 'human nature.' Such considerations may show how naïve it is to assume that all social laws must be derivable, in principle, from the psychology of 'human nature.'"[38]

Because engaging in competition costs money, it is always purposeful, even if its motivation is idealized or otherwise misunderstood. In fact, it is common for theorists to focus precisely on the subjective and transient functions of fashion in relation to architecture; in other words, to examine how a building's form reinforces or upends its physical or historic context, what stylistic modifications or transgressions have been employed, what intentions can be surmised, what emotions or feelings are engendered by its formal presence, or what ironic references to bygone styles or other cultural domains are evoked. A meta-theory of architecture looks instead at fashion's stable and overarching meta-function as a means of competition: to transform mere building into architecture.

EPILOGUE:
ARCHITECTURAL EDUCATION

The education of architects, derived in large part from Beaux-Arts practice, has three primary characteristics:

First, the program is typically divided into four or five distinct areas: design; technical courses (e.g., statics, environmental control systems, etc.); history and theory; professional practice; and electives in the liberal arts. In addition, there are often special elective programs which address other topics (e.g., computation and digital fabrication, community design, etc.). However, as researchers for the Architectural Research Centers Consortium recognized in 1982, design is clearly prioritized: "It is probably fair to say that architectural education focuses primarily on design and technology, with a strong emphasis or tradition in the studio experience."[1]

Second, design studio classes seem quite open-ended, as if each professor could decide to teach just about anything at any point in the undergraduate or graduate curriculum. In fact, the names of the courses (Studio #1, Studio #2, and so on) often reveal their indifference to any particular content. Furthermore, design instructors do not "teach." Instead, the form their instruction takes is criticism. Only after students produce do instructors respond with their "crits." This reluctance to explicitly "teach architecture" in the design studio has its most revealing (and wonderfully arrogant) formulation in the mission statement of the department of architecture at Cornell University, where the idea of internalizing the proper attitude within a landscape of constantly shifting stylistic tendencies—rather than learning any concrete strategies or practices—is made clear: "We do not teach architecture; instead we try to teach students how to learn about architecture (witness, for example, the inordinate number of Cornell alumni teaching in architecture programs). Rather than train architects who think of buildings as autonomous objects frozen in an assigned ideology, our goal is to produce architects who are capable of making independent judgments rooted in an ever-changing context of architectural thought."[2]

Third, questions involving technology, energy, economics, etc. are treated rather superficially. Specific functional or utilitarian issues are sometimes discussed—especially when the design brief foregrounds these issues as candidates for *expressive* elaboration—but the actual object to be judged is still the building as a work of art, as architecture. For Veblen, addressing ostensibly useful questions is nothing more than a smokescreen employed to soft-sell fashionable (wasteful) content. Writing about fashionable clothing or *dress*, he argues that "the principle of conspicuous waste requires an obviously futile expenditure; and the resulting conspicuous expensiveness of dress is therefore intrinsically ugly. Hence we find that in all innovations in dress, *each added or altered detail strives to avoid instant condemnation by showing some ostensible purpose*, at the same time that the requirement of conspicuous waste prevents the purposefulness of these innovations from becoming anything more than a somewhat transparent pretense."[3] In an earlier chapter, Veblen grudgingly admits the possibility that "ugliness" is not necessarily the outcome of all wasteful expenditures, but still foregrounds waste as the essential element in the service of luxury: "If beauty or comfort is achieved—and it is a more or less fortuitous circumstance if they are—they must be achieved by means and methods that commend themselves to the *great economic law of wasted effort*."[4]

The idea that waste is an important element of architectural design not only precedes Veblen, but survives, intact, well into the 21st century. But unlike Veblen's negative and caustic analysis, some influential theorists, both before and after him, turn his critique upside-down. John Ruskin, for example, criticizes the "modern" interest in efficiency by extolling the virtues of apparently wasteful expenditures, writing that the "Spirit of Sacrifice . . . is a spirit, for instance, which of two marbles, equally beautiful, applicable and durable, would choose the more costly because it was so, and of two kinds of decoration, equally effective, would choose the more elaborate because it was so, in order that it might in the same compass present more cost and more thought. It is therefore most unreasoning and enthusiastic, and perhaps best negatively defined, as the opposite of the prevalent feeling of modern times, which desires to produce the largest results at the least cost."[5]

On the other hand, the Dutch architect Rem Koolhaas acts more like Veblen's acolyte. Referring to his own work for the luxury Italian fashion house Prada, for example, Koolhaas remarks: "At the time we started collaborating, everything in the world of art and fashion was polished. Everything was smooth, so we felt that Prada must be rough. *We put an emphasis on concepts like waste. In real estate terms, the ultimate luxury is wasted space*."[6] Compare this with Veblen's "great economic law of wasted effort" in the service of luxury.

These characteristics of architectural pedagogy arise from the dual nature of architecture (embodying both "fashion" and "utility"); from the use of fashion to transform mere building into architecture; from the need for fashion in the world of competition; and from the necessity to compete, using fashion, when socially produced wealth takes the form of private property. The design studio's separation from technical areas of instruction reflects the dual nature of architecture as art and mere construction for utility. Because these two aspects of the profession occupy opposite poles of a contradiction, it is usually expedient to deal with them separately in school, so that their synthesis can occur in practice according to the particular needs of a given situation. That this contradiction is misunderstood as being a problem of the educational system is the cause of the recurring debate among educators about how technology can be better integrated into studio instruction.

Tension between the "art" and "science" of architecture is often acknowledged, even if the negative consequences are underestimated:

It is widely perceived today that there is an intrinsic tension between freedom of ideas in architectural education and the pragmatics of negotiation in the building process. Architecture remains one of the few professions that still allow dreams, but all designs, banal or avant-garde, must endure constraints of reality and seemingly unbearable compromises when put to realization. To their credit, architecture schools largely privilege abstract thinking in the design studio. This discrepancy between the education of architects and the practice of architecture produces an obscure yet revealing dynamic between the two realms, and it is this disjunction that enables the distance necessary to stretch and expand the boundaries of the architectural vocation.[7]

Yet it seems clear, even to those who value the types of abstract thinking encouraged within design studio pedagogy, that somehow—at some point—such abstractions must be reconciled with real conditions encountered when projects are actually constructed and occupied. What is less clear in such formulations are the specific aspects of "reality" which ought to be addressed, if at all, within the academic studio, and the proper means to accomplish this synthesis.

In fact, the types of building technology issues that might impinge upon a purely formal or expressive design pedagogy are quite numerous, and include things like structure (strength, stiffness, and efficiency); control of air, rain water, vapor, and heat at the building perimeter; fire (and other life) safety issues; energy use; production of global warming gases (carbon footprint); daylighting and electric lighting; site orientation issues (sun, wind, drainage); acoustic isolation and interior acoustic environments; toxicity of building materials; use of renewable materials and renewable (or on-site) energy; reduction or recycling of potable water and waste water; and so on.

All of these issues need not be addressed in every design studio, and some are almost never critical in terms of influencing or altering the conceptual basis for the design; that is, some technical issues can safely be left out of schematic design without compromising the viability of the scheme as it is further developed. For example, the ubiquitous use of electricity within buildings (at least when generated off-site) is never considered within schematic design, in spite of being perhaps the most fundamental of all the technologies necessary for the functioning of modern buildings. This is because buildings, no matter how they are formally configured, can accommodate panel boxes, conduit, switches, and outlets in routine ways that have almost no impact on the design concept or on a project's overall cost. Electrical contractors, in fact, routinely run conduit from panel boxes to switches, lighting fixtures, and so on based on nothing more than abstract drawings with curved arrows pointing in general directions, leaving the specific pathways for the field installer to work out; and architects routinely let electrical engineers determine the pattern of outlets, or sometimes even of lighting, well after schematic design decisions have been made. In this case, the *technology* can be "added" to the *design*.

Such a model (technology added to design) is often extrapolated to encompass a much greater range of technological decisions. For example, Mohsen Mostafavi, former Dean of the College of Architecture, Art, and Planning at Cornell University, describes an integrative design studio project at Cornell as follows: "We asked a group of students whether, as an experiment, they would be prepared to continue working on their old project, the one they had supposedly finished, and to *take it to another level of development*.[8] By "another level of development," Mostafavi means factoring in issues of building technology not ordinarily considered within the design studio. However, while it may be rational to "add" certain technologies to projects that were conceived without prior consideration of building technology issues, framing this as a general model for pedagogy or practice is both dangerous and counterproductive.

This strategy—"adding" technology to design—presumes a kind of symmetry between the process of abstract design and the requirements of building technology. That is, it is presumed that one can begin at either pole of the art–science duality and still end up with a viable building. But this is a false symmetry based on numerous logical errors including a misplaced confidence in the power of science to compensate for any a priori design decisions. In other words, some aspects of building technology are so fundamental, and also so sensitive to unusual or peculiar geometric manipulation, that their underlying logic must inform, if not precede, a schematic design process that prioritizes abstract form and expression.

Yet even when integrative design—defined as the "*ability* to make design decisions within a complex architectural project while demonstrating broad integration and consideration of environmental stewardship, technical documentation, accessibility, site conditions, life safety, environmental systems, structural systems, and building envelope systems and assemblies"[9]—is mandated by accreditation agencies, the technical content to be integrated is treated superficially. Technical subjects are, after all, fairly complex, and cannot be rigorously taught within the architectural curriculum. Furthermore, there are mechanical engineers, structural engineers, energy consultants, technical representatives from industry, and so on, to supply the actual expertise in any building project for which the architect is hired. So just as the purpose of the architect is not to provide technical skill (engineers are trained to do that), the purpose of technical courses in architectural schools is not to train technicians. In order to create architecture, a minimum of knowledge is needed in the technical areas so that the architect can at least communicate with technical consultants. In addition, the need for utility in buildings requires that the architect be familiar, in a general way, with the latest structural and mechanical systems, since the need for "fashion" does not eliminate the competition for more efficient, utilitarian, economical buildings.

The design studio, then, is left with the task of teaching the "art" of architecture. Unfortunately, art cannot be taught (if it could be taught, too many people might learn it, and it would become useless as a means of competition). For that reason, design instructors do not teach—they *criticize*. The content and form of their criticism has been studied by numerous researchers, who typically find both "intuitive" and "rational" components, corresponding to the "art" and "science" of architecture—the idea being that "as a general rule, the main aim of design is to satisfy human needs, but the enjoyment of architectural aesthetics is also an important goal."[10] Yet it is equally clear that the refinement of formal qualities— appearance—is prioritized by both critics and students. For example, the AIAS Studio Culture Task Force concluded in 2002 that "the current studio culture rewards students with the 'best looking' projects."[11] Peggy Deamer reaches the same conclusion in her discussion of first-year design, arguing that "the role of form and aesthetics cannot be overlooked. No matter how smart a student's concept is, if it isn't visually appealing, no one will pay attention."[12]

Other researchers, notably Donald Schön, scrutinize types of reflection *in* (or *on*) action that take place within professional (including architectural) culture, hyphenating the terms (i.e., "reflection-in-action") to give some rather commonplace observations the appearance of profundity. Thus, we learn that baseball pitchers and "good" jazz musicians have a "feel for the ball" or a "feel for the music" that allows the former to win and the latter to successfully improvise.[13] Such theories can be easily refuted (e.g., when both the pitcher and the batter opposing each other in a given game are conscientiously "reflecting-in-action," one of them will still lose), as they fail to account for the world of competition that, by its very nature, creates winners and losers in every domain.

Architecture students quickly learn how to compete in the studio context. Architect Harris Stone describes the behavior of the top students in his class at Harvard: "After the assignment was given out, they immediately went to the architectural library and found out how the currently popular architects had dealt with this or a similar problem . . . They got good grades learning how to take advantage of the work of others while I got bad grades trying to understand and work things out for myself."[14] Mr. Stone correctly sees what it is that students who are competing need to know about fashion ("the currently popular architects"), but fails to understand the purpose of fashion in architecture. This leads him to try to "work things out" for himself—that is, solve problems *he* thinks are important. If society isn't interested in his problems, at least his self-image as a moral individual remains intact (". . . while I got bad grades").

The purpose of this type of instruction is to force the student to internalize, not only the current fashion, but the very idea of fashion: that the existence *of* fashion is the important thing. This development of artistic consciousness is no easy task, since it cannot be "taught" like other subjects. The preferred method is therefore to subject the student uninterruptedly, for a period of up to five years, to the form of abuse described above, knowing that few will survive the ordeal without either learning to play the game or finding some other non-design niche within the profession. And if this method of criticism by individual instructors isn't enough, its extension into the end-of-term "jury" system provides an unassailable verdict for the still-wavering student.

For this reason, a systematically structured design curriculum is not required and, in fact, rarely exists. Since fashion changes, it is impractical to make a long-term commitment to one particular style, such as would be required in developing a curriculum. The fact that competition requires that a body of knowledge be learned within each particular style (if it were too easy, anyone could do it) may, however, result in some actual instruction occurring within the design studio, but only if the instructor determines that the preferred method of criticism is failing to get some crucial point across. The usual design "lecture" consists of an examination of the work of up-and-coming or established architects, so that even those students who don't know where the library is can internalize the constituents of fashion.

Louis Sullivan understood that the purpose of architecture has little to do with satisfying basic technical or programmatic needs. For example, he characterized the actual technology and functioning of tall office buildings—where "all in evidence is materialistic, an exhibition of force . . . the joint product of the speculator, the engineer, the builder"—as something almost trivial and certainly unworthy of his architectural passion. Rather, the question he asked about architecture took aim at a different problem— that of formal expression: "How shall we impart to this sterile pile, this crude, harsh, brutal agglomeration, this stark, staring exclamation of eternal strife, the graciousness of those higher forms of sensibility and culture that rest on the lower and fiercer passions?"[15]

In reaction to this design studio ethos—one that prioritizes "higher forms of sensibility"—special programs invariably spring up in architecture schools to investigate how architecture might be changed to be "more responsive" to precisely those things strategically left out. Sociological programs look into what people want and how they behave in the built environment. Solar power and daylighting programs show that a sustainable world is just around the corner. Community activists and advocates go into "the community" with the offer of free design services for those unable to pay, or they solicit opinions about what should be built in their neighborhoods. Numerous research projects are proposed to study everything from the "design process" to "disaster planning" since even "incremental improvements in the ways we design and construct environments can have enormous total benefits."[16]

Yet since none of these programs are concerned with why architecture takes the form it does in our society, but attribute its alleged "shortcomings" to lack of information, faulty methodology, or inequality in its application, they can at best serve as public relations efforts for their particular architectural schools, or act as means of getting funds from outside sources. And the difficulty in convincing the state or private industry to give money for these projects, compared to the research budgets of other departments in the university, is perhaps the best indication of what architecture is and isn't useful for. In any case, architectural pedagogy, having found a form adequate to its purpose, has little need for outside help.

* * *

Of all the many technological systems that fall loosely under the umbrellas of building technology and environmental science, the most important for both pedagogy and practice, at least in terms of their relationship to abstract and formal design decisions, are the control layers and cladding systems that together comprise building enclosure systems, constraining in various ways the movement of air, vapor, rainwater, and heat between the outside and inside of buildings. There are many specific requirements and attributes that characterize each control layer but the most fundamental—common to all four layers—is continuity. As discussed in Chapter 11, if continuity of all four control layers is maintained, and if control layers are properly configured so that, for example, materials that absorb water are able to dry out, vapor does not condense, rainwater is directed out of cavities, air leakage is limited, and heat loss is minimized, then the overwhelming majority of building failures will be prevented.

Conversely, if control layer continuity is made difficult or impossible because of formal or expressive design decisions that abstract from the underlying logic of such enclosure systems, then the probability of experiencing various types of building failure will increase. Unfortunately, many of the formal design conceits that prevail within schools of architecture (and in practice)—even and especially those that fetishize "materiality," or are based on abstract compositions of figure-ground or solid-void, or are derived from complex geometric or generative manipulations, or are otherwise governed by peculiar manipulations of site, surface, or mass— work against such continuity. Complexity and peculiarity, qualities that characterize many of these compositions, correlate strongly with various types of building failure.

The idea that changes in the nature of both abstraction and building technology have contributed to a virtual epidemic of non-structural building failure relies on probabilistic reasoning rather than on some definitively causal smoking gun and, for that reason, is relatively difficult to grasp.[17] Moreover, the problem and its causes remain largely invisible. This is because even well publicized instances of non-structural building failure can be easily dismissed as exceptional cases, pointing not to a general crisis but only to the hubris of a few architectural superstars. The bulk of evidence that might otherwise point to a bigger problem is largely unavailable, and so cannot be systematically compiled and analyzed. Manufacturers are not required, and are not generally interested, in publishing data about the reliability of their products, even if there were standards for how to do this. For one thing, competition with other manufacturers, and the absence of mandatory disclosure based on established protocols, favors hyperbole over accuracy. In addition, manufacturers are often unwilling to evaluate or describe the behavior of their products in relation to adjacent or connecting products over which they have no control.

It is this context that provides cover for an architectural pedagogy that supports bad building practices, one in which design studio instruction leads the way, with ancillary courses in history, theory, and technology—to the extent that they reinforce the heroic tendencies of formal expression— equally complicit.

It does not help that architectural critics educated primarily in the history and connoisseurship of culture and form can be counted on neither to understand architecture from the standpoint of building science, nor to challenge it on that basis. They tend, therefore, to lend support to a mode of education and practice that reinforces their own educated prejudices. Control layers are fundamental to the functionality of buildings. Because the probability of control layer failure is directly correlated with the proliferation of discontinuities in both geometry and material that are characteristic of complex and peculiar designs, and because the education of architects (reflecting and enabling the intense competition among practicing architects for recognition based upon increasingly complex and peculiar formal manipulation) often abstracts from the underlying logic of control layer design, one can conclude that architectural design pedagogy is complicit in the epidemic of building failure within the U.S.

Hannes Meyer famously attempted to devalue the role of the artist while emphasizing functional and technological issues within the curriculum of the Bauhaus. Such an extreme formulation of the art–science duality is only marginally relevant to the argument advanced here, since there is no reason to "abolish" or even to denigrate the role of artistic expression within the design process. Even if—as Meyer wrote in 1928—"the idea of the 'composition of a dock' is enough to make a cat laugh,"[18] such a finding should not be extrapolated into the realm of human cognition. To an extent unique among all creatures, humans construct—and, in doing so, *compose*—our world irrespective of any desire, however rational, to prioritize function and technology. The American neuroanthropologist Terrence Deacon argues that not only is the "compulsion to treat objects or actions as signs" a characteristic of the "*human aesthetic faculty*," but, most importantly: "We almost can't help ourselves."[19]

The question, therefore, is not whether art should be eliminated from architecture—art is unavoidable. The more important question considered herein is whether and how the art of architecture can adjust its trajectory so that it aligns with the most fundamental requirements of building science.

NOTES

PREFACE

1 Marx, "Letters from the Deutsch-Französische Jahrbücher."

INTRODUCTION

1 Schumacher, *Autopoiesis of Architecture*, 222.
2 Durand, *Précis of the Lectures*, 133.
3 *LEED Reference Guide v4*, 739.
4 Ford, *My Life and Work*, 113.
5 Mumford, "Function and Expression," 106.

1 HEALTH, SAFETY, AND WELFARE

1 "The Architects Sketch."
2 The architect's schematic renderings can be found at: Daniel Aloi, "Rand to House Luminous, Voluminous Fine Arts Library," *Cornell Chronicle*, January 25, 2018, https://news.cornell.edu/stories/2018/01/rand-house-luminous-voluminous-fine-arts-library.
3 Tobriner, "History of Building Codes."
4 "Fourteenth Amendment," (my italics).
5 Barnett, "Proper Scope of Police Power," 475.
6 "Village of Euclid v. Ambler."
7 Held and Hill, *The Democratic State* (in Chapter 5, "The Ideal Collective Capitalist—The Social State"); bold font in the original for the words "ideal collective capitalist" and "social state" has been removed.
8 Philip Shabecoff, "Reagan Order on Cost-Benefit Analysis Stirs Economic and Political Debate," *New York Times*, November 7, 1981.
9 A short, unpublished, version of what follows was presented by the author as "What Sustainability

Sustains," *Hawaii International Conference on Arts & Humanities*, January 2008.
10 Robert Pear, "Business Lobby Presses Agenda Before '08 Vote," *New York Times*, December 2, 2007, https://www.nytimes.com/2007/12/02/washington/02lobby.html.
11 Held and Hill, *The Democratic State* (in Chapter 4, "Justice—Protection of Person and Property—Morality"); bold font in the original for the words "morality" and "virtue" has been removed.
12 Janda, Berry, and Goldman, *The Challenge of Democracy*, 9.

2 STRUCTURE

1 Wikipedia, s.v. "Structural System," last modified April 6, 2019, 04:38, https://en.wikipedia.org/wiki/Structural_system.
2 William Rashbaum, "City Inquiry into Concrete Testing Widens," *New York Times*, August 17, 2009, https://www.nytimes.com/2009/08/18/nyregion/18concrete.html.
3 Makiko Inoue and Hisako Ueno, "Kobe Steel's Chief to Step Down as It Discloses Wider Quality Problems," *New York Times*, March 6, 2018, https://www.nytimes.com/2018/03/06/business/kobe-steel-ceo-resigns.html.
4 MacGregor, "Safety and Limit States," 489.
5 My discussion of steel vs. reinforced concrete safety factors is based on Ochshorn, *Structural Elements*, 342–43.

3 FIRE SAFETY

1 A short, unpublished version of this introductory paragraph and the historical overview found later in this chapter were presented by the

author as "What Sustainability Sustains," *Hawaii International Conference on Arts & Humanities*, January 2008.

2 Ahrens, "U.S. Experience with Sprinklers."

3 Licht, "Fire Protection Balance."

4 "Smoking," *National Fire Protection Association*, accessed January 7, 2020, http://www.nfpa.org/Public-Education/By-topic/Top-causes-of-fire/Smoking.

5 Rasmussen, *London: The Unique City*, 99.

6 Reddaway, *The Rebuilding of London*, 22.

7 Hoffer, *Seven Fires*, 21–31.

8 Reddaway, *The Rebuilding of London*, 31.

9 Wermiel, *The Fireproof Building*, 4.

10 Hoffer, *Seven Fires*, 32.

11 Reddaway, *The Rebuilding of London*, 33.

12 Wermiel, *The Fireproof Building*, 173–74.

13 Reddaway, *The Rebuilding of London*, 49.

14 Wermiel, *The Fireproof Building*, 10.

15 Wermiel, *The Fireproof Building*, 132–33.

16 Wermiel, *The Fireproof Building*, 191.

17 Licht, *Impact of Building Code Changes*.

18 Shulte, "Report on the World Trade Center," 16.

19 Robert Faturechi, "The Fire Sprinkler War, State by State," *ProPublica*, June 22, 2016, https://www.propublica.org/article/the-fire-sprinkler-war-state-by-state.

20 Haynes, "Fire Loss in the United States."

21 Statista, "Number of Owner Occupied Housing Units in the United States from 1975 to 2018," accessed November 10, 2019, https://www.statista.com/statistics/187576/housing-units-occupied-by-owner-in-the-us-since-1975/.

22 Viscusi, "The Value of Life."

23 Hall, Jr., "Total Cost of Fire," 24.

24 Brown, "Economic Analysis of Sprinkler Systems."

25 David Kirkpatrick, Danny Hakim, and James Glanz, "Why Grenfell Tower Burned: Regulators Put Cost Before Safety," *New York Times*, June 24, 2017 (my italics).

4 ACCESSIBILITY

1 A short, unpublished version of this chapter, excluding the discussion of protruding objects, was presented by the author as "What Sustainability Sustains," *Hawaii International Conference on Arts & Humanities*, January 2008.

2 Young, *Equality of Opportunity*, 5.

3 Dana Priest and Anna Hull, "Soldiers Face Neglect, Frustration at Army's Top Medical Facility," *Washington Post*, February 18, 2007.

4 Young, *Equality of Opportunity*, 10.

5 *Protruding Objects*, U.S. Access Board.

6 Young, *Equality of Opportunity*, 12 (ellipses in the original).

7 Young, *Equality of Opportunity*, 11.

8 Young, *Equality of Opportunity*, 2 (ellipses in the original).

9 Young, *Equality of Opportunity*, 3.

10 Mezey, *Disabling Interpretations*, 109–10.

11 Colker, *The Disability Pendulum*, 170.

12 Mezey, *Disabling Interpretations*, 110.

13 Mezey, *Disabling Interpretations*, 111–12.

14 "Milstein Hall Cornell University," OMA Office Work, http://oma.eu/projects/milstein-hall-cornell-university.

15 Le Corbusier and Jeanneret, "Five Points Towards a New Architecture," 100.

16 Ben Rosenberg, P.E. LEED AP (Senior Engineer, Robert Silman Assoc., Structural Engineers, New York), in videotaped interview with the author, June 9, 2011, https://youtu.be/xQP-e3OWSGE.

5 SUSTAINABILITY

1 Murphy, *The Green Tragedy*, 1–2.

2 Wilson, *Half-Earth*, 201.

3 Wilson, *Half-Earth*, 224.

4 Laitos, *The Right of Nonuse*, 4.

5 Laitos, *The Right of Nonuse*, 5.

6 Diamond, *Collapse*, 11.

7 Brundtland, *Our Common Future* (see part I, sec. 3).

8 A short, unpublished version of parts of this chapter, beginning with this paragraph, was presented by the author as "What Sustainability Sustains," *Hawaii International Conference on Arts & Humanities*, January 2008.

9 *LEED Reference Guide v4*, 4.

10 *LEED Reference Guide v4*, 4.

11   *LEED Reference Guide v4*, 4.
12   "U.S. Energy Facts Explained," see un-numbered figure titled "U.S. Energy Consumption by Source and Sector, 2018."
13   Zhou, Tutterow, Harris, and Bostrom, "Promoting Energy-Efficient Buildings." See Table ES-1 titled "Lighting and HVAC Energy Saving Potential in the Manufacturing Sector (TBtu)," 3.
14   "Today in Energy." See un-numbered chart titled "U.S. Household End-Use Energy Consumption by Fuel (2015)."
15   "Commercial Buildings Energy Consumption Survey." See Table 5, Major Fuel Consumption by End Use; and Table 6, Electricity Consumption by End Use.
16   *LEED Reference Guide v4*, 4.
17   *LEED Reference Guide v2.2*, 259 (my italics).
18   *LEED Reference Guide v2.2*, 188.
19   Shelton, "Greening the White House," 32–33.
20   *LEED Reference Guide v2.2*, 41.
21   Garreau, *Edge City*.
22   *LEED Reference Guide v2.2*, 315.
23   Ingersoll, "Second Nature," 145.
24   Alex Williams, "Buying into the Green Movement," *New York Times*, July 1, 2007, https://www.nytimes.com/2007/07/01/fashion/01green.html.
25   Andrew C. Revkin, "Carbon-Neutral Is Hip, But Is It Green?" *New York Times*, April 29, 2007, https://www.nytimes.com/2007/04/29/weekinreview/29revkin.html.
26   Michael Barbaro, "At Wal-Mart, Lessons in Self-Help," *New York Times*, April 5, 2007, https://www.nytimes.com/2007/04/05/business/05improve.html.
27   MacDonald and Deru, "The Wal-Mart Experience."
28   Jason Hickel, "Exposing the Great 'Poverty Reduction' Lie," *Al Jazeera*, August 21, 2014, https://www.aljazeera.com/indepth/opinion/2014/08/exposing-great-poverty-reductio-201481211590729809.html.

6   LIGHT AND AIR

1   Plunz, *History of Housing in New York City*.
2   Fisk, Faulkner, and Sullivan, "Accuracy of CO_2 Sensors."
3   Lstiburek, "Energy Flow Across Enclosures," 64 (footnote).
4   "Can 'Ghosts' Cause Bad Air? Poor Indoor Air Quality and 'Sightings,'" *ScienceDaily*, March 31, 2015, https://www.sciencedaily.com/releases/2015/03/150331121251.htm.
5   Freud, "The 'Uncanny,'" 241.
6   Vidler, *The Architectural Uncanny*, 11.
7   Marino, Nucara, and Pietrafesa, "Window-to-Wall Ratio."
8   Uraine et al., "Indoor Lighting Power Densities," 151 (see Table 75).
9   ASHRAE, *Advanced Energy Design Guide*.
10   Plunz, *History of Housing in New York City*, xxxii.
11   International Conference of Building Officials, *Uniform Building Code Vol. I* (Pasadena: ICBO, 1970), 81.
12   As of this writing, habitable rooms in dwellings are still required to have both natural lighting and ventilation in New York City, which has a municipal building code that is different, in this respect, from the IBC, from which it is derived, as well as the New York State Building Code.
13   Matter of Application of Jacobs, 98 N.Y. 98.
14   Furner, "Defining the Public Good," 244.
15   Matter of Application of Jacobs, 98 N.Y. 98.
16   Matter of Application of Jacobs, 98 N.Y. 98.
17   Byrne, "A Hobbesian Bundle," 735–36.
18   Eric Posner, "The Far-Reaching Threats of a Conservative Court," *New York Times*, October 23, 2018, https://www.nytimes.com/2018/10/23/opinion/supreme-court-brett-kavanaugh-trump-.html.

7   SECURITY

1   Foucault, *Discipline and Punish*, 172.
2   Brian Krebs, "Target Hackers Broke in Via HVAC Company," *Krebs on Security*, February 14, 2014, https://krebsonsecurity.com/2014/02/target-hackers-broke-in-via-hvac-company/.
3   Lee Mathews, "Hackers Use DDoS Attack to Cut Heat to Apartments," *Forbes*, November 7, 2016, https://www.forbes.com/sites/leemathews/2016/11/07/ddos-attack-leaves-finnish-apartments-without-heat/.

4   Szlósarczyk et al., "Towards Suppressing Attacks," 407.

5   Anthony Caruana, "Building Management Systems—Be Afraid, Be Very Afraid," *CSO Online*, May 26, 2016, accessed November 19, 2019, https://www.cso.com.au/article/600538/building-management-systems-afraid-very-afraid/.

6   GSA, *The Site Security Design Guide*, 76.

7   GSA, *The Site Security Design Guide*, 25.

8   GSA, *The Site Security Design Guide*, 5.

9   See, for example, Jacobs, *The Death and Life of Great American Cities*, and Newman, *Defensible Space*.

10 Hillier, "In Defense of Space," 541.

11 Lang and Moleski, *Functionalism Revisited*, 117.

12 Jacobs, *The Death and Life*, 32. "Yet Los Angeles cannot, any more than any other great city, evade the truth that, being a city, it is composed of strangers not all of whom are nice."

13 Emily Badger, "Redlining: Still a Thing," *Washington Post*, May 28, 2015, https://www.washingtonpost.com/news/wonk/wp/2015/05/28/evidence-that-banks-still-deny-black-borrowers-just-as-they-did-50-years-ago/.

14 Coates, *Between the World and Me*, 89–90 (my italics).

15 Wikipedia, s.v. "Shooting of Trayvon Martin," last modified November 18, 2019, 22:06, https://en.wikipedia.org/wiki/Shooting_of_Trayvon_Martin.

8   FUNCTION AS PATTERN

1   Alexander, Ishikawa, and Silverstein, *A Pattern Language*. See also Alexander, *The Timeless Way of Building*.

2   Wright, *Modern Architecture*, 27.

3   Wright, *An Organic Architecture*, 36 (my italics).

4   Wright, *An Autobiography*, 2nd edition, 489.

5   Wright, *An Autobiography*, 2nd edition, 395.

6   Wright, *An Autobiography*, 2nd edition, 157.

7   Wright, *An Autobiography*, 1st edition, 160.

8   Wright, *An Autobiography*, 2nd edition, 157.

9   Chermayeff and Alexander, *Community and Privacy*, 114–15.

10 Alexander, *Notes on the Synthesis of Form*, 7 (my italics).

11 Alexander, *Notes on the Synthesis of Form*, v.

12 Wright, *An Organic Architecture*, 34.

13 Alexander, *The Timeless Way of Building*, 247.

14 De Zurko, *Origins of Functionalist Theory*, 181.

15 Wolff, *Elements of Architecture*, quoted in De Zurko, *Origins of Functionalist Theory*, 181.

16 Alexander, Ishikawa, and Silverstein, *A Pattern Language*, 834.

17 Alexander, *The Timeless Way of Building*, 234.

18 Alexander, *The Timeless Way of Building*, 17 ("quality without a name") and 26 ("subtle kind of freedom").

19 Alexander, *The Timeless Way of Building*, 292.

20 Beck, Emery, and Greenberg, *Anxiety Disorders and Phobias*.

21 Alexander, Ishikawa, and Silverstein, *A Pattern Language*, 115.

22 Sullivan, "The Tall Office Building," 406.

23 Marcuse, *Reason and Revolution*, 9.

24 Marcuse, *Reason and Revolution*, 25.

25 Alexander, *The Timeless Way of Building*, 301 (my italics).

26 Alexander, *The Timeless Way of Building*, 88.

27 Michael Nichols and Christopher K. Walker, "'Separatist,'" *New York Times*, September 9, 2015, https://www.nytimes.com/2015/09/09/opinion/separatist.html.

28 Malcolm X, "Racial Separation," 57.

29 Alexander, Ishikawa, and Silverstein, *A Pattern Language*, 76.

30 Gegenstandpunkt, "Racism in the USA."

31 Alexander, *The Timeless Way of Building*, 114–15 (ellipses in original).

32 Alexander, *The Timeless Way of Building*, 265.

33 Alexander, *The Timeless Way of Building*, 86.

34 Jean Hannah Edelstein, "Young People Are Growing Ever More Depressed. Is Modern Life to Blame?" *The Guardian*, March 16, 2016, https://www.theguardian.com/commentisfree/2016/mar/16/depression-mental-health-modern-life-young.

35 Chermayeff and Alexander, *Community and Privacy*, 236.

36 Steil et al., "Contrasting Concepts."

37 Steil et al., "Contrasting Concepts."

9 INTRODUCTORY CONCEPTS

1 A version of this chapter was previously published as Ochshorn, "Utility's Evil Twin."
2 Scott Brown, "The Function of a Table," 154.
3 "Function," in Forty, *Words and Buildings*, 181.
4 Joshua Rothman, "Why J. Crew's Vision of Preppy America Failed," *New Yorker*, May 3, 2017, http://www.newyorker.com/business/currency/why-j-crews-vision-of-preppy-america-failed.
5 Vanessa Friedman, "Melania Trump, Agent of Coat Chaos," *New York Times*, June 21, 2018, https://www.nytimes.com/2018/06/21/style/zara-jacket-melania-trump.html.
6 Austin Frakt, "Why Your Doctor's White Coat Can Be a Threat to Your Health," *New York Times*, April 29, 2019, https://www.nytimes.com/2019/04/29/upshot/doctors-white-coat-bacteria.html.
7 Osgood, Suci, and Tannenbaum, *The Measurement of Meaning*, 290.
8 Gelernter, *Sources of Architectural Form*, 118, 130–31, 147, 149.
9 Fromm, *Man for Himself*, 55.
10 "Psychology: Introduction," in GegenStandpunkt, *Psychology of the Private Individual*.
11 Gombrich, *Art and Illusion*, 127.
12 Norberg-Schulz, *Intentions in Architecture*, 22.
13 Giedion is quoted in Harries, *The Ethical Function of Architecture*, 2.
14 Harries, *The Ethical Function of Architecture*, 24.
15 "Function," in Forty, *Words and Buildings*, 187.
16 Koolhaas, "Preface," in Balmond, *Informal*.
17 Steil et al., "Contrasting Concepts." I cannot validate this attribution with a citation to the original quote by Le Corbusier, although there are numerous secondary references, all saying essentially the same thing, and probably each assuming that their own unattributed source was accurate. This one is from Peter Eisenman.
18 Garbett, *Rudimentary Treatise*, 9. Quoted in De Zurko, *Origins of Functionalist Theory*, 140–41.
19 Steil et al., "Contrasting Concepts."
20 Marcuse, *The Aesthetic Dimension*, xi, 9 (my italics).
21 Leach, "Architecture or Revolution," 114.
22 Norberg-Schulz, *Intentions in Architecture*, 17.
23 Norberg-Schulz, *Intentions in Architecture*, 71.
24 Norberg-Schulz, *Intentions in Architecture*, 72, 79.
25 Wölfflin, *Renaissance and Baroque*, 77. Quoted in Vidler, *The Architectural Uncanny*, 72.
26 Roskam, *Improvised City*, 13.

10 EXPRESSION OF UTILITY

1 Gwilt, *Encyclopedia of Architecture*, 796, quoted in De Zurko, *Origins of Functionalist Theory*, 122.
2 Coleridge, *Essays and Lectures on Shakespeare*, 46–47, quoted in De Zurko, *Origins of Functionalist Theory*, 118.
3 Wright, "In the Cause of Architecture, Second Paper," 406 (see footnote).
4 Wright, *An Organic Architecture*, 4.
5 Vitruvius, *The Ten Books on Architecture*, 84.
6 Forty, "Function," in *Words and Buildings*, 185, 187.
7 Forty, "Function," in *Words and Buildings*, 187 (ellipsis in Forty's excerpt, not in the original text).
8 Marx, "Results of the Immediate Process," 1019.
9 Tell, "The Rise and Fall of a Mechanical Rhetoric," 163–64.
10 Mallgrave, *Gottfried Semper*, 220.
11 Panofsky, *Gothic Architecture and Scholasticism*, 43–44.
12 Alan Chimacoff and Klaus Herdeg, "Two Cornell Professors: 'A Promise Unfulfilled,'" *The Cornell Daily Sun*, May 4, 1973. The same article, slightly revised, appears ten years later in Herdeg, *The Decorated Diagram*.
13 Herdeg, *The Decorated Diagram*, 18.
14 Stephan Burgdorff and Bernhard Zand (interviewers), "An Obsessive Compulsion towards the Spectacular," *Spiegel International*, July 18, 2008 (my italics), https://www.spiegel.de/international/world/rem-koolhaas-an-obsessive-compulsion-towards-the-spectacular-a-566655.html.
15 Movingmaster, "Mocking the Monument: CCTV snapshots," *MovingCities.org*, December 10, 2008, https://movingcities.org/movingmemos/mocking-the-monument-cctv-snapshots/.
16 Jonnes, *Eiffel's Tower*, 26–27.
17 Jonnes, *Eiffel's Tower*, 311.

18 Osgood, Suci, and Tannenbaum, *The Measurement of Meaning*, 293.

19 Koolhaas and Obrist, "China Interview," in *Rem Koolhaas, The Conversation Series*, 6.

20 Koolhaas, "Universal Modernization Patent," 511.

21 Koolhaas and Obrist, "China Interview," in *Rem Koolhaas, The Conversation Series*, 6.

22 Koolhaas and Obrist, "Between-Cities Interview," in *Rem Koolhaas, The Conversation Series*, 51–52.

23 Venturi, Scott-Brown, and Izenour, *Learning from Las Vegas*, 64.

11 MODERNIST ABSTRACTION AND DYSFUNCTION

1 Parts of this chapter have been previously published in Ochshorn, "Architecture's Dysfunctional Couple" and Ochshorn, "Designing Building Failures."

2 Hegel, *Lectures on The History of Philosophy*, 25. Hegel argued, in the context of French representations of the absolute, that "to make abstractions hold good in actuality means to destroy reality."

3 Joseph Lstiburek, "But I Was So Much Younger Then (I'm So Much Older Than That Now)," BSI-065, *Building Science Insights*, https://www.buildingscience.com/documents/insights/bsi-065-i-was-younger-then.

4 Robin Pogrebin, "Extreme Makeover: Museum Edition," *New York Times*, September 18, 2005, https://www.nytimes.com/2005/09/18/arts/design/extreme-makeover-museum-edition.html.

5 John A. Hawkinson, "MIT Settles with Gehry over Stata Ctr. Defects," *The Tech*, online edition, March 19, 2010, https://thetech.com/2010/03/19/statasuit-v130-n14.

6 Campbell, *Pathways to Bliss*, 132–33.

7 Robin Pogrebin, "Extreme Makeover: Museum Edition," *New York Times*, September 18, 2005, https://www.nytimes.com/2005/09/18/arts/design/extreme-makeover-museum-edition.html.

8 Le Corbusier, "Trois Rappels," 92, translated and republished in Le Corbusier, *Towards a New Architecture*.

9 Piet Mondrian, *L'Architecture Vivante*, Autumn, 1925, 11, quoted in Collins, *Concrete*, 281.

10 [Fitzmaurice], *Principles of Modern Building*, 198.

11 [Fitzmaurice], *Principles of Modern Building*, 81.

12 Deborah Snoonian, "Sleuthing Out Building Failure," *Architectural Record*, August 2000, 168.

13 Yorke, *The Modern House*, 55.

14 "Building Failure Patterns and Their Implications," *The Architects' Journal*, February 5, 1975, 308.

15 Ramsey and Sleeper, "Preface," in Ramsey and Sleeper, *Architectural Graphic Standards*.

16 Lawton and Brown, "Considering the Use of Polyethylene Vapour Barriers."

17 William B. Rose, "Moisture Control in the Modern Building Envelope: History of the Vapor Barrier in the U.S., 1923–52," *APT Bulletin* 28, no. 4 (1997): 13–19.

18 Ramsey and Sleeper, "Preface," in Ramsey and Sleeper, *Architectural Graphic Standards*.

19 Le Corbusier, *Towards a New Architecture*, 1.

20 Balmond with Smith, *Informal*, 64.

21 Ben Folds, "Rockin' the Suburbs," *Rockin' the Suburbs*, Audio CD, Sony, 2001. Permission for the use of this quotation is gratefully acknowledged.

12 EXPRESSION OF STRUCTURE

1 Billington, *The Tower and the Bridge*, 5.

2 Thornton and Tomasetti, *Exposed Structure in Building Design*, 154.

3 Balmond Studio, "Informal," http://www.balmondstudio.com/work/informal.php.

4 Billington, *Robert Maillart*, 15.

5 Gombrich, *Art and Illusion*, 21.

6 Gombrich, *Art and Illusion*, 373–74.

7 Thompson, *On Growth and Form*, 16.

8 Gibson, *The Ecological Approach to Visual Perception*, 10.

9 Solomonson, *The Chicago Tribune Tower Competition*, 122.

10 Anthony Vidler, "'The big Greek column will be built': Adolf Loos and the Sign of Classicism," *Skyline*, October 1982, 16–17, quoted

in Solomonson, *The Chicago Tribune Tower Competition*, 118.

11 Solomonson, *The Chicago Tribune Tower Competition*, 118.

12 Bonta, *Architecture and Its Interpretation*, 23.

13 Banham, *The New Brutalism*, 17–18.

14 Krohn, *Mies van der Rohe*. Krohn does not compile these statistics, but his documentation of Mies's I.I.T. buildings provides the evidence.

15 Brady, "Iron in the Soul," 153.

16 Schulze, *Mies van der Rohe*, 226.

17 Sullivan, *The Autobiography of an Idea*, 314.

18 Claude Bragdon, "Foreword," in Sullivan, *The Autobiography of an Idea*, 5.

19 Howard, Jr., *Structure, An Architect's Approach*, 242.

20 Koolhaas, "Preface," in Balmond, *Informal*, 9.

21 Nicholas Kusnetz, "These Are the Toughest Emissions to Cut, and a Big Chunk of the Climate Problem," *Inside Climate News*, June 28, 2018, https://insideclimatenews.org/news/28062018/global-warming-pollution-industrial-sources-cement-steel-trade-solutions-technology-shipping.

22 Balmond, *Informal*, 62.

23 Sherrie Negrea, "Steel Framework Nearly Complete for Milstein Hall," *Cornell Chronicle*, June 14, 2010, http://news.cornell.edu/stories/2010/06/steel-framework-nearly-complete-milstein-hall.

24 LeBlanc, *The Architecture Traveler*, 134.

25 Sherrie Negrea, "Steel Framework Nearly Complete for Milstein Hall," *Cornell Chronicle*, June 14, 2010, http://news.cornell.edu/stories/2010/06/steel-framework-nearly-complete-milstein-hall.

26 Krohn, *Mies van der Rohe*, 110.

27 Banham, *The New Brutalism*, 19.

28 Wikiarquitectura, "Hunstanton School," https://en.wikiarquitectura.com/building/hunstanton-school/.

29 Lstiburek, "Thermal Bridge Redux," 60.

30 Robert Gutman, "House VI," in Cuff and Wriedt, eds., *Architecture from the Outside In*, 123, originally published in *Progressive Architecture* 58, no. 6 (June 1977): 65–67.

31 Robert Gutman, "House VI," in Cuff and Wriedt, eds., *Architecture from the Outside In*, 122, originally published in *Progressive Architecture* 58, no. 6 (June 1977): 65–67.

13 EXPRESSION OF SUSTAINABILITY

1 Emily York, "Businesses See Advantage in Green Buildings," *Phys.org*, September 2, 2010, https://phys.org/news/2010-09-businesses-advantage-green.html.

2 Rob Esmay, "Can't We Just Dye the Smoke Green," *New Yorker*, May 14, 2007, 101.

3 McDonough Architects, *The Hannover Principles*, 10. To remain consistent with the title of the book, the German spelling, "Hannover," rather than the American or English "Hanover," will be used throughout this chapter.

4 McDonough Architects, *The Hannover Principles*, 10.

5 Shapiro, *The Evolution of Rights in Liberal Theory*, 302–3.

6 Held and Hill, *The Democratic State* (in Chapter 2, "Sovereignty—The People—Constitutional Rights—Representation"); bold font in the original for the words "human rights" has been removed.

7 McDonough Architects, *The Hannover Principles*, 8.

8 Ana Swanson and Brad Plumer, "Trump's Solar Tariffs Are Clouding the Industry's Future," *New York Times*, January 23, 2018, https://www.nytimes.com/2018/01/23/us/politics/trump-solar-tariffs.html.

9 Barack Obama, "Text: Obama's Remarks on Solar Energy," *New York Times*, May 27, 2009, https://www.nytimes.com/2009/05/27/us/politics/27obama.text.html.

10 Editorial Board, "Is the Paris Climate Accord Too Little, Too Late?" *Los Angeles Times*, April 22, 2016, https://www.latimes.com/opinion/editorials/la-ed-0422-climate-change-accord-20160422-story.html.

11 McDonough Architects, *The Hannover Principles*, 8.

12 McDonough Architects, *The Hannover Principles*, 8–9.

13 Deborah Solomon, "Calling Mr. Green," *New York Times*, May 20, 2007, https://www.nytimes.com/2007/05/20/magazine/20wwln-Q4-t.html.

14 McDonough Architects, *The Hannover Principles*, 9.

15 McDonough Architects, *The Hannover Principles*, 9.

16 Petroski, *Design Paradigms*, 7.

17 McDonough Architects, *The Hannover Principles*, 10–12.

18 Ingersoll, "Second Nature: On the Social Bond of Ecology and Architecture," in Dutton and Mann, *Reconstructing Architecture*, 146.

19 McDonough Architects, *The Hannover Principles*, 24.

20 McDonough Architects, *The Hannover Principles*, 28.

21 McDonough Architects, *The Hannover Principles*, 29.

22 McDonough Architects, *The Hannover Principles*, 30.

23 McDonough Architects, *The Hannover Principles*, 31.

24 McDonough Architects, *The Hannover Principles*, 86.

25 McDonough Architects, *The Hannover Principles*, 86.

26 McDonough Architects, *The Hannover Principles*, 99.

27 McDonough Architects, *The Hannover Principles*, 101.

28 McDonough Architects, *The Hannover Principles*, 102.

29 McDonough Architects, *The Hannover Principles*, 102.

30 Vidler, *The Architectural Uncanny*, 65.

31 McDonough Architects, *The Hannover Principles*, 15.

32 McDonough Architects, *The Hannover Principles*, 17.

33 McDonough Architects, *The Hannover Principles*, 19, (my italics).

34 McDonough Architects, *The Hannover Principles*, 48.

35 McDonough Architects, *The Hannover Principles*, 66–67.

36 McDonough Architects, *The Hannover Principles*, 107.

37 Ursula Sautter, "Expensive Exposure," *Time*, June 12, 2000, http://content.time.com/time/world/article/0,8599,2051112,00.html.

14 THE COMMUNAL BEING AND THE PRIVATE INDIVIDUAL

1 Marx, "On the Jewish Question," 220.

2 Sahotsky, "The Roman Construction Process," 46 (my italics).

3 Curatorial wall text describing the work of Jackson Pollock (1912–1956) in the Metropolitan Museum of Art's "Epic Abstraction: Pollock to Herrera" show in New York City that opened December 17, 2018. Transcribed by the author.

4 Howell-Ardila, "Berlin's Search for a 'Democratic' Architecture," 63.

5 Howell-Ardila, "Berlin's Search for a 'Democratic' Architecture," 75.

6 Elizabeth Greenspan, "Daniel Libeskind's World Trade Center Change of Heart," *New Yorker*, August 28, 2013, https://www.newyorker.com/business/currency/daniel-libeskinds-world-trade-center-change-of-heart.

7 Wikipedia, s.v. "541," last modified January 15, 2019, 10:37, https://en.wikipedia.org/wiki/541.

8 Michael Kimmelman, "A Soaring Emblem of New York, and Its Upside-Down Priorities," *New York Times*, November 29, 2014, https://www.nytimes.com/2014/11/30/nyregion/is-one-world-trade-center-rises-in-lower-manhattan-a-design-success.html.

9 Held and Hill, *The Democratic State* (in Chapter 1, "Freedom and Equality—Private Property—Abstract Free Will").

10 Sudjic with Jones, *Architecture and Democracy*, 8 (my italics).

11 Sudjic with Jones, *Architecture and Democracy*, 20–21 (my italics).

12 Mimi Zeiger, "Koolhaas May Think We're Past the Time of Manifestos, But That's No Reason to Play Dumb," *Dezeen*, December 12, 2014, https://www.dezeen.com/2014/12/12/mimi-zeiger-opinion-urban-unrest-police-violence-race-architecture-urbanism-ferguson/.

13 Ockman, "What Is Democratic Architecture?" 71.

14 Aaron Betsky, "Railroad Stations Are Our Contemporary Architecture of Democracy," *Dezeen*, May 17, 2016, https://www.dezeen.com/2016/05/17/railroad-stations-architecture-democracy-transport-aaron-betsky-opinion/.

15 Koolhaas, "Junkspace," 179.

16 Ockman, "What Is Democratic Architecture," 67.

17 Sullivan, "The Young Man in Architecture," 118.

18 Gans, "How Can Architecture Be Democratic?" 119.

19 Fox, "The Uncertain Relationship between Transparency and Accountability," 665.

20 Hollyer, Rosendorff, and Vreeland, "Democracy and Transparency," 1191.

21 Fox, "The Uncertain Relationship between Transparency and Accountability," 663–64.

22 Foster + Partners, Projects, "1999—Berlin, Germany: Reichstag, New German Parliament," https://www.fosterandpartners.com/projects/reichstag-new-german-parliament/.

23 Elkadi, *Cultures of Glass Architecture*, 48.

24 Conradi, "Transparente Architektur = Demokratie?" quoted in Howell-Ardila, "Berlin's Search for a 'Democratic' Architecture," 81.

25 Wright, *An Organic Architecture*, 28–29.

26 Wright, *An Organic Architecture*, 27.

27 Wright, "Broadacre City: A New Community Plan," 246.

28 Norberg-Schulz, *Intentions in Architecture*, 118–19.

29 "Neue Rechte am Bau?" (New Right-Wing in Architecture?), *Der Spiegel* 45 (1995): 244. Quoted in Howell-Ardila, "Berlin's Search for a 'Democratic' Architecture," 79.

30 Rookwood and Pearson, "The Hoolifan."

31 Gegenstandpunkt, "The People: A Terrible Abstraction," first paragraph.

32 Allison Arieff, "Affordable Housing that Doesn't Scream 'Affordable,'" *CityLab*, October 21, 2011, https://www.bloomberg.com/news/articles/2011-10-21/affordable-housing-that-doesn-t-scream-affordable.

15 FASHIONABLE BUILDING

1 Marx, *Grundrisse*, 650–51.

2 "Pecunia," *Legal Dictionary*, http://legal-dictionary.thefreedictionary.com/pecunia (my italics).

3 Lang and Moleski, "Preface," *Functionalism Revisited*, xvii.

4 Contemporary equivalents of the AIA's "How to Win" seminars from the early 1980s include Enoch Sears, "Marketing for Architects: The Authoritative Guide (with Case Studies)," https://www.businessofarchitecture.com/marketing-for-architects/, and Stasiowski, *Architect's Essentials of Winning Proposals*, sponsored by the AIA.

5 "Fashion," *Merriam-Webster Dictionary*, https://www.merriam-webster.com/dictionary/fashion.

6 Prum, *The Evolution of Beauty*, 11–12.

7 "Gertrude McFuzz," in Dr. Seuss, *Yertle the Turtle and Other Stories*.

8 Gombrich, "The Logic of Vanity Fair."

9 Val Warke, "'In' Architecture: Observing the Meanings of Fashion," in Fausch et al., eds., *Architecture: In Fashion*, 133.

10 Schumacher, *Autopoiesis of Architecture*, 134.

11 Val Warke, "'In' Architecture: Observing the Meanings of Fashion," in Fausch et al., eds., *Architecture: In Fashion*, 133–34.

12 Veblen, *The Theory of the Leisure Class*, 97.

13 Gombrich, "The Logic of Vanity Fair."

14 "Conversation with Graves," 112.

15 Robert Guenther, "In Architects' Circles, Post-Modernist Design Is a Bone of Contention," *Wall Street Journal* 63, no. 204 (August 1, 1983), 7.

16 Paul Goldberger, "Gracious Living: Frank Gehry's Swirling Apartment Tower," *The New Yorker*, March 7, 2011, 72–74, https://www.newyorker.com/magazine/2011/03/07/gracious-living-paul-goldberger.

17 Anne Field, "Buildings Designed by 'Starchitects' Pay Off Big," *Crain's New York Business.com*, November 27, 2011, https://www.crainsnewyork.com/article/20111127/REAL_ESTATE02/311279985/buildings-designed-by-starchitects-pay-off-big.

18 Paul Goldberger, "High Design at a Profit," *New York Times*, November 14, 1976, https://www.nytimes.com/1976/11/14/archives/high-design-at-a-profit.html.

19 Paul Goldberger, "Gracious Living: Frank Gehry's Swirling Apartment Tower," *The New Yorker*, March 7, 2011, 72–74, https://www.newyorker.com/magazine/2011/03/07/gracious-living-paul-goldberger.

20 James Gardner, "Gehry Undone: Spruce Street Building Billows to Nowhere," December 1, 2010, *RealDeal.com*, https://therealdeal.com/issues_articles/james-gardner-gehry-undone/.

21 Hegel, *Reason in History*, 17.

22 Gombrich, "The Logic of Vanity Fair."

23 "Introduction," in Marx, *Grundrisse*, 91.

24 Venturi, Scott-Brown, and Izenour, *Learning from Las Vegas*, 64. The authors famously suggest that, along with "decorated sheds" (discussed in Chapter 10), the contortion of buildings into "ducks" provides a means for "symbolic and representational elements" to become embedded in architecture.

25 Marx, *Capital, Volume II*, 201.

26 Ruskin, *The Seven Lamps of Architecture*, 15.

27 Mumford, "Function and Expression in Architecture," 109.

28 Robert Guenther, "In Architects' Circles, Post-Modernist Design Is a Bone of Contention," *Wall Street Journal* 63, no. 204 (August 1, 1983), 7.

29 Sloan, *My Years with General Motors*, 64.

30 Edmondson, *Ice Cream Social*, vii.

31 Veblen, *The Theory of the Leisure Class*. See especially Chapter 6, "Pecuniary Canons of Taste."

32 Held and Hill, *The Democratic State* (in Chapter 1, "Freedom and Equality—Private Property—Abstract Free Will").

33 Lang and Moleski, *Functionalism Revisited*, xvii.

34 "Ancient Egypt, an Introduction," *Kahn Academy*, https://www.khanacademy.org/humanities/ap-art-history/ancient-mediterranean-ap/ancient-egypt-ap/a/ancient-egypt-an-introduction.

35 Mahall and Serbest, *How Architecture Learned to Speculate*, 114.

36 Gegenstandpunkt, "The System of Free Competition and What It Is About," Section 1.

37 Marx, "Preface," in *A Contribution to the Critique of Political Economy*.

38 "Marx's Method: The Autonomy of Sociology," in Popper, *The Open Society and Its Enemies*, 86.

EPILOGUE: ARCHITECTURAL EDUCATION

1   Michael Joroff, James Snyder, and John Templer, "Introduction," in Joroff et al., *An Agenda for Architectural Research*, 3.

2   "Department of Architecture Program Mission," *Courses of Study*, Ithaca, NY: Cornell University, 2010–11, 136, https://ecommons.cornell.edu/bitstream/handle/1813/38676/COS_v102_2010_2011_03.pdf.

3   Veblen, *The Theory of the Leisure Class*, 176–77 (my italics).

4   Veblen, *The Theory of the Leisure Class*, 82–83 (my italics)

5   Ruskin, *The Seven Lamps of Architecture*, 17.

6   Jack Self, "OMA AMO w/for Prada," 032c, February 16, 2017, https://032c.com/oma-prada (my italics).

7   Angela Pang, "Implementing Architecture: Cornell and the Education of Architects," *Architecture and Urbanism (a+u)*, no. 428, May 2006: 9.

8   Seng Kuan and Angela Pang, "Education in Process: New Directions at Cornell," *Architecture and Urbanism (a+u)*, no. 428, May 2006: 18 (my italics).

9   *NAAB Procedures for Accreditation*: *Professional Degree Programs in Architecture 2015 Edition*, s.v. "Student Performance Criteria," approved May 6, 2015, https://www.naab.org/wp-content/uploads/2016/03/Full-Document.pdf.

10 Bashier, "Reflections on Architectural Design Education," 427.

11 Koch et al., *The Redesign of Studio Culture*, 11.

12 Deamer, "First Year: The Fictions of Studio Design," 11.

13 Schön, *The Reflective Practitioner*, 54–56.

14 Stone, *Workbook of an Unsuccessful Architect*, 175.

15 Sullivan, "The Tall Office Building," 403.

16 James Snyder, "Preface," in Joroff et al., *An Agenda for Architectural Research*, iii.

17 This discussion of building failure and pedagogy is based on Ochshorn, *Architecture's Dysfunctional Couple*.

18 Hannes Meyer, "Bauen," quoted in Hays, *Modernism and the Posthumanist Subject*, 158–59.

19 Terrence Deacon, "The Aesthetic Faculty," in Turner, ed., *The Artful Mind*, 25 (italics in original).

BIBLIOGRAPHY

Ahrens, Marty. "U.S. Experience with Sprinklers." *NFPA Research* 7, no. 17 (July 2017): 1–35. https://www.nfpa.org/-/media/Files/News-and-Research/Fire-statistics-and-reports/Suppression/ossprinklers.pdf.

Alexander, Christopher. *Notes on the Synthesis of Form.* Cambridge, MA: Harvard University Press, 1973.

Alexander, Christopher, Sara Ishikawa, and Murray Silverstein. *A Pattern Language: Towns, Buildings, Construction.* New York: Oxford University Press, 1977.

Alexander, Christopher. *The Timeless Way of Building.* New York: Oxford University Press, 1979.

"The Architects Sketch." *Monty Python's Flying Circus* episode 17, "The Buzz Aldrin Show" (1970). Transcript accessed November 9, 2019. http://www.montypython.net/scripts/architec.php.

ASHRAE. *Advanced Energy Design Guide for Small to Medium Office Buildings.* Atlanta: ASHRAE, 2019.

Balmond, Cecil, with Jannuzzi Smith. *Informal*, edited by Christian Brensing. Munich: Prestel, 2002.

Banham, Reyner. *The New Brutalism: Ethic or Aesthetic?* London: The Associated Press, 1966.

Barnett, Randy E. "The Proper Scope of the Police Power." *Notre Dame Law Review* 79 (2004): 429–95. https://scholarship.law.georgetown.edu/facpub/508.

Bashier, Fathi. "Reflections on Architectural Design Education: The Return of Rationalism in the Studio." *Frontiers of Architectural Research* 3 (2014): 424–30. http://dx.doi.org/10.1016/j.foar.2014.08.004.

Beck, Aaron, Gary Emery, and Ruth L. Greenberg. *Anxiety Disorders and Phobias: A Cognitive Perspective.* New York: Basic Books, 1985.

Billington, David P. *Robert Maillart and the Art of Reinforced Concrete.* Cambridge, MA: MIT Press, 1990.

Billington, David P. *The Tower and the Bridge: The New Art of Structural Engineering.* New York: Basic Books, 1983.

Bonta, Juan Pablo. *Architecture and Its Interpretation: A Study of Expressive Systems in Architecture.* New York: Rizzoli, 1979.

Brady, Noel. "Iron in the Soul." *Building Material*, no. 20 (2016): 151–69. https://www.jstor.org/stable/26445107.

Brown, Hayden. "Economic Analysis of Residential Fire Sprinkler Systems." NISTIR 7277, U.S. Department of Commerce Technology Administration, National Institute of Standards and Technology, Office of Applied Economics, Building and Fire Research Laboratory, Gaithersburg, Maryland (December 2005). https://tsapps.nist.gov/publication/get_pdf.cfm?pub_id=860095.

Brundtland, Gro Harlem. *Report of the World Commission on Environment and Development: Our Common Future.* World Commission on Environment and Development, 1987. http://www.un-documents.net/our-common-future.pdf.

Byrne, J. Peter. "A Hobbesian Bundle of Lockean Sticks: The Property Rights Legacy of Justice Scalia." *Vermont Law Review* 41 (2017): 733–62. https://scholarship.law.georgetown.edu/facpub/1976.

Campbell, Joseph. *Pathways to Bliss: Mythology and Personal Transformation*, edited by David Kudler. Novato, CA: New World Library, 2004.

Chermayeff, Serge, and Christopher Alexander. *Community and Privacy: Toward a New Architecture of Humanism.* New York: Doubleday & Co., 1963.

Coates, Ta-Nehisi. *Between the World and Me.* New York: Spiegel & Grau, 2015.

Coleridge, Samuel Taylor. "Shakspeare [sic], a Poet Generally." In *Coleridge's Essays and Lectures on Shakespeare & Some Other Old Poets & Dramatists*, edited by Ernest Rhys, 38–47. London: J.M. Dent & Sons, 1907. Reprinted 1914.

Colker, Ruth. *The Disability Pendulum: The First Decade of the Americans with Disabilities Act*. New York: New York University Press, 2005.

Collins, Peter. *Concrete: The Vision of a New Architecture*, 2nd ed. Montreal: McGill-Queen's University Press, 2004.

"Commercial Buildings Energy Consumption Survey (CBECS)." U.S. Energy Information Agency (EIA). Release date, March 18, 2016. https://www.eia.gov/consumption/commercial/reports/2012/energyusage/.

Conradi, Peter. "Transparente Architektur = Demokratie?" *Der Architekt* 9 (1995): 539–42.

"Conversation with Graves." *Progressive Architecture* 64, no. 2 (February 1983): 108–15.

Cuff, Dana, and John Wriedt, eds. *Architecture from the Outside In: Selected Essays by Robert Gutman*. New York: Princeton Architectural Press, 2010.

Deamer, Peggy. "First Year: The Fictions of Studio Design." *Perspecta* 36 (2005): 10–16.

De Zurko, Edward Robert. *Origins of Functionalist Theory*. New York: Columbia University Press, 1957.

Diamond, Jared. *Collapse: How Societies Choose to Fail or Succeed*. New York: Penguin Books, 2005.

Durand, Jean-Nicolas-Louis. *Précis of the Lectures on Architecture*. Translated by David Britt. Los Angeles: The Getty Research Institute, 2000.

Dutton, Thomas A., and Lian Hurst Mann, eds. *Reconstructing Architecture: Critical Discourses and Social Practices*. Minneapolis: University of Minnesota Press, 1996.

Edmondson, Brad. *Ice Cream Social: The Struggle for the Soul of Ben & Jerry*. San Francisco: Berrett-Koehler Publishers, 2013.

Elkadi, Hisham. *Cultures of Glass Architecture*. Aldershot: Ashgate Publishing, 2006.

Fausch, Deborah, Paulette Singley, Rodolphe El-Khoury, and Zvi Efrat, eds. *Architecture: In Fashion*. New York: Princeton Architectural Press, 1994.

Fisk, William, David Faulkner, and Douglas Sullivan. "Accuracy of CO_2 Sensors." *IAQ Applications* 9, no. 3 (October 2008). https://www.osti.gov/servlets/purl/941429.

[Fitzmaurice, R.] *Principles of Modern Building Vol. 1*, 3rd ed. London: Dept. of Scientific and Industrial Research (Building Research Station), Her Majesty's Stationery Office, 1959.

Ford, Henry, with Samuel Crowther. *My Life and Work*. Garden City, NY: Garden City Publishing Co., 1922.

Forty, Adrian. *Words and Buildings: A Vocabulary of Architecture*. London: Thames & Hudson, 2000.

Foucault, Michel. *Discipline and Punish: The Birth of the Prison*. Translated from the French by Alan Sheridan. New York: Vintage Books, 1995. First published in 1977 by Allen Lane (London).

"Fourteenth Amendment." Legal Information Institute. Cornell Law School. https://www.law.cornell.edu/constitution/amendmentxiv.

Fox, John. *Understanding Capital Volume II*, 1985. https://www.marxists.org/subject/economy/authors/fox/ucv2-ch20.htm.

Fox, Jonathan. "The Uncertain Relationship between Transparency and Accountability." *Development in Practice* 17, no. 4–5 (August 2007): 663–71. https://escholarship.org/uc/item/8c25c3z4.

Freud, Sigmund. "The 'Uncanny.'" In *The Standard Edition of the Complete Psychological Works of Sigmund Freud: An Infantile Neurosis and Other Works* XVII (1917–1919). Translated by James Strachey, 219–52. London: Hogarth Press, 1953.

Fromm, Erich. *Man for Himself*. New York: Rinehart and Co., 1947.

Furner, Mary. "Defining the Public Good in the U.S. Gilded Age, 1883–1898: 'Freedom of Contract' versus 'Internal Police' in the Tortured History of Employment Law and Regulation." *The Journal of the Gilded Age and Progressive Era* 17, no. 2 (April 2018): 241–75. https://doi.org/10.1017/S1537781417000822.

Gans, Herbert J. "How Can Architecture Be Democratic?" *Dissent* 59, no. 1 (Winter 2012): 119. https://doi.org/10.1353/dss.2012.0001.

Garbett, Edward Lacy. *Rudimentary Treatise on the Principles of Design in Architecture as Deducible from Nature and Exemplified in the Works of the Greek and Gothic Architects* (No. 18 in Weale's Rudimentary Series). London: John Weale, 1850.

Garreau, Joel. *Edge City: Life on the New Frontier*. New York: Doubleday, 1991.

Gegenstandpunkt. "The People: A Terrible Abstraction." Translated from *Gegenstandpunkt: Politische Vierteljahreszeitschrift 1–06*. Munich: Gegenstandpunkt Verlag, 2006. https://en.gegenstandpunkt.com/.

Gegenstandpunkt. *Psychology of the Private Individual: Critique of Bourgeois Consciousness.* https://en.gegenstandpunkt.com/. Translated from *Die Psychologie des Bürgerlichen Individuums.* Munich: Gegenstandpunkt Verlag, 2003–2009.

Gegenstandpunkt. "Racism in the USA—Where It Comes From and Why It Won't Go Away." Translated from *Gegenstandpunkt: Politische Vierteljahreszeitschrift 1–15*. Munich: Gegenstandpunkt Verlag, 2015. https://en.gegenstandpunkt.com/.

Gegenstandpunkt. "The System of Free Competition and What It Is About." Translated from *Gegenstandpunkt: Politische Vierteljahreszeitschrift 3–17*. Munich: Gegenstandpunkt Verlag, 2017. https://en.gegenstandpunkt.com/articles/system-free-competition-and-what-it-about.

Gelernter, Mark. *Sources of Architectural Form: A Critical History of Western Design Theory.* Manchester: Manchester University Press, 1995.

Gibson, James J. *The Ecological Approach to Visual Perception.* Boston: Houghton Mifflin Co., 1979.

Gombrich, E.H. *Art and Illusion: A Study in the Psychology of Pictorial Representation.* Princeton: Princeton University Press, 1960.

Gombrich, E.H. "The Logic of Vanity Fair: Alternatives to Historicism in the Study of Fashions, Style and Taste." In Paul Arthur Schilpp, ed., *The Philosophy of Karl Popper*, Volume 14 of *Library of Living Philosophers*. Chicago: Open Court, 1974. http://www.the-rathouse.com/2012/Gombrich.html.

GSA. *The Site Security Design Guide.* Washington, DC: U.S. General Services Administration, Public Buildings Service, June 2007. https://www.wbdg.org/FFC/GSA/site_security_dg.pdf.

Gwilt, Joseph. *The Encyclopedia of Architecture: Historical, Theoretical, and Practical* (The Classic 1867 Edition). New York: Crown Publishers, Inc., 1982.

Hall, Jr., John R. "The Total Cost of Fire in the United States." National Fire Protection Association Fire Analysis and Research Division. Quincy, MA: NFPA, March 2014.

Harries, Karsten. *The Ethical Function of Architecture.* Cambridge, MA: MIT Press, 1997.

Haynes, Hylton. "Fire Loss in the United States During 2016." *NFPA Research* (September 2017).

Hays, K. Michael. *Modernism and the Posthumanist Subject: The Architecture of Hannes Meyer and Ludwig Hilberseimer.* Cambridge, MA: MIT Press, 1992.

Hegel, Georg Wilhelm Friedrich. *Lectures on The History of Philosophy* (Volume III). Translated from the German by E.S. Haldane and Frances H. Simone. London: Kegan Paul, Trench, Trübner & Co., 1896. First published in German by editor Eduard Gans in 1837.

Hegel, Georg Wilhelm Friedrich. *Reason in History: A General Introduction to the Philosophy of History.* Translated from the German by Robert S. Hartman. Indianapolis: Bobbs-Merrill Educational Publishing, 1953. First published in German, but without the passage quoted, by editor Eduard Gans in 1837. Hartman's translation is based in part on Hegel's *Einleitung in die Philosophie der Weltgeschichte*, edited by Georg Lasson, which includes the quoted passage from additional handwritten lecture notes, published 1917 by Verlag von Felix Meiner (Leipzig).

Held, Karl, and Audrey Hill. *The Democratic State: Critique of Bourgeois Sovereignty.* Munich: Gegenstandpunkt-Verlag, 1993. https://en.gegenstandpunkt.com/books/democratic-state.

Herdeg, Klaus. *The Decorated Diagram: Harvard Architecture and the Failure of the Bauhaus Legacy.* Cambridge, MA: MIT Press, 1983.

Hillier, Bill. "In Defense of Space." *RIBA Journal* 80, no. 11 (November 1973): 539–44.

Hoffer, Peter Charles. *Seven Fires: The Urban Infernos that Reshaped America.* New York: Public Affairs, 2006.

Hollyer, James R., B. Peter Rosendorff, and James Raymond Vreeland. "Democracy and Transparency." *The Journal of Politics* 73, no. 4

(October 2011): 1191–1205. https://www.jstor.org/stable/10.1017/s0022381611000880.

Howard, Jr., Seymour. *Structure, An Architect's Approach*. New York: McGraw-Hill, 1966.

Howell-Ardila, Deborah. "Berlin's Search for a 'Democratic' Architecture: Post-World War II and Post-unification." *German Politics & Society* 16, no. 3 (48) (Fall 1998): 62–85. https://www.jstor.org/stable/23737374.

Ingersoll, Richard. "Second Nature: On the Social Bond of Ecology and Architecture." In *Reconstructing Architecture: Critical Discourses and Social Practices*, edited by Thomas A. Dutton and Lian Hurst Mann, 119–57. Minneapolis: University of Minnesota Press, 1996.

Jacobs, Jane. *The Death and Life of Great American Cities*. New York: Vintage Books, 1961.

Janda, Kenneth, Jeffrey M. Berry, and Jerry Goldman. *The Challenge of Democracy: American Government in Global Politics*, 11th ed. Independence, KY: Cengage Publishers, 2011.

Jonnes, Jill. *Eiffel's Tower: And the World's Fair Where Buffalo Bill Beguiled Paris, the Artists Quarreled, and Thomas Edison Became a Count*. New York: Viking, 2009.

Joroff, Michael, and John Templer. *An Agenda for Architectural Research 1982*, edited by James Snyder. N.p.: The Architectural Research Centers Consortium, Inc., 1982.

Koch, Aaron, Katherine Schwennsen, Thomas Dutton, and Deanna Smith. *The Redesign of Studio Culture. A Report of the AIAS Studio Culture Task Force*. Washington, DC: The American Institute of Architecture Students, 2002.

Koolhaas, Rem, and Hans Ulrich Obrist. *Rem Koolhaas, The Conversation Series*. Cologne: Verlag der Buchhandlung Walther König, 2006.

Koolhaas, Rem. "Universal Modernization Patent, Skyscraper Loop (2002)." In *Content*, edited by Brendan McGetrick (Rem Koolhaas, editor-in-chief). Cologne: Taschen, 2004.

Koolhaas, Rem. "Junkspace." *October*. 100, Obsolescence (Spring 2002): 175–90.

Krohn, Carsten. *Mies van der Rohe: The Built Work*. Basel: Birkhäuser, 2014.

Laitos, Jan G. *The Right of Nonuse*. New York: Oxford University Press, 2012.

Lang, Jon, and Walter Moleski. *Functionalism Revisited: Architectural Theory and Practice and the Behavioral Sciences*. Aldershot: Ashgate Publishing, 2010.

Lawton, Mark, and William Brown. "Considering the Use of Polyethylene Vapour Barriers in Temperate Climates." *Proceedings of the Ninth Canadian Conference on Building Science and Technology (Design and Construction of Durable Building Envelopes)*. Vancouver (February 2003).

Leach, Neil. "Architecture or Revolution." In *Architecture and Revolution: Contemporary Perspectives on Central and Eastern Europe*, edited by Neil Leach, 112–26. London: Routledge, 1999.

LeBlanc, Sydney. *The Architecture Traveler: A Guide to 250 Key 20th Century American Buildings*. New York: W.W. Norton, 2000.

Le Corbusier and Pierre Jeanneret. "Five Points Towards a New Architecture." In *Programs and Manifestos on 20th-Century Architecture*, edited by Ulrich Conrads, 99–101. Cambridge, MA: MIT Press, 1971.

Le Corbusier. *Towards a New Architecture*. New York: Dover Publications, 1986. Based on work originally published by John Rodker, London, in 1931, translated from the 13th French edition by Frederick Etchells. Originally published as *Vers une architecture* in 1923 based primarily on essays first published in *L'Esprit Nouveau* starting in 1921.

Le Corbusier. "Trois Rappels à MM. Les Architectes, Premiere Rappel: Le Volume." *L'Esprit Nouveau* 1 (October 1920): 91–96.

LEED Leadership in Energy and Environmental Design: New Construction Reference Guide v2.2. Washington, DC: U.S. Green Building Council, 2006, 3rd ed. (October 2007).

LEED Leadership in Energy and Environmental Design: Reference Guide for Building Design and Construction v4. Washington, DC: U.S. Green Building Council, 2013.

Licht, Richard. "Clarifying the Issue of Fire Protection Balance." *Fire Engineering* 156, no. 11 (November

1, 2003). White paper version (n.d.). https://nfca-online.org/lichtwhitepaper.pdf.

Licht, Richard. "The Impact of Building Code Changes on Fire Service Safety." *Fire Engineering* 158, no. 4 (April 1, 2005). Modified version (n.d.). https://www.dhi.org/shared/forms/PDFforms/codes/impactobuildingcodechanges.pdf.

Lstiburek, Joseph. "Energy Flow Across Enclosures." *ASHRAE Journal* 50, no. 8 (August 2008): 60–62, 64–65.

Lstiburek, Joseph. "Thermal Bridge Redux." *ASHRAE Journal* 54, no. 7 (July 2012): 60–66.

MacDonald, Michael, and Michael Deru. "The Wal-Mart Experience, Part One." *ASHRAE Journal* 49, no. 9 (September 2007): 14–25.

MacGregor, J.G. "Safety and Limit States Design for Reinforced Concrete." *Canadian Journal of Civil Engineering* 3, no. 4 (December 1976): 484–513. https://doi.org/10.1139/l76-055.

Mahall, Mona, and Asli Serbest. *How Architecture Learned to Speculate*. Stuttgart: Gerd de Bruyn, 2009.

Mainstone, Rowland. *Developments in Structural Form*. Cambridge, MA: MIT Press, 1975.

Mallgrave, Harry Francis. *Gottfried Semper: Architect of the Nineteenth Century*. New Haven: Yale University Press, 1996.

Marcuse, Herbert. *The Aesthetic Dimension: Toward a Critique of Marxist Aesthetics*. Boston: Beacon Press, 1978.

Marcuse, Herbert. *Reason and Revolution: Hegel and the Rise of Social Theory*, 2nd ed. London: Routledge & Kegan Paul, Ltd., 1960. First edition published in 1941.

Marino, C., A. Nucara, and M. Pietrafesa. "Does Window-to-Wall Ratio Have a Significant Effect on the Energy Consumption of Buildings? A Parametric Analysis in Italian Climate Conditions." *Journal of Building Engineering* 13 (2017): 169–83. http://dx.doi.org/10.1016/j.jobe.2017.08.001.

Marx, Karl. *Capital: A Critique of Political Economy, Volume II*. Transcribed from first English edition of 1907. Moscow: Progress Publishers, 1956. https://libcom.org/files/Capital-Volume-II.pdf.

Marx, Karl. *Grundrisse: Foundations of the Critique of Political Economy*. New York: Vintage Books, 1973. Written 1857–1861.

Marx, Karl. *A Contribution to the Critique of Political Economy*. Translated by S.W. Ryazanskaya. Moscow: Progress Publishers, 1977. First published in 1859. https://www.marxists.org/archive/marx/works/1859/critique-pol-economy/.

Marx, Karl. "Letters from the Deutsch-Französische Jahrbücher: Marx to Ruge." Written September 1843. First published February 1844. https://www.marxists.org/archive/marx/works/1843/letters/43_09.htm.

Marx, Karl. "On the Jewish Question." In *Karl Marx, Early Writings*. Translated by Rodney Livingstone and Gregor Benton. New York: Vintage Books, 1975. Written in 1843.

Marx, Karl. "Results of the Immediate Process of Production" (*Resultate*). In *Karl Marx, Capital: A Critique of Political Economy, Volume I*. Translated by Ben Fowkes. New York: Vintage Books, 1977. First published in 1933 and believed to have been written by Marx between 1863 and 1866.

Matter of Application of Jacobs. 98 N.Y. 98 (Court of Appeals of the State of New York, 1885). https://casetext.com/case/matter-of-application-of-jacobs.

McDonough, William, Architects. *The Hannover Principles: Design for Sustainability*, 1992. Fifth "special" edition, 1999 ("A version of the final document issued by the City of Hannover in 1992.") ISBN: 1-55963-634-3.

Mezey, Susan Gluck. *Disabling Interpretations: The Americans with Disabilities Act in Federal Court*. Pittsburgh, PA: University of Pittsburgh Press, 2005.

Mumford, Lewis. "Function and Expression in Architecture." *Architectural Record* 110, no. 5 (1951): 106–12.

Murphy, Pat. *The Green Tragedy: LEED's Lost Decade*. Yellow Springs, OH: Arthur Morgan Institute for Community Solutions, 2009.

Newman, Oscar. *Defensible Space: Crime Prevention Through Urban Design*. New York: Macmillan, 1972.

Norberg-Schulz, Christian. *Intentions in Architecture*. Cambridge, MA: MIT Press, 1965.

Ochshorn, Jonathan. "Architecture's Dysfunctional Couple: Design and Technology at the

Crossroads." *International Journal of Design Education* 7, no. 4 (2014): 35–46.

Ochshorn, Jonathan. "Designing Building Failures." *Proceedings of the 2006 Building Technology Educators' Symposium*, edited by Deborah J. Oakley and Ryan E. Smith (August 3–5, 2006): 313–26. https://btes.org/BTES_2006/2006_BTES_Proceedings_Complete.pdf.

Ochshorn, Jonathan. *Structural Elements for Architects and Builders: Design of Columns, Beams, and Tension Elements in Wood, Steel, and Reinforced Concrete*, 2nd ed. Champaign, IL: Common Ground Research Networks, 2015. doi:10.18848/978-1-61229-802-3/CGP.

Ochshorn, Jonathan. "Utility's Evil Twin: The Function of *Venustas* and the Fear of Reality." *Cornell Journal of Architecture Vol. 11*, edited by Val Warke (March 2020). Actar Birkhäuser Distribution.

Ockman, Joan. "What Is Democratic Architecture? The Public Life of Buildings." *Dissent* 58, no. 4 (Fall 2011): 65–72. https://doi.org/10.1353/dss.2011.0100.

Osgood, Charles E., George Suci, and Percy Tannenbaum. *The Measurement of Meaning*. Urbana: University of Illinois Press, 1975. First published in 1957.

Panofsky, Erwin. *Gothic Architecture and Scholasticism*. New York: New American Library, 1976. First published in 1951.

Petroski, Henry. *Design Paradigms: Case Studies of Error and Judgment in Engineering*. Cambridge: Cambridge University Press, 1994.

Plunz, Richard. *A History of Housing in New York City: Dwelling Type and Social Change in the American Metropolis*. New York: Columbia University Press, 1990.

Popper, Karl. *The Open Society and Its Enemies, Volume II: The High Tide of Prophecy: Hegel, Marx, and the Aftermath*. London: Routledge, 1945.

Protruding Objects. U.S. Access Board Technical Guide. Washington, DC: United States Access Board, February 2014. https://www.access-board.gov/attachments/article/1002/protruding%20objects.pdf.

Prum, Richard. *The Evolution of Beauty: How Darwin's Forgotten Theory of Mate Choice Shapes the Animal World—and Us*. New York: Doubleday, 2017.

Ramsey, Charles, and Harold Sleeper. *Architectural Graphic Standards*, 1932 facsimile edition. New York: John Wiley & Sons, 1990.

Rasmussen, Steen Eiler. *London: The Unique City*. New York: The Macmillan Company, 1937.

Reddaway, T.F. *The Rebuilding of London After the Great Fire*. London: Jonathan Cape, 1940.

Rookwood, Joel, and Geoff Pearson. "The Hoolifan: Positive Fan Attitudes to Football 'Hooliganism.'" *International Review for the Sociology of Sport* 47, no. 2 (2010): 149–64.

Roskam, Cole. *Improvised City: Architecture and Governance in Shanghai, 1843–1937*. Seattle: University of Washington Press, 2019.

Ruskin, John. *The Seven Lamps of Architecture*. New York: Noonday Press, 1974. First published in 1849.

Sahotsky, Brian. "The Roman Construction Process: Building the Basilica of Maxentius." PhD diss., University of California, Los Angeles, 2016. https://escholarship.org/uc/item/39b230f1.

Schön, Donald. *The Reflective Practitioner: How Professionals Think in Action*. New York: Basic Books, 1983.

Schulze, Franz. *Mies van der Rohe: A Critical Biography*. Chicago: University of Chicago Press, 1985.

Schumacher, Patrik. *Autopoiesis of Architecture*. Chichester: John Wiley & Sons, 2011.

Scott Brown, Denise. "The Function of a Table." *Architectural Design* 37 (April 1967): 154.

Seuss, Dr. *Yertle the Turtle and Other Stories*. New York: Random House, 1958.

Shapiro, Ian. *The Evolution of Rights in Liberal Theory*. Cambridge: Cambridge University Press, 1986.

Shelton, Tod. "Greening the White House: Executive Mansion as Symbol of Sustainability." *Journal of Architectural Education (JAE)* 60, no. 4 (May 2007): 31–38.

Shulte, Richard. "The Report on the World Trade Center Incident: A Critique." *Plumbing Engineer* 30, no. 8 (August 2002).

Sloan, Alfred P. *My Years with General Motors*. Garden City, NY: Doubleday & Co., 1964.

Solomonson, Katherine. *The Chicago Tribune Tower Competition: Skyscraper Design and Cultural*

Change in the 1920s. Chicago: University of Chicago Press, 2001.

Stasiowski, Frank. *Architect's Essentials of Winning Proposals.* New York: Wiley, 2003.

Steil, Lucien, Brian Hanson, Michael Mehaffy, and Nikos Salingaros, eds. "Contrasting Concepts of Harmony in Architecture: The 1982 Debate Between Christopher Alexander and Peter Eisenman." *Katarxis*, no. 3 (September 2004). http://www.katarxis3.com/Alexander_Eisenman_Debate.htm.

Stone, Harris. *Workbook of an Unsuccessful Architect.* New York: Monthly Review Press, 1973.

Sudjic, Deyan, with Helen Jones. *Architecture and Democracy.* London: Lawrence King, 2001.

Sullivan, Louis. *The Autobiography of an Idea.* Mineola, NY: Dover Publications, 1956.

Sullivan, Louis. "The Tall Office Building Artistically Considered." *Lippincott's Magazine* (March 1896): 403–9. https://archive.org/details/tallofficebuildioosull.

Sullivan, Louis. "The Young Man in Architecture." *The Brickbuilder* 9, no. 6 (June 1900): 115–19. https://babel.hathitrust.org/cgi/pt?id=uc1.co42015741&view=1up&seq=10.

Szlósarczyk, Sebastian, Steffen Wendzel, Jaspreet Kaur, Michael Meier, and Frank Schubert. "Towards Suppressing Attacks on and Improving Resilience of Building Automation Systems— An Approach Exemplified Using BACnet." *GI Sicherheit.* LNI 228 (March 2014): 407–18.

Tell, Dave. "The Rise and Fall of a Mechanical Rhetoric, or, What Grain Elevators Teach Us About Postmodernism." *Quarterly Journal of Speech* 100, no. 2 (May 2014): 163–85. https://doi.org/10.1080/00335630.2014.939992.

Thompson, D'Arcy Wentworth. *On Growth and Form, A New Edition.* Cambridge: Cambridge University Press, 1945. First edition published in 1917.

Thornton, Charles H., and Richard L. Tomasetti (contributor). *Exposed Structure in Building Design.* New York: McGraw Hill, 1993.

Tobriner, Stephen. "The History of Building Codes to the 1920s." *Proceedings of the Structural Engineers Association of California*, *1984 Convention.* Monterey, CA (October 18–20, 1984). Released as:

CEDR-02-8. Center for Environmental Design Research, Berkeley, CA (October 1984).

"Today in Energy." U.S. Energy Information Agency (EIA). November 7, 2018. https://www.eia.gov/todayinenergy/detail.php?id=37433.

Turner, Mark, ed. *The Artful Mind: Cognitive Science and the Riddle of Human Creativity.* Oxford: Oxford University Press, 2006. DOI: 10.1093/acprof:oso/9780195306361.001.0001.

Uraine, Christopher, Mike McGaraghan, Bernie Bauer, and Jon McHugh. "Indoor Lighting Power Densities—Final Report." Codes and Standards Enhancement (CASE) Initiative, 2019 California Building Energy Efficiency Standards (September 2017). http://title24stakeholders.com/wp-content/uploads/2017/09/2019-T24-CASE-Report_NR-Indoor-Light-Sources_Final_Semalber-2017.pdf.

"U.S. Energy Facts Explained." U.S. Energy Information Agency (EIA). Last updated August 28, 2019. https://www.eia.gov/energyexplained/us-energy-facts/.

Veblen, Thorstein. "The Economic Theory of Woman's Dress." *The Popular Science Monthly* 46 (1894): 198–205. http://www.modetheorie.de/fileadmin/Texte/v/Veblen-The_Economic_Theory_of_Fashion_1894.pdf.

Veblen, Thorstein. *The Theory of the Leisure Class.* New York: The Modern Library, 1961. First published in 1899.

Venturi, Robert, Denise Scott Brown, and Steven Izenour. *Learning from Las Vegas.* Cambridge, MA: MIT Press, 1972.

Vidler, Anthony. *The Architectural Uncanny: Essays in the Modern Unhomely.* Cambridge, MA: MIT Press, 1992.

"Village of Euclid v. Ambler Realty Co." *Legal Information Institute.* Cornell Law School. https://www.law.cornell.edu/supremecourt/text/272/365.

Viscusi, W. Kip. "The Value of Life." Harvard John M. Olin Center for Law, Economics, and Business Discussion Paper No. 517, Harvard Law School, Cambridge, MA, June 2005. http://www.law.harvard.edu/programs/olin_center/papers/pdf/Viscusi_517.pdf.

Vitruvius. *The Ten Books on Architecture.* Translated by Morris Hicky Morgan. Cambridge, MA: Harvard University Press, 1914. http://www.chenarch.

com/images/arch-texts/0000-Vitruvius-50BC-Ten-Books-of-Architecture.pdf.

Wermiel, Sara E. *The Fireproof Building: Technology and Public Safety in the Nineteenth-Century American City*. Baltimore: The Johns Hopkins University Press, 2000.

Wilson, Edward O. *Half-Earth: Our Planet's Fight for Life*. New York: Liveright Publishing Corporation, 2016.

Wölfflin, Heinrich. *Renaissance and Baroque*. Ithaca, NY: Cornell University Press, 1966.

Wright, Frank Lloyd. *An Autobiography*, 1st ed. London: Longmans, Green and Company, 1932.

Wright, Frank Lloyd. *An Autobiography*, 2nd ed. San Francisco: Pomegranate 2005. First published in 1943 by Duell, Sloan and Pearce (New York).

Wright, Frank Lloyd. "Broadacre City: A New Community Plan." *Architectural Record* 77 (April 1935): 243–54.

Wright, Frank Lloyd. "In the Cause of Architecture, Second Paper." *Architectural Record* 35 (May 1914): 405–13.

Wright, Frank Lloyd. *Modern Architecture: Being the Kahn Lectures for 1930*. Carbondale: Southern Illinois University Press, 1931.

Wright, Frank Lloyd. *An Organic Architecture: The Architecture of Democracy*. The Sir George Watson Lectures on the Sulgrave Manor Board for 1939. Cambridge, MA: MIT Press, 1970. First published in 1939 by Lund Humphries (London).

X, Malcolm. "Racial Separation." In *Civil Rights: Great Speeches in History*, edited by Jill Karson. Farmington Hills, MI: Greenhaven Press, 2003.

Yorke, R. S. *The Modern House*. London: The Architectural Press, 1934.

Young, Jonathan M. *Equality of Opportunity: The Making of the Americans with Disabilities Act*. Washington, DC: National Council on Disability, 2010. First published 1997. https://ncd.gov/publications/2010/equality_of_Opportunity_The_Making_of_the_Americans_with_Disabilities_Act.

Zhou, Aiming, Vestal Tutterow, Jeffrey Harris, and Paul Bostrom. "Promoting Energy-Efficient Buildings in the Industrial Sector." Alliance to Save Energy (2009). https://pdfs.semanticscholar.org/7524/ccaf107fa9dba2ee42e072949fd6d0f2e921.pdf.

INDEX

ILLUSTRATION CREDITS

1.1 Photo by the author; circle "A" insert photoshopped by the author based on schematic renderings published in Daniel Aloi, "Rand to House Luminous, Voluminous Fine Arts Library," *Cornell Chronicle*, January 25, 2018, https://news. cornell.edu/stories/2018/01/rand-house-luminous-voluminous-fine-arts-library.

3.1 (*Top*) Old St. Paul's Burning by Wenceslaus Hollar (1607–1677) accessed at https://en.wikipedia.org/wiki/Thomas_ Farriner. (*Below*) Destroyed Buildings in the Aftermath of the 1871 Great Chicago Fire, unknown photographer, https://commons. wikimedia.org/wiki/File:1871_Great_ Chicago_Fire_destroyed_buildings.jpg.

4.1 Underlying image drawn by author based on "Limits of Protruding Objects," in the United States Access Board's Guide to the ADA Standards (Chapter 3, Protruding Objects), https://www.access-board.gov/ guidelines-and-standards/buildings-and-sites/about-the-ada-standards/ guide-to-the-ada-standards/chapter-3-protruding-objects. Blind woman with cane is a public domain vector illustration, https://publicdomainvectors.org/en/free-clipart/Vector-image-of-a-blind-woman-walking/5745.html.

4.2 Photos by Matthew Carbone, https:// www.matthewcarbone.com/, matt@ matthewcarbone.com, from "Milstein Hall at Cornell University / OMA," November 1, 2011, ArchDaily, https://www. archdaily.com/179854/milstein-hall-at-cornell-university-oma-2/. Photographer's permission gratefully acknowledged.

4.3 & 4.4 Photos by the author.

5.1 NASA, "Carbon Dioxide," April 2020, https://climate.nasa.gov/vital-signs/ carbon-dioxide/.

6.1 Drawn by author based in part on data provided in C. Marino, A. Nucara, and M. Pietrafesa, "Does Window-to-Wall Ratio Have a Significant Effect on the Energy Consumption of Buildings? A Parametric Analysis in Italian Climate Conditions," *Journal of Building Engineering* 13 (2017): 169–83, http://dx.doi. org/10.1016/j.jobe.2017.08.001.

7.1 Plan of Jeremy Bentham's panopticon prison, drawn by Willey

Reveley in 1791, https://commons. wikimedia.org/wiki/File:Panopticon.jpg.

7.2 Partially redrawn by the author based on Diagram 2.1, "Guidelines for Elements and Innovation," *GSA Site Security Design Guide*, https://www.gsa.gov/cdnstatic/ GSA_Chapter_Two_8-8-07.pdf.

9.1 Photo of Town Hall of Logroño by Miguel Angel Nieto, edited into grayscale with perspective correction by the author, https://commons.wikimedia. org/wiki/File:Ayuntamiento_de_ Logro%C3%B1o.jpg.

9.2 Drawing by the author based on models of unbuilt projects by (*right*) Venturi and Rauch, D'Agostino House, https://usmodernist.org/venturi.htm; and (*left*) Eisenman Architects, House I, https:// eisenmanarchitects.com/House-I-1968.

10.1 Photo and annotations by the author.

10.2 Photo and drawing by the author (photo edited to remove background building; drawing based on similar, though unattributed, renderings).

10.3 Photo by the author.

10.4, 10.5 & 10.6 Drawings by the author.

10.7 Photos and photoshopping by the author.

10.8 Photo of Palazzo Farnese by Peter1936F, https://commons.wikimedia. org/wiki/File:Palazzo_Farnese_Fassade. jpg, edited into grayscale with bottom image photoshopped by the author to remove decorative elements.

11.1 Photo of Wexner Center by Ibagli, https://commons.wikimedia.org/wiki/ File:OSU_Wexner_Center.jpg; photo of Stata Center by Tony Webster from Portland, Oregon, https://commons. wikimedia.org/wiki/File:Ray_and_ Maria_Stata_Center_-_MIT,_Cambridge_ (16868722144).jpg; both images edited into grayscale by the author.

12.1 Drawings by the author.

12.2 Photo of Temple of Zeus by Michael Nicht, https://commons.wikimedia.org/ wiki/File:Temple_of_Zeus_at_Olympia_ (Doric_column).jpg, edited into grayscale

with perspective correction by the author; insert Tribune Tower rendering by Adolph Loos, https://www.loc.gov/item/2017645480/.

12.3 Photo by Hedrich-Blessing, first published in *Mies van der Rohe*, an exhibition catalog/book written by Philip Johnson and published by the Museum of Modern Art in 1947; image scanned from Reyner Banham, *The New Brutalism: Ethic or Aesthetic*, London: The Associated Press, 1966, 29 and reproduced twice, with the right image photoshopped by the author to show the building's construction. Original photo, HB-09969-A, in Hedrich-Blessing Collection of the Chicago History Museum.

12.4 Photo (*left*) of Prudential Building, 28 Church Street, Buffalo, Erie County, NY, Reproduction Number: HABS NY,15-BUF,6--1, Library of Congress Prints and Photographs Division, https://www.loc.gov/pictures/ item/ny0204.photos.116403p/. Photo (*right*) of Prudential Building under construction from William Harvey Birkmire, *The Planning and Construction of High Office-Buildings*, 4th edition, New York: J. Wiley, 1906, 107.

12.5 Photo (*left*) of Hancock Center, Chicago by Joe Ravi, https://commons. wikimedia.org/wiki/Category:Photographs _by_User:Jovianeye#/media/File:John_ Hancock_Center_2.jpg. Photo (*right*) of Citicorp Center, NYC, by the author. Drawings (*center*) by the author.

12.6 Photo by Gunnar Klack, https:// commons.wikimedia.org/wiki/File: Washington-Dulles-International-Airport-Eero-Saarinen-04-2014.jpg, edited into grayscale by the author.

12.7 Graph and diagrams by the author.

12.8 Photo by the author.

12.9 Photo by Paperclips0701, https://commons.wikimedia.org/wiki/ File:AquaTower2009_02_08_image2.jpg.

12.10 & 12.11 Photos by the author.

14.1 Drawings by the author.

15.1 Photo by Petr Kratochvil, https:// www.publicdomainpictures.net/en/view-image.php?image=284022&picture=-, edited into grayscale by the author.